# Note by Note

Ankur Bhardwaj is a journalist with *Business Standard*. Passionate about films, food and politics, he has an innate understanding of India because of his wide-ranging experience in myriad jobs dealing with technology. A lapsed MBA from Haryana, he has moved from selling telephones in Punjab and Uttar Pradesh to selling ideas to readers across India.

Seema Chishti is a journalist with *The Indian Express*. Having worked as a television and radio broadcaster with BBC in the UK, she has been riding the technology curve in reverse having finally moved to print journalism in India. Surrounded by politics, she is deeply interested in Indian society, its contradictions and its interactions across caste, class and region. She brings her understanding of society to her writings on Indian politics and culture.

Sushant Singh is a journalist with *The Indian Express*. He writes on matters of strategy, defence, foreign policy and politics. He is interested in all things political and social, and his twenty years as an army officer have given him a unique lens on India. He attributes his love for politics and poetry to his early years in Agra. He has authored *Mission Overseas*, a book on three overseas missions of the Indian armed forces.

# Note by Note

## THE INDIA STORY 1947–2017

Ankur Bhardwaj
Seema Chishti
Sushant Singh

HarperCollins *Publishers* India

First published in India in 2018 by
HarperCollins *Publishers*

Building 10, Tower A, 4th Floor, DLF Cyber City, Phase II,

Gurugram Haryana – 122002, India
www.harpercollins.co.in

2 4 6 8 10 9 7 5 3 1



P-ISBN: 978-93-5277-010-6
E-ISBN: 978-93-5277-011-3



Typeset in 11/14.2 Linden Hill at
Manipal Digital Systems, Manipal

Printed and bound at

MicroPrints India, New Delhi

To the founders of the grandest experiment of our times – the Republic of India. And to the people who have turned this experiment into a successful and living reality.

# Contents

## 1980s: Hard Drive in Tough Times



## 1990s: Old Battles, New Direction



## 2000s: India Shining

# Foreword

SONGS have been an essential part of popular Indian cinema since the advent of sound in 1928. The Indian 'talkie' film started to sing even before it began to talk. Each of the early talkies were studded with at least seven songs while the film version of the mid-nineteenth-century play *Indra Sabha* produced in 1932 had a staggering seventy songs!

Songs in Indian films usually function as a means to reveal the feelings, thoughts and desires of the characters in the narrative (most often sung by the characters themselves) or are used to comment on the way a situation may develop in a story or indicate the direction the narrative might take. Frequently they are used as punctuations between scenes and sequences; to highlight a situation or to anticipate a turn in the plot.

Film songs, particularly those written by some of our great contemporary poets, have either through metaphor or simile tended to reflect upon our everyday existential, social, national and universal concerns.

*Note by Note: The India Story* 1947–2017 is a unique rendering of the eventful and often turbulent seventy-year journey of independent India with a film song representing each of those years. Songs that encapsulate and hold up an oblique mirror to the significant events of the year – events that profoundly impacted our people in the continuing historic journey of our nation.

10 April 2018 Shyam Benegal

# Introduction

IS *Note by Note* a book of Hindi film songs? Or is it a book on India since Independence? No, it is neither. Reading *Note by Note* is like looking into the old-fashioned bioscope where the vignettes of India's story over the past seven decades are played to Hindi film music. Or you can call it a travelogue of India's journey since Independence, where Hindi film music is a constant accompaniment as you move from one milestone to another.

The connection between Hindi film music and independent India's evolution seems tenuous but a closer scrutiny shows that one is reflected in the other; on occasions, they even influence each other. In fact, Hindi film music's relationship with India is the same as its relationship with an individual film. The songs exist independently on their own but are also part of the larger story. More often than not, the music is integral to the story; but at times, it sounds out of place, even though it would still be a great earworm by itself.

*Note by Note* provides for each of the seventy-one eventful years since Independence, a Hindi film song which was composed, heard, sung and spoken about in that year. Though intricately linked, this song is not just meant as an anthem for that year – it also links the story of India over the years. Flowing with the tale of the song is also the story of each of independent India's seventy-one years: the two mostly run parallel, merging and diverging at moments in history. Each of the seventy-one chapters in the book is a harmonious synthesis of Hindi film song and modern Indian history, a note about India's journey. It is the rhythm of modern Indian history played to the beat of Hindi film music.

*Note by Note* is as much a story of songs as it is of what India experienced in the last seven decades. In charting the course of each year, we have tried to pick a melody which would enable us to understand the overall mood and groove of that year. The songs picked for each year may not always have been the most popular or the best known, and sometimes the choice has been agonizingly hard to make. The criteria for picking a tune has been varied, but overall, the endeavour has been to spot one signature song that goes with the major events unfolding in India at the time, sometimes by just the sheer contrast of the events to the tone and mood of the song. As a shaper of mood, witness of its times, each of the seventy-one songs in the book emerges as a parable for that year.

Through all the vicissitudes and twists of the past seven decades, in looking at each year, there is also a story to be told and a thought to be shared. Every year, there is a story of political change, social emancipation and economic growth which has been forgotten, pushed to the recesses of our memories. Those memories need to be refreshed. It is the story of independent India, with the flavour of Hindi film music, 'not wholly or in full measure, but very substantially'.

♫

In 1947, as the subcontinent was torn into two, India went on to find its feet, its spirit and its moorings. It was perhaps only in part, as India's first prime minister Jawaharlal Nehru remarked, but substantially – a young nation reached out to embrace its destiny and achieve a sense of being one, even if it was not a perfect entity. As the colonial yoke was thrown off and India settled down, a decade of hope and expectation, a search for a *Naya Daur* followed. India dreamt big then, both domestically and globally, for all its characterization as a large and hopelessly diverse poor country; a 'functioning anarchy', as John Kenneth Galbraith, former US ambassador to India and a renowned economist, called it.

Nothing captures the extraordinary flight of India's soaring ambitions than the modern, progressive Constitution given by its own people, whereby India became a republic in 1950. Institutions fundamental to India's governance like the Planning Commission came into existence, even as the internal map of India was redrawn to satisfy the emerging demand for linguistic states. Even these states began their own nascent experiments with democracy: Kerala could boast of the world's first elected communist government. It was in the 1950s that the big dams, the power plants, the steel mills were all built even as India's space programme began to take shape; the IITs were also born then.

The decade of the 1960s brought with it two wars with two neighbours, each of which left India a little shaken. This decade saw the demise of that colossus, Jawaharlal Nehru. The seeds of the green revolution were sown, and the politics of the country saw the emergence of short-lived non-Congress governments in many states. But it also freed Indira Gandhi from the shackles of her party and she emerged as a leader in her own right.

Politically, it was the 1970s that gave New Delhi the first break from single-party rule and India got its first non-Congress government at the Centre. It followed the first and only rupture in India's so far unbroken and regular record with democracy: Emergency resulted in the rhythm of the five-yearly elections being disrupted. But it was a decade in which India won a war, tested a nuclear device, nationalized its banks and achieved self-sufficiency in food-grain production.

The events of the 1980s were to leave their mark on India for decades. Sikh militancy, assassination of a prime minister, anti-Sikh riots and the unrest in Kashmir: all pushed India to the brink. In the heartland, centred over an existing mosque in Ayodhya in Uttar Pradesh (UP), religious divides were fomented by a growing movement that argued that India's largest community was actually being sidelined and minorities being pampered. The contestation and strife in the air got a bigger push as middle castes in north India pushed for more. It was about riots, shutdowns and turmoil, happening barely a few years after Rajiv Gandhi won an unprecedented and overwhelming electoral mandate in 1984. But his legacy was also about giving India a big push towards modernity – communications and computers were to transform the country's future.

The 1990s was a challenging decade mirroring the cataclysmic changes in the world. As the Second World collapsed like a house of cards, India too opened its economy and sought greater integration. It was a move perhaps inevitable, but it left a bitter-sweet taste in the mouth. Politics too, as late V.P. Singh put it, began to mirror the 'social coalition' that India was. Unprecedented to and fros between parties and coalition governments became the norm. Babri Masjid was destroyed, preceded by a series of events that had devastating consequences and cost thousands of lives. Rajiv Gandhi was assassinated in this decade, sending shock waves and pushing the Congress party back to the drawing board for picking leaders.

In the first decade of the new millennium, India saw its first non-Congress government to almost last a full term when Atal Bihari Vajpayee demitted office in 2004. India suffered a jolt in 2002 when Gujarat witnessed riots that killed nearly 2,000 persons. In 2004 though, Congress regained power, but only at the head of a coalition – a historical first for the party. In a period of high economic growth and growing bonhomie with the United States, a decade of rule by the United Progressive Alliance (UPA) also revitalized the promise of rights that India had given to its people in the Constitution: rights to livelihood, dignity, information, employment and food were enacted.

The second decade of the twenty-first century has been a continuation of the roller-coaster ride of a nation in the making, as a single party again got into the saddle with Narendra Modi as prime minister. The journey continues.

♫

All through these past seven decades, it was not as if the Hindi film music was on a slow tempo. It struck a beat to match and reflect what India was going through. In the 1940s and 1950s, desire was spoken of in muted terms – from behind a veil and in hushed tones, via haunting restraint and classical ragas or via ghazals. If social and political turbulence marked the 1960s, jazz and rock influences in Hindi film music spoke to that mood.

In the 1970s, as social change began to reveal itself, deep questions about single-motherhood, faith and morality wove their way into songs. The 1970s and the 1980s saw a quickening of the Indian heartbeat and even the angry young man could not dispense with the need to sing in his films. A phase of banal and crass lyrics seemed to reflect similar tones in political exhortations.

As India arrived economically and socially on the world scene, myriad influences, beats and music found expression in musical scores. As India fell in love with all that is shiny, disposable and glittering, there was loudness and lyrics to match, but there were also throwback moments, holding onto nostalgia, so much so that most films made soon had titles which were taken from old Hindi film songs.

A very significant part of the logic – and turbulence – was the city of Bombay. It was a city of commerce, academics and politics. This was where extremes of incomes lived, worked and thrived; this was where a nascent film world was kicking into life and blossoming. It was neither an 'industry' then nor pure commerce, but a series of creative experiments with a new and exciting medium. Seven decades ago, there were other cities where films were being made – Lahore, for instance – but little remained of those centres while Bombay flourished year after year.

The fate of Lahore and Bombay film industries mirrors the trajectory of India and Pakistan in the last seven decades. A commercially viable, widely acceptable, creative industry was not possible in an inward-looking Pakistani society while an inclusive India, which boasted of its diversity in religions, languages, people and cultures, provided the enriching environment for the Hindi film industry to flourish.

The early years after Independence were a great time for the Bombay film industry, a time when poets came there, some to make a fortune and others to make a living, but most came to find fellowship in creating a new metric and lyric: the Hindi film song. It is because of this influence that the language of Hindi films, particularly its songs, was Hindustani and not

Hindi. It clearly was not the sarkari Hindi that led someone to famously quip: *Ab aap samacharon mein Hindi suniye*, a sharp pun on the opening line of All India Radio's news bulletins: *Ab aap Hindi mein samachar suniye* – but it was Hindustani, with a heavy influence of Urdu. The Urdu influence was always restricted by its commercial acceptability. Sahir's famous nazm '*Kabhi Kabhi*' had to be rewritten in a simpler language to become a popular Hindi film song.

The issue of pure Hindi as a language was somehow also linked to the purity of Hindi film music. In 1952, All India Radio stopped broadcasting Hindi film music, along with any music featuring the harmonium. This was because the then information and broadcasting minister, B.V. Keskar, an austere Brahmin and classical music purist, thought the Hindi film music of that time was vulgar, cheap and overly westernized. This led to the birth of the Hindi film music service of Radio Ceylon, which was a station originally set up by the Government of Ceylon – now Sri Lanka – as an Asia-wide commercial service. For a couple of decades, Indians got their fix of Hindi film music from Radio Ceylon, listening to it on Short Wave radio where the quality of broadcast was rather uneven. The station pioneered a weekly countdown of Hindi filmi songs, called the *Binaca Geetmala*, which was as famous for its songs as it was for its signature host, Ameen Sayani.

Even though the *Binaca Geetmala* was based on a Binaca Countdown show of English music on Radio Ceylon, the Hindi film song was a unique thing, not seen anywhere else in the world, till the music video (via MTV) caught on in the 1980s. The story in each film was broken by song sequences, mouthed by stars on screen, providing both relief in the story and yet, being very much a part of the tale. It started with stars singing but soon, another intriguing innovation, the 'playback', came in and the film song became a separate entity though it remained a part of the main story. And, of course, it was wildly popular and remains so even today.

From the day films incorporated sound and became 'talkies', they held an inexorable draw over Indian lives. Films of all kinds – mythologicals, historicals, action dramas, musicals, love stories, family dramas – were made. Some saw them, some did not. But what stayed and touched all lives was the Hindi film song. It reflected and absorbed what it was to be India and Indian, in its various dimensions. Political and social turmoil, love, separation, the impossibility of love, India's poverty, injustices, struggles and its other stark realities found a voice, literally, in the Hindi film song.

There were other glorious and worthy film and film music traditions, some would say far worthier, e.g., Bengali, Tamil and Marathi films. Somehow, maybe because Hindi had a larger market, or because Bombay was home to several traditions – folk and local – the Hindi film song ended up representing the idea of the song of India better than others.

'Change is the only constant' is an overused cliché but like all clichés, it contains a grain of truth. As India has changed – dramatically, many will say – in the last seven decades, there are a few things that have remained constant. And they have remained constant because they have also changed with time. Hindi film music is one of them, a tradition unique to India. You can imagine an India without cricket – after all, hockey was more popular till the 1970s – but you cannot imagine an India without Hindi film music.

♫

There is scarcely a generation in India which has not grown up on Hindi film music. It is as much a matter of discussion and disagreement when you put a couple of Indians together, as is perhaps politics. Was Sahir a greater lyricist than Shailendra? Was Mohammed Rafi a more versatile singer than Kishore Kumar? Did Khayyam not get his due as a composer? Why does a Dev Anand or a Rajesh Khanna have the best songs over decades? Did Lata Mangeshkar kill all competition over the years? How did the music decline in the 1990s? Why are older film songs more memorable than the new ones? The questions never end.

In a way, they mirror the questions being asked about India's journey in the last seven decades. Was Nehru as great as everyone says he was? Did Shastri get his due in India's political history? Will Indira Gandhi be remembered for the Bangladesh War or for the Emergency? What is the legacy of the Janata experiments? Was the BJP's rise inevitable after the demolition of Babri Masjid? How did India defeat its various insurgencies?

When did the Indian economy turn around? Did UPA turn far too left in a society not receptive to those ideas? The questions are endless.

If the questions run parallel, so do the answers. The journey of Hindi film music uniquely mirrors the life story of independent India. *Note by Note* moves on parallel lines, highlighting the connection between the twin tracks. The Hindi film song is India's background score – noticed at times, unnoticed at others but always present – often adding to the drama but at times, also jarring with the events. Songs written for their times, sometimes to push India along a certain way, just reflecting the zeitgeist at others, provide the perfect motif to accompany the India story.

♫

Modern India, like the proverbial Rome, was not built in a day. It is a unique experiment in crafting an idea of a citizenry, of nationhood, without a single language or religion, but coming together for progressive values and ideas. India-watchers in the early decades believed it would not last more than a few years. Yet, for all its turbulence, turmoil and chaos, India has flourished to cock a snook at those who predicted its demise well before it got going.

This book is about an India which was thought of and built, brick by brick and life by life, through a difficult struggle and a conscious accommodation of a myriad identities. Unlike the Soviet Union, another multi-national and multi-ethnic idea fused together after the Bolshevik revolution, the idea of India did not emerge through a violent revolution. The idea of an electoral democracy, however imperfect, of each adult citizen electing her representatives every five years was equally revolutionary though.

The bold ideas and dramatic vision reflected in the Constitution did not emerge suddenly; they had been discussed, debated and fine-tuned in the years of freedom struggle. The high ideals are not a marker of our failures but of the dreams that we need to aspire to, of the goals we need to strive for. Much was thought of, achieved and done in the past seven decades. Much was not – plenty of dreams were interrupted – and there is much we have to answer for.

Year by year, it is note by note, a small tribute to those who dared to dream and then do; and to all those who eventually built India through the early years of instability and kept the faith – whether in the role of nation-builders, leaders, workers, entrepreneurs, students, teachers, soldiers, generals, artists, or those who felt outside the system and yet kept the faith – in this idea of India.

The songwriters, singers and musicians gave us well beyond three minutes of songs. They gave us joy, reflection, delight, melancholy and the words and tunes to articulate some of our deepest desires, delights and nightmares.

Something intangible and tough to capture, but something very much present, constitutes the stuff that binds India and makes it tick. Essentially, this book is a tribute to India and the exceptional republic that it has been – made and shaped by every single Indian in her own way.

# Prologue

IF India didn't exist, no one would have the imagination to invent it. It was that bold and radical an idea, well ahead of its times in 1947. Jawaharlal Nehru's evocative description of India as 'an ancient palimpsest on which layer upon layer of thought and reverie had been inscribed, and yet no succeeding layer had completely hidden or erased what had been written previously' often masquerades the astounding fact that 1947 did represent a major break from the past.

Not only was this land mass brought together as India for the first time, a people beset by poverty, massive illiteracy and with such huge diversity on a subcontinental scale chose to be a democracy. The ideals did not emerge suddenly but were rooted in the decades-long movement for independence, which has no parallels in its audacious idealism and willingness to dream.

Neither was the world a kind place in 1947, having suffered greatly during the Second World War. India was born in such turbulent times, in the first flushes of the end of colonialism, but it refused to consider itself a victim in any manner. For Indians, it was an opportunity to break from the past, to shape their future and make their dreams come alive. It was a moment of glorious hope. Although the past still clung on to the present, guiding it and at times threatening to haunt India's future.

There is no doubt that 15 August 1947 was a turning point in India's journey. But as Nehru reminded us in his famous midnight speech then, 'Yet the turning point is past, and history begins anew for us, the history which we shall live and act and others will write about.' It is time to recount the history that Indians have lived and acted in the past seven decades.

# 1940s
# Birth Pangs of a Nation

## Jiya Beqaraar Hai

Turmoil, hope, audacity and baby steps towards its tryst with destiny

1 and 2. Millions of people migrated to and from the newly created Pakistan after the Partition of India in August 1947. Lakhs of them perished in the communal rioting during Partition.

3. Mahatma Gandhi was assassinated on 30 January 1948. People pay their last respects to the departed leader.

4. Jawaharlal Nehru delivering his midnight speech in the Central Hall of parliament to mark India's 'tryst with destiny' in August 1947.

1.

2.

3.

4.

# 1947: *Afsana Likh Rahee Hoon*

*Afsana likh rahee hoon*
*Dil e beqaraar ka*
*Aankhon mein rang bhar ke*
*Tere intezaar ka*

Lyricist: Shakeel Badayuni
Music: Naushad
Singer: Uma Devi
Film: *Dard*

TIME froze, in the meltdown that was 1947. The British packed their bags and rolled out, back to Blighty. And a dawn of unbelievable possibilities broke out in India.

A luminous morning that promised the bright light of freedom did not come without its shadows. The clouds hovering above may have been darker than what India's founding fathers had hoped for. They carried in them the agony of Partition, the pain of separation as the country was divided into two nations: India and Pakistan. But the phrase 'the empire on which the sun never sets' got a fitting burial, well after dark on that day in August.

Yes, 15 August 1947 did spell Freedom in several languages: Swatantrata, Azaadi, Sudandiram, Swadhinata. It was no Russian Revolution and India's transformation would be stuck with the label of being a social democratic one. But there was little to be sanguine about that day.

It was a new day and a new way.

*'Afsana likh rahee hoon'* is arguably the most memorable melody of 1947, it is hummed – with a familiar ring to it – even today. It is anything but easy to pick a song that tells or encapsulates the 1947 story. Events headier and more surprising than a Bombay blockbuster were unfolding in real time in the subcontinent. The afsana (story) of India itself would begin to unfold this year. And what a start it got too. In August, Mahatma Gandhi and Khan Abdul Ghaffar Khan were in Calcutta trying to stop the communal mayhem and Jawaharlal Nehru was in Delhi. Each hoping to cement the idea of a modern India amidst all the turmoil – both together, yet apart.

So – midwifed in both agony and hope – did India's afsana get under way.

Uma Devi (better known as Tun Tun, perhaps the first comedienne of Hindi cinema) sang the words of Shakeel Badayuni to the music of Naushad in the film *Dard*. She wanted to be an actress. Having lost her parents early, she ran away from home, landed at Naushad's door and insisted he secure her a break. He said he could not make it work for her as an actress, but sensing that she could carry a tune, he suggested playback.

Shakeel Badayuni, who was to become known as one of Bombay's finest lyricists, had just arrived in the city in 1946. Naushad was also new at the trade and scoffed at in early reviews. But *Dard* went on to become a huge hit.

Coming from the stable of Kardar Studios, directed by the well-established A.R. Kardar, *Dard* was what you might call a 'Muslim social' with two women in love with a doctor and one woman (played by the beauteous Suraiya) eventually, dying. A.R. Kardar, apart from being a phenomenon himself in film terms, would be spoken of in many conversations later: the first cricket Test captain of neighbouring Pakistan was his brother, and another brother, whom he cast as the star in *Dard*, migrated to Pakistan too. In many ways, the Kardar story itself is the story of twinned yet partitioned brothers.

Despite the turmoil, it is a wonder that so many Hindi films were made and Hindi film songs continued to be popular. The year was about both hope with the shaking off of the imperial yoke as well as bloodshed and mayhem that the division of the land brought about.

This was the year when the music colossus K.L. Saigal died, marking the end of an era. His last film *Parwana* was released in that year. Mohammed Rafi started his climb, with his first hit in *Jugnu* with Noor Jehan – '*Badla wafa ka*'. Soon after recording her songs for *Jugnu*, Noor Jehan left for Pakistan – marking another big milestone. Geeta Dutt started her rapid ascent to stardom with her songs for *Do Bhai*.

India, in 1947, was buzzing at an unbelievable pace; in the middle of a 'tryst' and a churn that was to shake its core.

The previous year had seen relations between the Congress and the Muslim League break down almost completely. The interim government with Jawaharlal Nehru as prime minister and Liaquat Ali Khan as finance minister was not working. The British Cabinet Mission continued discussions, and in February 1947, the British prime minister Clement Attlee announced that British rule would end by June 1948.

It was the appointment of Lord Louis Mountbatten – the cousin of the King Emperor – as viceroy with more autonomy than his predecessor Lord Wavell, that further (and alarmingly) speeded up things. In June 1947, Lord Mountbatten announced the agreement of a formula whereby the date for the transfer of power to two successor states was brought forward to 15 August 1947. 'Ten weeks would suffice for the constitutional, social, military and infrastructural vivisection of a subcontinent' as historian John Keay put it sardonically.

The Indian Independence Act, 1947, passed by the British Parliament on 4 July 1947, reads: 'As from the fifteenth day of August, nineteen hundred and forty-seven, two independent Dominions shall be set up in India, to be known respectively as India and Pakistan.'

Lord Mountbatten's picking of an early date, 15 August, historians point out, was prompted by his own personal history. Mountbatten later claimed, as quoted in *Freedom at Midnight*: 'The date I chose came out of the blue. I chose it in reply to a question. I was determined to show I was master of the whole event. When they asked had we set a date, I knew it had to be soon. I hadn't worked it out exactly then – I thought it had to be about August or September and I then went out to the 15th August. Why? Because it was the second anniversary of Japan's surrender.'

The separation of India and Pakistan had a human cost of catastrophic dimensions, being the largest exodus in human history involving ten million people. At least one million died. Much is made of the 'unfinished business' of Kashmir, but little attention is paid to how much else was botched up as the British packed their bags.

International boundaries were not made available by Sir Cyril Radcliffe's Boundary Commission till 17 August, two days *after* 15 August. The hurry with which the British decided to depart from India is clear in how Radcliffe came to India only on 8 July 1947, with just five weeks to make sure that two commissions, one for Punjab and the other for Bengal, drew their lines. But boundaries in hearts and heads were firmly etched by then and people fled in fear, whether they wanted to or not.

A ceremony in Karachi was overseen by Muhammad Ali Jinnah, the Quaid-i-Azam (supreme leader) of the new country on 14 August. Lord Mountbatten attended, flying back for the Indian event on the night. Interestingly, Pakistan, officially for a few years, was okay with acknowledging that 15 August was when it too got its freedom – postage stamps issued as late as July 1948 bear witness to that. But later, anxious to be seen seceding from British India and *not* independent India, it advanced its Yaum-e-Azadi to 14 August. In India, its first prime minister gave his most memorable 'tryst with destiny' speech 'at the stroke of the midnight hour' and heralded the dawn of freedom. His calm articulation of the idea of India and the importance of the moment in world history was to be among the first steps that he took to situate India boldly on the world stage.

While the entire country was on fire, Punjab and Bengal, being actually partitioned, bore the brunt of the violence. Art, fiction and cinema were to echo the pain for generations. Whether in Sadaat Hasan Manto's stories, Bhishm and Balraj Sahni's recollections or in Ritwik Ghatak's memorable scenes from *Meghe Dhaka Tara* or Khushwant Singh's *Train to Pakistan*, the sense of loss was felt and expressedly so, as the full import of 1947 dawned on both India and its new neighbour.

Film-musically speaking, two other notable events took place this year. In the grimness that 1947 represented, 'fun and frolic (too) were legitimised', as author Ganesh Anantharaman puts it, when C. Ramachandra composed '*Aana meri jaan Sunday ke Sunday*' for *Shehnai*. And Lata Mangeshkar, the voice that would go on to sing for four generations at least, went on to find her feet in Bombay, with her debut for Hindi films in *Aap Ki Sewa Mein*.

# 1948: *Saari Duniya Ke Sartaj*

*Desh hua aazad magar*
*Na pahna tune taaj*
*Tera amar rahega raaz*
*Sari duniya ke sartaj*

Lyrics: Ishwar Chandra Kapoor
Music: Pandit Gobindram
Singer: Shamshad Begum
Film: *Ghar Ki Izzat*

SHAMSHAD Begum belted out a patriotic song in *Ghar Ki Izzat* in 1948, complete with visuals of Mahatma Gandhi and blooming buds, commending the Mahatma for not wearing the crown despite struggling so hard to win freedom. But the song was an afterthought.

In Ram Daryani's *Ghar Ki Izzat*, starring Dilip Kumar and Mumtaz Shanti, the plot about a subservient Indian son, unable to protect his wife from his mother's taunts and taking to drinking, could be the seeds of the first questions being raised about joint families not being the best of places for young women married into them. But as Mahatma Gandhi's assassination on 30 January so haunted the nation, it was felt necessary to add this song. Ishwar Chandra Kapoor wrote the words and Pandit Gobindram did the score.

It was a mediocre film which was trashed by reviewers at the time. *Filmindia*, April 1949, is scathing, calling it one of 'idiotic stories', 'trash supreme' and 'reactionary'. Even the Gandhi tribute is sneered at.

But 1948, so close to the horrors of the bloody Partition that had split the subcontinent, bore witness to serious consequences inside India too.

January was when the Mahatma, already at odds with the way Partition happened and shaken by his inability to stall communal rioting in Bengal and Punjab, was facing the worst ever attacks with the Hindu Mahasabha and the Rashtriya Swayamsevak Sangh (RSS) whipping up passions against him. While Muslim communalists of the subcontinent felt vindicated and had got a nation, Hindu communalists felt rapped hard on their knuckles at watching a modern, secular state take shape under the persuasion and direction of the Congress, which stood steadfast for an India, unlike Pakistan, which was not majoritarian.

The deputy prime minister, Vallabhbhai Patel, when he berated the RSS after banning it in the aftermath of Gandhi's assassination by Nathuram Godse, spoke of the hatred that was fomented both actively on the streets and through whisper campaigns. An assassination attempt was made on the Mahatma just days before his murder by the same forces who tried to paint him as 'pro-Muslim'. On 20 January, one Madanlal Pahwa threw a bomb which exploded some 20 metres away from where Gandhi was sitting.

But the assassination of Gandhi, resulting in the RSS being shunned and banned had another significance for independent India. Says A.G. Noorani in *The RSS and the BJP, A Division of Labour*: 'The Sangh Parivar profited enormously by the partition of India. Gandhi's assassination arrested that trend. The damage caused by this self-inflicted wound has not yet healed. It took the RSS–BJP 30 years to achieve some respectability – thanks to the Emergency – and 40 years to come close to acquiring power at the centre.'

The year 1948 could not shake off the shadow of the eventful predecessor year as the battle for Kashmir intensified with Pakistan. Started as tribal raids in October 1947, it was a regular battle all through this year (ending only in 1949). Ramachandra Guha juxtaposes the competing views about the accession of Kashmir well when he speaks of how 'on the Indian side the finger is pointed at the British Governor-General, who dragged the case to the UN and at the British general of the Indian army, who stopped his troops from going into northern Kashmir. But the Pakistanis blame Mountbatten too, who they think conspired with Radcliffe to give Indians the district of Gurdaspur, which gave New Delhi a road into Kashmir.

Kashmir became, with important symbols like Sheikh Abdullah and Brigadier Mohammad Usman of the Indian Army (who bravely defended a bold attack by Pakistan in Nowshera and later died in July), a way of India differentiating its own secular, modern self-image from that of a theocratic and narrowly conceived idea of Pakistan.

The Government of India succeeded in getting the princely state of Junagadh to accede to India in November, after it rescinded its accession to Pakistan. The state of Hyderabad joined the Indian Union in September, though in this case it was a more violent struggle with the Nizam resisting the accession for long. Telangana, where communists along with peasants were successfully waging a struggle, continued to simmer and the struggle was to die out only three years later.

The Communist Party of India, the leading opposition force of the time, changed colour, as General Secretary P.C. Joshi gave way to B.T. Ranadive in Calcutta in 1948. Apart from the sea change in the personalities of the leaders, the resolve earlier demonstrated by Joshi to bat against Hindu revivalist forces in the aftermath of Gandhi's assassination gave way to a much narrower party line, urging that the Congress regime be attacked through general strikes and peasant uprisings.

While the Industrial Disputes Act had been enacted a year earlier, the Factories Act and the Minimum Wages Act were among those that were enacted now to ensure fair wages and protection to the working class, a major countervailing force in the country at the time. Other significant economic laws that explicitly protected workers included the Coal Mines Provident Fund and Miscellaneous Provisions Act and the Employees' State Insurance Act.

In hindsight, 1948 was to prove to be a landmark year when things which would shape Bombay music eventually found their place – writer Sahir Ludhianvi decided to leave Lahore and settle in Bombay. Music director O.P. Nayyar migrated to India. Ghulam Haider, the big-ticket composer and music director, who decided to go to Pakistan, made his last film *Shaheed* this year.

It is a big year for Raj Kapoor and Dev Anand too, who were to rule the hearts and Hindi cinema for some decades. Raj Kapoor made his directorial debut with the film *Aag*, which was also produced by him under the banner of RK Films. The film was not a hit but it showcased for the first time the legendary pairing on screen of Raj Kapoor and Nargis. In *Ziddi*, Dev Anand experienced his first hit, greatly propelled by the music. Kishore Kumar debuted as a singer in this one, though clearly reeling under the K.L. Saigal influence, in songs like '*Marne ki duaaen kyun maangoon*'; he would find his own voice a little later.

This was the year when independent India sent a contingent of seveny-nine men to compete in the London Olympics – the first Olympics after the end of the Second World War. The hockey team met England in the finals. This was the first time they were playing hockey with their erstwhile 'masters' but were able to skilfully wrest the Gold.

# 1949: *Jiya Beqaraar Hai*

*Jiya beqaraar hai*
*Aayi bahaar hai*
*Aaja more balma*
*Tera intezar hai*

Lyrics: Hasrat Jaipuri
Music: Shankar–Jaikishan
Singer: Lata Mangeshkar
Film: *Barsaat*

AS the 1940s drew to a close, Nargis would find herself falling and hanging on the right arm of director/actor Raj Kapoor, set to be her co-star for many more ventures. This languid and sensual moment would go on to be immortalized as the logo for Raj Kapoor's RK Films. Also debuting in this hit musical, *Barsaat*, were music directors Shankar and Jaikishan. The film went on to be the top grosser ever in Hindi cinema until then. This was Raj Kapoor's second film under his independent banner and his first big hit.

'*Jiya beqaraar hai/Aayi bahaar hai/Aaja more balma/Tera intezar hai*', a group song led by Lata Mangeshkar, with its easy use of folk phrases, broke away from just classical, ghazal or other strictly conventional forms that were the norm then. The wait and longing sit easy with the otherwise cheerful tone of the song and almost seem emblematic of the mood in the nation – waiting, yet hopeful as it pushed back the demons it needed to fight in the two years after Independence and put its head down to the tedious task of nation building.

The year climaxes with the Preamble to the Constitution being formalized on 26 November. 'We, the People' were finally sovereigns, de facto, breaking free from the clutches of off-shore monarchs. India was on the road to be a republic. Motley princely states effectively gave up rights as the Preamble signalled their coming under the framework of a modern, democratic republic, where office was not to be inherited.

This was the last year since the British Crown took charge of India in 1858 that an Act passed in the British Parliament would decide matters in India. It set the stage clearly for India to rule itself, which it would start to do the following year.

It is not as if India was to be free of problems that had so scarred its horizon just after Independence. Far from it. It was to just start coming into its own and get beset with different issues to wrestle with.

The year 1949 saw the fierce but democratic and illuminating debates of the Constituent Assembly intensify, with one subject, the language issue, becoming quite prominent as Hindi speakers faced off with non-Hindi speakers on the question of national versus official language. Both sides fought their corner but importantly no national language was agreed upon. English would be continued. B.R. Ambedkar, the chairman of the drafting committee of the Constitution, remarked on conclusion of the debate: 'Let us remember that after all if Hindi has to be accepted by them (people of south Indian states) they must accept it, not we for them; and after all what is it which has evoked so much controversy? I was wondering why we should take so much time, so much discussion over a small matter.'

But language was to be anything but 'a small matter'. Resurgence of movements of linguistic autonomy were fired up at this time. The Samyukta Karnataka, Samyukta Maharashtra and the Aikya Kerala movements along with Mahagujarat became very popular. Prime Minister Jawaharlal Nehru, not easy with the idea of linguistic divisions, was somewhat stunned by the ferocity with which these movements picked up steam, seeking to unify respective language speakers. Things got hotter when demands for a Sikh state combining language and religion reared their head.

This year saw the protracted fighting over Kashmir draw to a close with a ceasefire negotiated by the UN Commission for India and Pakistan. The Karachi Agreement established a ceasefire line on 27 July. Another significant event this year was a first – the appointment of an Indian as the commander-in-chief of the Indian Army. Gen. K.M. Cariappa, who would become one of the only two field marshals India has had, took charge on 15 January, which day is now commemorated as Army Day.

November was also to record the hanging of Nathuram Godse and Narayan Apte for the assassination of Mahatma Gandhi. The ban on the RSS imposed by Vallabhai Patel, then deputy PM, in the aftermath of Mahatma Gandhi's killing, was lifted this year, on the condition that its head, M.S. Golwalkar, agree to 'ask his men to profess loyalty to the Constitution of India and the national flag and to restrict the Sangh's activities "to the cultural sphere abjuring violence or secrecy".' (Ramachandra Guha: *India After Gandhi*). It is a known fact that for decades later, it was not the tricolour that was hoisted from the Sangh headquarters in Nagpur but a saffron flag.

The year 1949 was also when the Reserve Bank of India (RBI) was nationalized.

Building blocks for a nation were in the process of being laid. Historians have reflected on how, after the Soviet Union, this was the largest exercise ever in making a nation with so many diverse elements like languages, ethnicities, religions and castes.

Scarcity of foreign exchange and the food crisis worried Prime Minister Nehru deeply. Inder Malhotra speaks of how 'In November that year Nehru made his first visit to the US amidst a tremendous welcome. During his talks with Harry Truman he did mention the scarcity of food in India. Truman's response was positive. But there were bureaucratic obstructions, resistance in the US Congress, procedural delays and other difficulties, including the American attempt to barter wheat for strategic materials. There could therefore be no agreement even though there was a glut of wheat in America. India said that the US was "ungracious" and "stingy". What annoyed New Delhi the most was that the US had tried to use food aid as a "policy lever". For their part, American officials complained that the Indian government had not "followed up" on Nehru's vague request to Truman.'

Musically, this year was about the runaway success of *Andaz* and *Barsaat* primarily because of their songs. *Dulari* marked Lata's steep climb up, and composer Naushad's successful journey continued. Actors like Raj Kapoor and Dev Anand realized the importance of songs to their fortunes and began to slowly play a role in deciding which singer and song would best work with them. On the one hand, this year saw the seriously melodious Mohammed Rafi sing a song elevating the wait for a beloved to a fine art in '*Suhaani raat dhal chuki, Na jaane tum kab aaoge*' (from *Dulari*). On the other hand, C. Ramachandra continued with his unconventional compositions, like '*Mere piya gaye Rangoon, Wahan se kiya hai telephoon*' (in *Patanga*), a song that in another millennium has made its way into play lists of people in their twenties.

# 1950s
# A Constitutional Revolution

## Suhana Safar

India draws up its Constitution. It lays the foundation for industry, planning and education.

1. The first Indian Institute of Technology (IIT) was inaugurated at Kharagpur in 1951.

2. The first General Elections were held in 1952: The Congress party with its election symbol of two bullocks was voted into power.

3. Temples of modern India: Jawaharlal Nehru visits the camp site of Hirakud dam.

4. Heart-throbs of the 1950s: Nargis, Raj Kapoor and Dilip Kumar in the film *Andaz*.

# 1950: *Gore Gore O Banke Chhore*

*Roz roz mulaqat achchhi nahin*
*Pyaar me aisi baat achchhi nahin*
*Thoda thoda milna thodi si judai*
*Sada chandni raat achchhi nahin*

Lyrics: Rajendra Krishan
Music: C. Ramachandra
Singers: Lata Mangeshkar and Amirbai Karnataki
Film: *Samadhi*

THE light-hearted, Western-sounding tune with a radiant and relaxed Ashok Kumar and Nalini Jaywant on screen and the young Lata Mangeshkar and Amirbai Karnataki singing, '*Gore gore, O banke chhore*' in many ways was an exception to the norm then. These were still the years when classical training and the classical touch were seen as being vital to a song's popularity and its longevity.

'*Gore gore*', essentially an unusual beat and sensibility being introduced in the film *Samadhi*, owed much to C. Ramachandra and the songwriter Rajendra Krishan whose partnership was legendary. Unique in their own role but quite special when they came together. Rajendra Krishan began life as a clerk in Simla but his wide reading of Hindi and Urdu poetry ever since his adolescence and his obvious talent ensured that a clerk's life could not hold him for long. He came to Bombay as a writer in the 1940s and started with screenplay and from 1947 also wrote songs for many movies. He was proficient in Tamil and tied up with AVM Productions. His close association with C. Ramachandra reflects very well in this song, though critics hint that it is inspired by a hit tune released in 1945. A 1951 Tamil film, *Or Iravu* (based on a play originally written by C.N. Annadurai – Anna) has a song '*O Samy*', based on the same tune. This was to happen time and again as Hindi and Tamil films retained strong and distinct personalities, yet mirrored a lot of aspects of the other, reflective of the differently coloured yet entangled threads of Madras and Bombay cinema.

The women leads in '*Gore gore*' dominate the stage with abandon and confidence, without any binding of gender roles and Ashok Kumar truly lights up the song. This song could well be seen in contrast to the important strides made by India in this crucial year. A sunny, flirtatious and joyous tune and tone – Western in spirit – may seem to be the wrong song to recall from this significant year. But its longevity, popularity, buoyancy and confidence make it perhaps the most suitable one as India took important steps towards defining itself and finally breaking free of colonial chains and the Indian Independence Act of 1947.

The Constitution of India was adopted on 26 January 1950. One of the longest Constitutions in the world, it grappled with India's complexities and its troubled immediate history with skill, compassion and foresight that remain a source of wonder to date. It was described as a 'seamless web' of democracy and social and economic reform. It was to herald a social revolution with its knitting together of several strands that comprised the idea of India.

Three essential things were the foundation: The Government of India Act of 1935, other Constitutions and finally, the Objectives Resolution adopted during the December 1946 Constituent Assembly session, which drew upon Congress resolutions from two decades ago. The essence of the Objectives Resolution was twofold, of deriving the authority and power of the Indian Union from the Indian people, as well as securing adequate safeguards for minorities, depressed and 'backward' classes, underdeveloped and tribal areas.

To be able to declare itself a sovereign, democratic republic was an idea way ahead of its time as far as India was concerned, and as the first president, Rajendra Prasad, stood on Republic Day to take the first salute, it was a historic day in the subcontinent, when India rose to confer on each of its citizens, rights as an individual but with a keen acknowledgement of her context and group identity as well.

The election of the president of the country was the stuff of much political jockeying between the two power centres in the country then, both close associates and favourites of Mahatma Gandhi – Jawaharlal Nehru and Vallabhbhai Patel. They had managed to sink their differences in the months following Gandhi's assassination, but significant differences in their world view emerged. While Nehru favoured Governor General C. Rajagopalachari as president, Patel wanted Rajendra Prasad, a fellow social conservative, for president. Nehru, it appears, was quite unaware of the support within the party for Prasad that Patel was able to drum up and when discussing the choice of the first president, Nehru was effectively outsmarted by Patel. Rajendra Prasad was sworn in as the Republic of India's first citizen.

The Election Commission of India came into being a day earlier, on 25 January, under Article 324 of the Constitution, as an autonomous one-member commission, with its task being the conduct of free and fair elections, and ensuring a smooth and bloodless transfer of power after elections. It is something India has managed at each interval, so far (except a brief delay in 1976–77) and this is something which most countries that secured their freedom around this time seem, even today, unable to accomplish.

The year 1950 is crucial for Indo-Pak relations too; both the countries formally committed themselves to a cessation of hostilities and agreed on the modalities of protecting the minorities in each country. On 8 April, the Nehru–Liaquat pact was signed. East Pakistan witnessed a record number of riots and a huge exodus of Bengali Hindus into India. With the bitterness of riots continuing, Prime Minister Nehru is supposed to have suggested to his counterpart that they visit the troubled areas together, but this was not seen as feasible by the Pakistani establishment. But Liaquat Ali agreed to come to Delhi and sign an agreement committing both countries to treating minorities in each country fairly. The areas considered were forced conversions, property rights and the rights of women who had been abducted in the violence of Partition.

If 1950 is important for India with the coming into force of the Constitution, the first amendment to it too came this year. On 26 January 1950, when the Supreme Court of India too was inaugurated, Chief Justice Harilal Kania said presciently, 'Different parts of the Constitution will act and react on each other and the Court will have to decide questions arising from such a situation.' As Granville Austen notes in his masterly *Working a Democratic Constitution*, about the first amendment, 'It may add clarity to sketch the course of the great confrontation that was now beginning between the Parliament and the Supreme Court over guardianship of the Constitution.'

It was also the year that Nehru's senior-most colleague, Deputy Prime Minister and Home Minister Sardar Patel, died (15 December), bringing to an end an interesting and eventful relationship that vividly coloured early India's politics, policies and its sense of self.

# 1951: *Awara Hoon*

*Abaad nahin barbaad sahi*
*Gaata hoon khushi ke geet magar*
*Zakhmon se bhara seena hai mera*
*Hansti hai magar yeh mast nazar*
*Duniya ... mein tere teer ka ya taqdeer ka maara hoon*
*Awara hoon, awara hoon*
*Ya gardish mein hoon aasmaan ka taara hoon*

Lyricist: Shailendra
Music: Shankar–Jaikishan
Singer: Mukesh
Film: *Awara*

THE year 1951 belonged to the soundtrack of *Awara*. Despite having such stiff and varied competition from songs as diverse and full of oomph like '*Saiyaan dil mein aana re*' (*Bahar*), '*Tadbeer se bigdi hui*' (*Baazi*), '*Shola jo bhadke*' (*Albela*), '*Tum na jane kis jahan mein kho gaye*' (*Sazaa*) or '*Bachpan ke din bhula na dena*' (*Deedar*), '*Awara hoon*' could be said to qualify as the true symbol of hope, a joyous statement of being who you are, easy and willing to bet on the future.

The combination of Shankar–Jaikishan, Shailendra and Mukesh (as the voice of Raj Kapoor) which began with this song was set to dominate the next decade or so. Raj Kapoor, with his rendition of the Chaplinesque Tramp, was a far cry from the rich or the angry or half-villain heroes that went on to dominate Hindi cinema in the later decades. He was penniless, new to the city, but comfortable in his skin and innocent, happy to define himself as a vagabond, light as the star even if he was down in the dumps.

Shankar–Jaikishan's music and lyrics by Hasrat Jaipuri and Shailendra formed a new school of music set to define most of the 1950s and provide a 'counterpoint to Naushad's classicism'. They drew their power from composing tunes that were 'hummed by the nation' as Ganesh Anantharaman says in *Bollywood Melodies*.

Raj Kapoor's onscreen presence and Mukesh beginning to be accepted as his 'voice' added more punch to this as one of the most memorable songs ever. It became popular in the Soviet Union, China, Japan and in Central Asia and, to this day, remains recognizable as the song from India; it is sung in the oddest of places across the globe.

The carefree, confident tune that marked Raj Kapoor's steps in the city found resonance in many of the significant events in India in this year. It was a momentous year, to say the least.

The first general elections, after India became a sovereign, democratic republic in 1950, were conducted over four months in 1951–52: from 25 October 1951 till 21 February 1952. Universal adult franchise was in play and 173 million voters above the age of twenty-one cast their vote. Simultaneous elections were held for the Lok Sabha and state assemblies. In all, 224,000 polling booths, one for almost every 1,000 voters, were set up after a careful house-to-house survey to register voters. With over 70 per cent of the electorate being illiterate, symbols were the key to identify candidates. People treated the elections almost as a festival, a celebration; and the percentage of invalid votes was very low – just 3 to 4 per cent.

The Communist Party of India and the Bharatiya Jana Sangh were the main opponents of the larger-than-life Congress, led by the even larger figure of Nehru. He displayed immense energy in the course of an arduous campaign wherein he continued with his practice of using his public addresses as a process of mass education, 'of teaching the masses that they had minds which they should use' to quote his biographer S. Gopal.

Events in faraway Korea also touched India at this time. The break-up of Korea into North and South divided by the 38th Parallel (latitude) in June 1950 continued to leave its traces on 1951. India, essentially Nehru, with his ideas about India's place in the world, batted aggressively for peace. At one point, India was the only communication link between North and South Korea. Newspapers in the US noted the crucial role this newly independent country was playing in this dangerous conflict. Nehru sharpened his ideas of active non-alignment, not merely as a principle of neutrality but of a thoughtful seeking of space outside the cold war. The Neutral National Repatriation Commission was founded, headed by Gen. Thimayya, and an Indian Custodian Force under him was made in-charge of the task of repatriating soldiers between the two sides. As Bipan Chandra et al. note in *India Since Independence*, India 'stoically faced first Chinese and Soviet hostility because she voted to declare N. Korea the initial aggressor. India then endured American wrath for refusing to go along with Western intervention in the war, and for refusing to declare China the aggressor.'

Independent India counted her own, in her first census since Independence, in 1951. Only 18 per cent of Indians were literate and life expectancy was just thirty-two years. Though Hindi, Punjabi and Urdu were counted as one language, Hindi speakers accounted for just over 42 per cent of the population. Telugu, Tamil, Marathi, Bangla and others constituted the other languages which would pose the other big question soon after, in this decade. India's magnificent diversity received recognition in the numbers the census threw up, as much as the realization that so much needed to be done.

This year saw the first amendment to the Constitution.

A prominent journalist, Romesh Thapar, protesting the banning of *Cross Roads*, a left-wing journal from Madras, approached the Supreme Court to secure his freedom of expression – his right to write what he wished to, as per Article 19 of the Constitution. The court upheld his right.

There was, simultaneously, another matter of proscribing cartoons in the *Organiser*, a right-wing publication. The Supreme Court interpreted this as a violation of Article 19, an overreach which allowed the state to act against what 'undermines the security of, or tends to overthrow, the State'.

The ruling of the Supreme Court led to an amendment by parliament – the famous first amendment to the Indian Constitution. This made freedom of speech subject to 'reasonable' restrictions and subject to 'public order'.

The Supreme Court upheld the rights of zamindars in another ruling, so as part of the first amendment the Constitution was reworded to ensure the validation of the zamindari abolition law. Also, parliament widened the remit of Article 15(3) to ensure that educationally, socially and economically backward sections get treated differently without in any way seeming to impact the principle of equality.

The First Five-Year Plan (for the years 1951 to 1956) was drawn up in this year. The Planning Commission, whose chairman was the prime minister, published its first Plan in July and this became the yardstick for allocating and apportioning resources across states and sectors.

Jawaharlal Nehru repeatedly stressed the importance of trained engineers and technical personnel for nation building. Keeping this in mind the first Indian Institute of Technology (IIT) was formally inaugurated by the then education minister Maulana Abul Kalam Azad on 18 August 1951. As its website states; 'IIT Kharagpur started its journey in the old Hijli Detention Camp where some of our great freedom fighters toiled and sacrificed their lives for the independence of our country. The history of IIT Kharagpur is thus intimately linked with the history of the Hijli Detention Camp. This is possibly one of the very few Institutions all over the world which started life in a prison house.'

The first Asian Games – based on the idea of an 'Asiad' where mutual strength, cooperation and excellence of the newly emerging and independent countries in Asia could find full expression – was held in Delhi in March 1951. Eleven countries and 489 athletes participated in the event held in the areas surrounding the Old Fort.

Prime Minister Nehru was an ardent champion of secularism, realizing that it was the backbone of a diverse India, and tried to keep religion out of state. But he and President Rajendra Prasad were not on the same page when it came to participating in the inauguration of the refurbished

Somnath Temple in Gujarat. It was Nehru's contention that as the head of state, Prasad must not extend his support for on overtly religious act such as the inauguration of a temple. Prasad disagreed and defied his prime minister and attended the function on 11 May 1951. This contentious discussion, of how far the Indian state must go in being religious, or avoiding association with religion, would continue in the years to come.

Monotosh Roy, a Dacca-born Indian body-builder, became the first Indian – and indeed Asian – to win the 'Mr Universe' title this year.

# 1952: *Mann Tadpat*

*Mann tadpat Hari darshan ko aaj*
*More tum bin bigde sagare kaaj*
*Ho binti karat hu rakhiyo laaj*
*Mann tadpat Hari darshan ko aaj*

Lyricist: Shakeel Badayuni
Music: Naushad
Singer: Mohammed Rafi
Film: *Baiju Bawra*

THE quintessential bhajan, based on the classical Raga Malkauns, rendered by the redoubtable Mohammed Rafi, among the most mellifluous and suitable voices for classical singing, this was a runaway hit in ways most unexpected.

In the last few years film music had seen a lot of experimentation with folk tunes and the verve and swing of jazz and pop tunes. But now, Naushad's ability and interest in classical music paid off. While all songs of *Baiju Bawra*, a film based on young Baiju's desire to defeat Akbar's court musician Tansen, worked very well together, this song has a recall value which few of this time do. It spoke eloquently to the times then and now. The fact that it is an invocation to Lord Hari, written, composed and sung by Muslims, has somehow added another dimension to its rich melody.

Naushad, whose strength lay in his grasp of classical tunes and themes, got a superb opportunity to lay out his wares and present his skills. Rafi's singing ensured that everything flowered beautifully. It is said that as the movie was marking its silver jubilee at the Broadway theatre in Bombay, Naushad was so moved that he told the producer of the film, Vijay Bhatt: 'I used to sleep on the pavement opposite the theatre when I first came to Bombay. It took me sixteen years to cross the road and get here.'

The success of *Baiju Bawra* and especially this song proved decisive in Naushad's life and he regained his confidence in classical music. He jettisoned 'the clarinet and accordion', welcoming the 'sarangi, jaltarang, violin, sitar and tabla', says G. Anantharaman in *Bollywood Melodies*. His second big score took a decade, with *Mughal-e-Azam*, but plenty of songs inspired by classical music followed in this decade with '*Mann ki been matwari baaje*', '*Insaf ka mandir hai yeh*', '*Madhuban mein Radhika nache re*' and more.

In a sense, this year also witnessed India's tryst with the classical and some seminal changes that shifted India into another gear.

Elections which began in October the previous year were completed this year; almost 46.6 per cent of the electorate voted and the first parliament of free India met on 13 May 1952. The elections were recognized worldwide as free, fair, representative and as having been conducted in an orderly manner. Sukumar Sen, India's first chief election commissioner, was called in as an adviser and expert by several Asian and African countries. The Congress party secured 364 seats and the communists emerged as the opposition, with twenty-three seats. The Jana Sangh secured three seats. The socialists and the Jana Sangh may not have done well, but the drawing in of all kinds of ideologies, deeply divided till just a few years ago, into the electoral framework was a very important achievement of the Indian system, especially so soon after the violence and turbulence of 1947.

India put in place much else of significance. The Cinematograph Act of 1952 ensured the setting up of the Central Board for Film Certification (CBFC). India held its first International Film Festival in January this year.

This was also the year when a Calendar Reform Committee was set up under the Council for Scientific and Industrial Research to even out all calendars and come up with one calendar that could be an Indian calendar. Meghnad Saha, the scientist, was the chairman of the committee. The committee submitted its report in 1955. Jawaharlal Nehru wrote in the preface of the report: 'They [different calendars] represent past political divisions in the country ... Now that we have attained Independence, it is obviously desirable that there should be a certain uniformity in the calendar for our civic, social, and other purposes, and this should be done on a scientific approach to this problem.' The unified national calendar (Saka Calendar) eventually came into being with effect from on 1 Chaitra 1879 or 22 March 1957.

Panchayati raj got a fillip of sorts. This year would be seen in hindsight as an important year for local self-government. The Community Development Programme was started nine months after the first general elections, in October 1952. The idea was to ensure that rural India gets attended to. This programme sought to provide the framework through which the administration would reach the district, tehsil and taluka level. It was to ensure that progress and development reached people in India's villages and development happens with their participation.

There was one more significant event which would shake up how the map of India would look. While most of India's national leadership was mindful of India's diversity and easy with allowing it to flower, language was one thing that had perhaps not got the attention it deserved. The first census had shown more Hindi/Hindustani speakers but there were other developed and proud languages. In the south too there was a strong sentiment that wanted to speak in its own voice, literally.

The first language movement was led by the Telugus for their own state, and Potti Sriramulu, a Gandhian, led the movement. The demand for a separate state for the Telugus was not new but had been on since 1910. But Potti's fast calling for a separate state for Telugu speakers unsettled all, and finally, his death on 16 December at the end of a three-month-long fast, brought the entire issue of the formation of linguistic states to a boil and led to the appointment of the First States Reorganisation Commission under Justice Fazl Ali next year.

The Indian cricket team, meanwhile, tasted its first ever Test victory, vs England, at Chepauk, in Madras. On 10 February, India beat the English by an innings and eight runs. Vinoo Mankad took eight wickets in the first innings with an economy rate of 1.41. Polly Umrigar and Pankaj Roy scored centuries. Vijay Hazare had the honour of captaining the first Indian side to be victorious in a Test ever, though the series was drawn at 1–1. The Pakistani cricket team too came to India in 1952 to play its first-ever matches after its formation.

In the 1952 Olympics, wrestler Khashabha Dadasaheb Jadhav became the first Indian ever to get an individual medal when he won the Bronze in Helsinki.

# 1953: *Mausam Beeta Jaaye*

*Apni kahaani chhod ja*
*Kuchh toh nishaani chhod ja*
*Kaun kahe is aur*
*Tu phir aaye na aaye*
*Mausam beeta jaaye*

Lyricist: Shailendra
Music: Salil Chowdhury
Singers: Manna Dey and Lata Mangeshkar
Film: *Do Bigha Zameen*

'MAUSAM *beeta jaaye*' – the season is adrift. This legendary song from an equally legendary film, *Do Bigha Zameen*, is full of pathos but it is premised on hope. It is the story of ordinary lives, made more ordinary by their tragic circumstances. Bimal Roy – inspired by Vittorio de Sica's *Bicycle Thief*, it is believed – introduced the cinema of realism with this film. It captures one of the truths of its times: the relationship of land and agriculture to Indians who owned little land – the drama heightened by the fact that a predominantly agricultural country was making rapid strides towards industrialization.

Struggling to hold on to what is precious and beautiful to him, the protagonist, played by Balraj Sahni, leaves his beloved land behind, hoping to gather enough money to repay his debts and keep his two bighas of land. That the end of the story is tragic is not quite evident in this song, as his fellow agriculturists till the land, plant crops and present a sunny picture of life in the village.

The tune is inspired by the dramatic and larger-than-life rhythm of the anthem of the Red Army in Russia at the time of the Second World War, '*Polyushko-polye*'. The music by Salil Chowdhury does full justice to the spirit of the anthem, of the reference to the plains calling out to the soldiers, even as they prepare for battle. It was no coincidence that this was picked from the Soviet Union's songbook; this was still a time of connecting with the idea of stirring changes inspired by the revolutionary changes in the USSR. Socialism, egalitarianism and radically breaking away from feudalism, with each Indian being equal to the other, were ideas that seemed immediately attainable.

*Do Bigha Zameen* was based on a short story written by Salil Chowdhury, called 'Rickshawallah', but the title of the film was picked from a poem by Rabindranath Tagore titled 'Dui Bigha Jomi'. This film, its theme, the song and its composition are a tribute to Bengal's themes and music and their imprint on Bombay cinema at this time.

This was a time when the zamindari system was being fought tooth and nail and a struggle was on to get legislation in various states to abolish it. Just two years ago, as the Supreme Court had upheld the right of the zamindars, the Constitution of India had to be amended to reiterate that legislation would be brought in to make landownership more equitable. *Do Bigha Zameen*, and more, would be something every Indian would be able to, ideally, dream about.

The year saw a first that was about higher aspirations, and literally so. The tallest peak in the world, Mt Everest, was scaled by an Indian and a New Zealander on 29 May. Tenzing Norgay and Edmund Hillary became the first to reach the heights and this made history in interesting ways, by setting a standard for ambition, endeavour and enterprise.

The Untouchability (Offence) Bill was passed this year. To finally outlaw untouchability in India was an important and progressive step and was made possible after years of campaigning, both social and political.

Indian Airlines and Air India were created in August through the Air Corporation Act, which oversaw the nationalization of India's airlines, one for inland travel and the other for international flights.

The year 1953 was to be very significant politically for events in two states at least. Andhra Pradesh became the first linguistic state to be carved out. This state for Telugu speakers had become an inevitability after the death of Potti Sriramulu after a three-month fast in 1952, but it had deeper consequences. Responding to the demands for linguistic states of their own from Marathi, Gujarati, Kannada and Malayalam speakers, the States Reorganization Commission recommended the division of India into linguistic units, which became basic administrative units. This was not something Nehru was very happy about, but it was an arrangement that was to serve India well and resolve the vexed 'language question' in large measure. Hindi chauvinists did not take kindly to it, but it had salutary consequences, overall.

The other state that was to experience changes was the state of Jammu and Kashmir. Relations between Sheikh Abdullah and Prime Minister Nehru were very strong but had started fraying and a break came this year as the Sheikh appeared to be veering towards full independence which made the Indian government jittery. The Sheikh publicly called for independence, which set off a chain of events leading to his ministerial colleagues and party men calling for his dismissal. Karan Singh, the Sadr-i-Riyasat, dismissed Abdullah and he was soon arrested. Hence, Kashmiris regard 1953 as a significant year as it shifted the ground on what autonomy meant for the state. Bakshi Ghulam Mohammed succeeded Sheikh Abdullah and inaugurated a difficult chapter for Kashmir.

The erstwhile PEPSU (Patiala and East Punjab States Union) was the first state to have a non-Congress government. Its chief minister, Gyan Singh Rarewala, resigned in March 1953, after an election tribunal struck down his election. He led the United Front in the state.

The First Backward Classes Commission headed by Kaka Kalelkar was set up this year. Decades later, the Second Backward Classes Commission, headed by B.P. Mandal, became politically sensitive, introducing the idea of reservation and quotas for socially, educationally and economically backward classes.

The University Grants Commission, which was to be the apex body for higher education, was set up this year. The Sangeet Natak Akademi came into being in January in 1953. The All India Khadi and Village Industries Board (renamed Commission in April 1957) too came into existence this year.

Hindustan Machine Tools (HMT) was set up in Bangalore at a place which had previously served as a hangar during the Second World War. HMT was to produce a variety of things, but most memorably, wrist watches.

The Archbishop of Bombay, the Karachi-born Valerian Gracias, became the first Indian to be named as a cardinal by the Vatican.

## 1954: *Tu Chhed Ek Baar, Mann Ka Sitar*

*Raat bani dulhan, bhigi hui palake*
*Bhini bhini kushboo se sagar chhalake*
*Aise me nainaa se, nainaa ho chaar*
*Zaraa nainaa ho chaar, raahi matavaale*

Lyricist: Qamar Jalalabadi
Music: Anil Biswas
Singers: Talat Mehmood and Suraiya
Film: *Waaris*

THE composer of this dulcet duet, Anil Biswas, or Anil-da, was also known as the 'composer's composer'. Critics recall him being firm; it was to be all about melody and well-rounded melodies. He 'did not care much about beats' that were becoming very important. Growing up in East Bengal, hearing both songs of Bhatiyali boatmen and those of his mother, who had trained as a classical musician, he was a child prodigy and learnt to sing at the age of four. He participated in the freedom movement, did time in jail too as a consequence and finally started composing music in the 1930s. Anil-da, they say, chose to just do the kind of music he wanted to do and retired when he felt he was out of tune with the times. This song (strongly reminiscent of '*Ore grihabasi, khol dwar khol*'), speaks of Rabindra Sangeet's indelible influence on Anil-da.

This remains among his finest compositions, and the voices of Talat and Suraiya lent it the right lightness of spirit and enhanced its sprightly but mellow mood.

The lyricist, Qamar Jalalabadi, was born Om Prakash Bhandari in Jalalabad and was given his pen name (Qamar, meaning moon) by a poet in his hometown who had served as a source of encouragement for him. Jalalabadi started work as a journalist, writing for Lahore-based newspapers after his graduation. He was versatile and he wrote all kinds of songs, romantic like this one, and poems exhorting people to action.

Hindi film songs of the time elaborately marked the absence of and yearning for the beloved. In its 'happy' version, this song is bold and racy, as both lovers are celebrating companionship and being together in a very uninhibited manner. The hero and heroine travel in a train, with the girl dressed as a man, blasé in a man's shirt, preferring to travel in a general compartment to dodge the ladies bogey.

This song which celebrates pure, unfettered love is an apt marker for this year, which saw the enactment of Special Marriage Act, 1954. This was a landmark legislation and it replaced the old Act III, 1872, which was found to be inadequate. This Act of Parliament provided for a civil marriage for people who had renounced all faith and did not intend to solemnize their union in the name of God. This provided for inter-faith as well as inter-caste marriages and also their registration, divorce and succession. This, in more ways than one, was a very progressive step and ahead of its time. By recognizing inter-caste and inter-faith weddings, the Indian state gave a huge push for progressive thought and integration.

This year was also important for a big step that the Indian government took with reference to hydel power and constructing dams. One of India's first river valley projects, the Bhakra dam, was inaugurated over the River Sutlej in 1954. This and the Nangal dam close by are referred to as the Bhakra Nangal project. At the inaugural speech here, Prime Minister Nehru challenged tradition by terming this project, along with scientific centres, steel factories and educational institutes, the 'temples of modern India'. This was an important part of the nation building that Nehru envisioned and was able to get going.

In hindsight, 1954 was to prove to be a significant year for Sino-Indian ties. India, on 29 April 1954, signed an agreement with China on trade and other activities between India and Tibet. Under this agreement, India gave up all extra-territorial rights and privileges that it had inherited from the British Raj and recognized Tibet as part of China. The question of Tibet has bedevilled the relations between India and China. However, in 2003, Prime Minister Atal Bihari Vajpayee reiterated the 1954 agreement and once again recognized Tibet as a part of the People's Republic of China.

The Bharat Ratna and the Padma awards (state awards to eminent persons in diverse fields) were inaugurated this year. The first Bharat Ratnas went to C. Rajagopalachari, S. Radhakrishnan and C.V. Raman.

The Indian cricket Test team made its maiden journey to Pakistan this year, stepping across the border under the captaincy of Vinoo Mankad on 28 December 1954. Pakistan's Test team was led by Abdul Kardar. All the matches in the series were drawn.

It was a year of plenty of activity in the cultural field as the National Film Awards were inaugurated – starting with the cinema of 1953. Marathi film *Shyamchi Aai*, directed by Pralhad Keshav Atre, won the gold medal for the Best Feature Film. In the documentary section, *Mahabalipuram*, in English, produced by the Films Division, got the gold medal. There were three categories to begin with: feature films, documentaries and childrens' film, across all languages. There was no gold medal for the childrens' film section this year.

The Sahitya Akademi, the Lalit Kala Akademi and the National Gallery of Modern Art too were set up and inaugurated this year. Films, literature, fine arts and modern art in India all got a fillip in 1954.

French India – or the French Indian territories – which were scattered across the eastern and western coasts – Pondicherry, Mahe, Karikal and Yanam – were handed over to India and were turned into a union territory called Pondicherry. Chandernagore (now Chandannagar) was integrated into West Bengal this year.

India had truly got going, and a lot of things that needed to be done with building a modern Indian nation, beyond even boundary fixing and managing basics, were on their way to being put in place.

# 1955: *Apalam Chapalam*

*Tedha-medha khel hai*
*Yeh pyaar jo main jaanati*
*Bhul ke bhi baat kabhi*
*Dil ki na maanati*

Lyrics: Rajendra Krishan
Music: C. Ramachandra
Singers: Lata Mangeshkar and Usha Mangeshkar
Film: *Azad*

THIS song exemplified the marvel of sisterhood, in many senses. Sayee and Subbulakshmi, teenaged sisters from Madras, students of Muthuswami Pillai, danced barely two years after their arangetram (first public performance) in a sparkling performance that brought the spring and skill of Bharatanatyam bang on to the film sets of *Azad*. But eventually, the film was to be seen as Dilip Kumar's film.

The lyricist and music director, the duo of Rajendra Krishan and C. Ramachandra, were to convert the phrase *apalam chapalam*, with its strong Tamil sensibility, into a simple but evocative Hindustani one, in a way that made this a most delicious song.

Sayee and Subbulakshmi did at least thirteen Tamil films and one more Hindi film. Apart from Bharatanatyam, they danced in Kathak and folk styles too, which at the time was unusual but was to herald an India where its diversity allowed even purists to borrow and share and go beyond the exploration of just one form or idea.

Adding to this memorable number were the voices of the Mangeshkar sisters. Usha, the least known of them, showcases her talent here with Lata at her playful best. Lata was to grow from here into the legend we now know her as.

*Azad* was a remake of the Tamil film, *Malaikkallan*, or Thief of the Hills, made a year ago, which introduced the idea of Robin Hood in Tamil cinema. The original Tamil film had dialogues by M. Karunanidhi and had M.G. Ramachandran (MGR) and Bhanumathi in the lead.

The year began with the ruling Congress party declaring in its session held in January at Avadi in Tamil Nadu that a 'socialistic pattern of society' was to be its goal. The First Five-Year Plan was in place by now and the high-minded goals of ensuring equality seemed to the party to point towards socialism as the way forward and this led the party to adopt the 'Avadi resolution'.

In April 1955, India participated in the Bandung Conference in Indonesia, a meeting of twenty-nine Asian and African countries, which would have repercussions on world politics for decades to come. It was a time of great possibilities as colonial rule had ended over large swathes of the world in the early and mid-twentieth century. Now, caught in the middle of a 'cold war', the Bandung Conference presented a new way of looking at the world. Led by Indonesia, India, Burma and Sri Lanka, a new framework of self-assertion and self-interest was sought to be created.

A ten-point charter, inspired by the UN Charter and Prime Minister Jawaharlal Nehru's Panchsheel/Five Principles (mutual respect for each other's territorial integrity and sovereignty; mutual non-aggression; mutual non-interference in each other's internal affairs, equality and cooperation for mutual benefit; and peaceful co-existence), was adopted unanimously. Non-alignment would face several challenges, but this was a key benchmark that made the world sit up and take notice of India and its political leadership, well before its GDP (gross domestic product), economics or 'middle class' made others take note. It was an exercise in enhancing India's goals for itself and its self-image; it helped India grow and come into its own. Decolonization got welded into the idea of who the people of these countries saw themselves as and what they wanted to be.

It also enhanced Prime Minister Nehru's charisma back home. He was awarded the Bharat Ratna this year by President Rajendra Prasad.

India got what is recognized as its first 'computer' in 1955. India's first computer was a small analogue device built in 1953 at the Indian Statistical Institute, based at Calcutta, which was used to solve linear equations. But this year, a British-built HEC-2M was imported from Britain for ₹10 lakh. The computer was a behemoth measuring 10 feet in length, 7 feet in breadth, and 6 feet in height. It had no keyboard, monitor, or even a processor, and was armed with a generous 3 KB worth of memory. Input was fed into it using punched cards and output was printed out via an attached printer. The computer took around 15 minutes to calculate the square root of a 16-digit number. But it was still used to solve complex differential equations (among other things) sent to the institute by Homi J. Bhabha of the Tata Institute of Fundamental Research (TIFR).

Narinder Singh Kapany, a lad born in Moga (Punjab), first went to work in the Indian Ordnance Factory Service, and then went on to study at the Imperial College, London. Kapany was to eventually coin the phrase 'fibre optics' in an article for *Scientific American* in 1960. But in this year, along with Harold Hopkins, he achieved a breakthrough in the field of image transmission through optical fibres.

It was in 1955 that the Imperial Bank of India, the largest commercial bank in the subcontinent, was turned into the State Bank of India.

The Indus Valley civilization, in many ways a mystery till today as its script has yet to be deciphered, unlike other river-valley civilizations that existed at the time, was proven to be much larger than imagined before. The dock at Lothal, the ancient site in the district of Ahmedabad in Gujarat, was discovered this year.

India's National Chess Championship was instituted at Eluru in Andhra Pradesh this year. The first championship was won by R.C. Sapre (Maharashtra) and D. Venkaiya (Andhra Pradesh).

Bharat Petroleum was to start the manufacture of liquefied petroleum gas (LPG) and start selling it in a cylinder from this year. The gas cylinder has been an important and almost indispensable part of India's journey from escaping the chulha and making cooking easier, something closely linked with freeing women from household chores.

The Hindu Marriage Act, 1955, came into force this year, codifying Hindu marriages and introducing several reformist measures. The process for this had started in the British period, and it was Jawaharlal Nehru's reformist zeal that took matters forward. Faced with severe criticism from the Hindu Right, led by Syama Prasad Mookerjee, who went on to found the Bharatiya Jana Sangh, Nehru had shelved plans till after the general elections. In protest, B.R. Ambedkar had resigned from the Union cabinet.

Nehru also faced opposition to the move from President Rajendra Prasad, a social conservative, but Nehru firmly believed it was essential to reform Hindu law as a precursor to reforming laws of minority communities. So, the bills postponed in the early 1950s started rolling out this year: bills on marriage; succession and inheritance; minority and guardianship; and adoption and maintenance. The Hindu Marriage Act was the first of the lot.

Nehru wrote in June 1955: 'Even though we have a multitude of problems and difficulties surround us and often appear to overwhelm, there is the air of hope in this country, a faith in our future and a certain reliance on the basic principles that have guided us thus far. There is the breath of the dawn, the feeling of the beginning of a new era in the long and chequered history of India.'

As a very Tamil-sounding, foot-tapping '*Apalam chapalam*' was being hummed by so many Hindi-speaking fans, the language dispute in India had become more pressing and would lead to a change in the map of India next year.

# 1956: Ae *Dil Hai Mushkil Jeena Yahaan*

*Ae dil hai mushkil jeena yahaan*
*Zara hatke zara bach ke*
*Yeh hai Bambai meri jaan*

Lyrics: Majrooh Sultanpuri
Music: O.P. Nayyar
Singers: Mohammed Rafi and Geeta Dutt
Film: *C.I.D.*

'A*E dil hai mushkil jeena yahaan*' was a product of a triumvirate which spelt box-office success in the 1950s: Mohammed Rafi singing for comedian Johnny Walker, with music by O.P. Nayyar. This particular song was not an original as it was based on '*Oh my darling, Clementine*', the upbeat American Western folk ballad. The tune provided the contrast to the lyrics of Majrooh Sultanpuri, which is a pessimistic commentary on the inhumanity of a large city and deals with the vagaries of urban life. Walker's jaunty walk and inimitable grin mitigate the poignancy and bring cheer to the viewer, who is taken on a tonga ride through Bombay's streets. Kumkum joins Walker in the latter half of the song and the playback for her is provided by Geeta Dutt.

The film was produced by Guru Dutt and marked the directorial debut of his long-time assistant, Raj Khosla. Dev Anand and Shakila were the lead pair, while the movie introduced Waheeda Rehman to Hindi films. As with most songs filmed on Walker in that era, they are intended to provide a comic relief from either the pessimistic mood of a *Pyaasa* or from the intensity of a thriller drama, as in the case of *C.I.D.* Walker, whose real name was Badruddin Jamaluddin Kazi, plays a pickpocket in the film – he keeps bumping against people and after each such collision, he ends up with the purse of the other person – but his philosophy about the city is profound.

Walker used to work as a BEST bus conductor in Bombay, regaling passengers with funny tales and cracking jokes while he issued them tickets. He had an inimitable way of calling out the names of the stops, which is supposed to have caught the eye of actor Balraj Sahni while travelling in a BEST bus. An amused Balraj, who was scripting the screenplay for Guru Dutt's *Baazi* (1951), recommended him to Dutt. Following a successful audition with Dutt as a drunkard, Kazi was immediately taken on board for *Baazi* though it was nearing completion. Expectedly, the role was that of a drunkard and Kazi was rechristened by a delighted Dutt as Johnny Walker, after Dutt's favourite whisky. Kazi, however, was an avowed teetotaller.

Meanwhile, not very far from Bombay, Dr B.R. Ambedkar chose to embrace Buddhism along with nearly two lakh followers, living his statement from 1935 that while he was born a Hindu, he wouldn't die one. In less than two months after converting to Buddhism, Ambedkar passed away. Before that, he witnessed the passage of the Hindu Succession Act in June. The Act, which recognized the right of inheritance of Hindu women along with the male successors when some property was left without a will, was part of Hindu Reform Bill Ambedkar had pushed very hard as a law minister but couldn't see through. Nehru split the bill into four separate ones and piloted them successfully, despite the opposition of the RSS, Hindu Mahasabha, Bharatiya Jana Sangh and conservative sections of the Congress party.

The States Reorganization Bill was passed by parliament in November. It provided for fourteen states and six centrally administered territories. It was based on the recommendations of the States Reorganization Commission formed in 1953, comprising Justice Fazl Ali, K.M. Panikkar and Hridaynath Kunzru, which had submitted its report in October 1955.

The commission's recommendations were broadly accepted by the government, with certain modifications.

The strongest reaction against the commission's recommendations and the Act came from Maharashtra where widespread rioting broke out and eighty people were killed in police firing in Bombay in January. Under pressure, the government decided in June 1956 to divide the Bombay state into two linguistic states of Maharashtra and Gujarat with Bombay city forming a separate, centrally administered Union territory, which was again opposed strongly by the Maharashtrians. In July, Nehru reverted to the formation of a greater, bilingual Bombay, which was now opposed by the people of both Maharashtra and Gujarat. C.D. Deshmukh, the then Union finance minister, resigned from the cabinet on the issue of Bombay not being given to Maharashtra; Gujaratis wanted Bombay in their own state. The matter would continue to fester, spawning violence and arson, besides loss of electoral support to the Congress party in Bombay.

This was the year Nehru responded very firmly to the violent secessionist movement in Nagaland, where separatists under A.Z. Phizo had declared the formation of an independent state in 1956. He sent the army to Nagaland to restore peace and order, hoping that a quick and strong military action would make the rebels realize that they were in a no-win situation. This would lead to the promulgation of Armed Forces Special Powers Act (AFSPA) in 1958 in the states of the north-east, which was based on the Armed Forces (Special Powers) Ordinance, 1942, which aimed 'to confer special powers upon certain officers of the Armed Forces'. Ironically, the 1942 Ordinance was promulgated by the British viceroy under Section 72 of the Government of India Act, 1935, to crush the Quit India movement launched by the Congress party.

The meeting at Brioni in Yugoslavia between President Josip Broz Tito of Yugoslavia, President Gamal Abdel Nasser of Egypt and Prime Minister Jawaharlal Nehru of India in January 1956 led to the formation of the Non-aligned Movement. When Egypt nationalized the Suez Canal in response to US and British pressure to abandon its non-aligned policy, India mooted a proposal that stipulated Egyptian control of the Canal, an advisory role for the users, and settlement of disputes in accordance with the UN Charter in

August at the London Conference, which met with widespread approval, including from Egypt. Later, when France and Britain got Israel to attack Egypt and landed their troops in Suez, Nehru called it 'naked aggression' and a 'reversion to the past colonial methods'. Indian troops participated in large numbers in the peacekeeping force as the withdrawal of Western forces took place under UN supervision.

When the Soviet Union sent its forces into Hungary in October, India refrained from issuing a formal condemnation although Nehru criticized the Soviet Union and did not send an ambassador to Budapest for two years to show his unhappiness. The Soviets reciprocated by abstaining when the Kashmir issue came up next at the UN Security Council. They reverted to their usual veto thereafter, but it highlighted the precarious situation India was in.

The Soviets readily came forward with assistance in the building of the Bhilai Steel Plant, as Western powers, especially the US, hesitated to help. India's need for industrialization, especially in heavy industry, brought India closer to the Soviet Union. This was all part of the Second Five-Year Plan which focused on industrial growth with a leading role for the public sector, as envisaged by P. C. Mahalanobis.

Life insurance business was nationalized in September, and India's most profitable and reputed public-sector company, the Oil and Natural Gas Commission (ONGC), was established the same month. In October, government-owned Ashoka Hotel was opened in New Delhi. India's first five-star deluxe hotel, it was built to accommodate delegates of the UNESCO at its first out-of-Europe session. Delhi also saw the opening of the All India Institute of Medical Sciences (AIIMS) – the construction of which was funded by the Government of New Zealand – which remains to date the country's premier medical institute.

This was the year in which the Indian hockey team, led by Balbir Singh (Sr), won another Gold at the Melbourne Olympics. The Australian cricket team also made its first visit to India for a three-Test series, winning it 2–0.

The main opposition party in the country, the Communist Party of India (CPI), made two major changes in its position at the Palghat (now Palakkad) Congress. It accepted that India had won independence in 1947 and was now a sovereign republic. The party now held that the government's policies were directed at building capitalism but by following anti-people policies and giving concessions to the imperialists. The party's main task was to build a 'democratic front' to replace Congress, but this was not to be anti-Congress as Congress contained many democrats who had to be won over and detached from their leaders.

Meanwhile, India entered the nuclear age when Apsara, its first nuclear reactor in Trombay, Bombay, also the first in Asia, went critical in August. The city also had the honour of having the first woman mayor, Sulochana Modi, whose tenure lasted only for three months. Bombay was the happening place, and the people had to live '*Zara hatke, zara bachke; yeh hai Bombay meri jaan*'.

# 1957: *Yeh Duniya Agar Mil Bhi Jaaye*

*Yeh mehlo, yeh takhto, yeh taajo ki duniya,*
*Yeh insaan ke dushman samaajo ki duniya,*
*Yeh daulat ke bhookhe riwaajo ki duniya,*
*Yeh duniya agar mil bhi jaaye toh kya hai?*

Lyrics: Sahir Ludhianvi
Music: S.D. Burman
Singer: Mohammed Rafi
Film: *Pyaasa*

*PYAASA* is widely regarded among the best Hindi films ever made. It was made within the conventions of Hindi cinema but it went beyond them. As a result, the film appeals to both Indian and international audiences. Rated by *Time* magazine among the top 100 must-watch films, it is rightfully celebrated for its storytelling, performances, camerawork, poetry, music, lyrics and wonderful songs. The film is about a jobless poet, played by Guru Dutt, also the director of the film, who is deemed a failure but becomes a huge success after he is mistakenly presumed dead. He arrives at his own memorial, only to denounce the world and walk away from it.

Sahir Ludhianvi, the film's lyricist, was a poet of great repute and the name of his book of poems, *Parchhaiyan*, was the name of the book in the film which makes the poet famous after his presumed death. Sahir's lyrics for *Pyaasa* are among the most famous and loved of all Hindi films, set to S.D. Burman's music and mostly sung by Mohammed Rafi and Geeta Dutt, Guru Dutt's wife. Unfortunately, this is the last time Burman and Sahir worked together, as they fell out in a clash of egos.

Rachel Dwyer has noted that the film has an extraordinary amount of Christian imagery and references, including in the song, '*Yeh duniya agar mil bhi jaaye*', which comes at the climax of the film as the poet decides to walk away from the world while his success is being celebrated at his memorial. In this great set piece, masterfully sung by Mohammed Rafi with little music, the chorus is a translation of Matthew 16.26: 'For what will it profit a man, if he gains the whole world, and loses his own soul?' In perhaps the most iconic visual from the movie, Guru Dutt appears in this song standing backlit in the door like Christ by the empty tomb. The song starts softly as a whisper, building up to a crescendo where the poet's desire to burn the world is also Biblical, Matthew 3.12: 'He will burn up the chaff with unquenchable fire...'

'*Yeh duniya agar mil bhi jaye*' remains a classic because of Guru Dutt's mastery over his craft: the picturization, aided by rhythmic editing, stark lighting and fluid camera movements of V.K. Murthy, which magnifies the impact of music and the lyrics manifold. It is the finest example of a film-maker seamlessly harmonizing the audio and video into a storyline. A dark and sombre film, *Pyaasa* was panned by reviewers when it was released and not many gave it a chance of succeeding at the box office. But it was a box-office success, in a year which also saw the release of *Naya Daur*, *Mother India* and *Musafir*.

The year marked a decade of India's independence, and *Pyaasa* captured Guru Dutt's reaction to the corruption and degradation around him, masterfully captured in the song '*Jinhe naaz hai Hind par woh kahaan hai*'. But his is a moral disgust rather than political – he shows his romantic, ineffectual response to the world that surrounds him by producing beautiful poetry.

The moral disgust at the political disappointment is best captured by the Mundhra affair, the first major financial scandal in independent India. On 4 September, Ram Subhag Singh, a Congress MP posed a question in the Lok Sabha about this incident based on an obscure newspaper report. It soon emerged that in June 1957 the Life Insurance Corporation (LIC) had bought ₹1.24 crore worth of fraudulent stock in six companies owned by Haridas Mundhra, a Calcutta-based businessman. The investment was the largest that LIC had made in its short history, but contrary to regulations, its investment committee had not been consulted on the decision.

The crusade to demand an explanation for LIC's decision was led, in an odd soap-operatic twist, by Feroze Gandhi, estranged son-in-law of Nehru. In hectoring speeches in the Lok Sabha, Feroze Gandhi charged that the principal finance secretary, H.M. Patel, and the finance minister, T.T. Krishnamachari, had pushed LIC's investment through. In response, in early 1958, Nehru appointed former chief justice of the Bombay High Court M.C. Chagla as a one-man commission of inquiry.

The hearings of the Chagla Commission were conducted in public; such huge crowds attended that loudspeakers had to be set up for people who remained outside the court room. Chagla worked remarkably fast and submitted his report in less than a month, indicting Krishnamachari, who resigned on 18 February 1958. Mundhra, arrested from the Claridges Hotel in New Delhi, went to prison for twenty-two years.

It only showed that the making of a new nation, however, was a prolonged and continuous process, which was open to challenges, interruption, disruption and even reversals. As Nehru said then, 'Personally, I feel that the biggest task of all is not only the economic development of India as a whole, but even more so the psychological and emotional integration of the people of India.'

One of those challenges revolved around the question of language. Following the submission of the report of the Official Language Commission in 1956, sharp differences on the official languages issue crept up. The commission had recommended that Hindi should start progressively replacing English in various functions of the Central government, with effective change taking place in 1965. Two members of the commission, from West Bengal and Tamil Nadu, dissented, alleging that other members had a pro-Hindi bias and that the use of English should continue.

The commission's report was sent for review to a special Joint Parliamentary Committee, but Ram Manohar Lohia's Samyukta Socialist Party and the Jana Sangh launched a militant movement, which continued for nearly two years. One of the agitational methods adopted by the followers of Lohia on a large scale was to deface English signboards of shops and in other places. Nehru, however, handled the matter with great caution and care, promising time and again that an official language could not and would not be imposed on any region of the country and the pace of imposition of Hindi would be determined keeping in view the wishes of the non-Hindi-speaking people.

Democratic system and processes were taking deeper root as the country saw the second general elections for the Lok Sabha and state assemblies, in which the voter turnout marginally improved to 47 per cent from 46 per cent in 1952. Nearly 193 million Indians were registered to vote, which included 94 per cent of adult women. The elections were held over a period of three weeks and cost the exchequer ₹45 million less than the previous one. The election was a referendum on the Congress party and its government, with Nehru being the chief campaigner and vote catcher for the party.

The Congress party again gained an overwhelming majority of seats in the Lok Sabha though with a diminished share of votes, and neither the Right nor the Left could pose a serious challenge to it despite denting the Congress hegemony in a few states. In fact, the Communist Party of India was able to form a government in Kerala, which was the first democratically elected communist government anywhere in the world. This government was dismissed by Nehru in 1959, a huge blemish on his stellar democratic record, and president's rule was imposed in the state.

After the general elections, Jayaprakash Narayan retired from politics, declaring that party politics was not suitable for India and advocated, instead, 'partyless democracy'. Nehru, meanwhile, was at the peak of his popularity and public approval, with his birthday being officially announced as the Children's Day of India.

A decade after Independence, India introduced the naya paisa – the prefix naya was removed in 1964 – as the decimal coinage was initiated via the Indian Coinage Act; postage stamps and postal stationary was also introduced in the decimal system. A new national calendar was also adopted which happened to be seventy-eight years behind the Christian era.

The National Book Trust was set up to produce good literature and ensure its availability at reasonable prices. The Central Warehousing Corporation and the Export Risk Insurance Corporation were set up this year.

To compete with Radio Ceylon, which mainly broadcast Hindi film songs, the All India Radio started a new service, Vividh Bharati, which was to gain great popularity.

It was the year when the first-ever Davis Cup match was played on Indian soil, which was won by the Indian team led by Ramanathan Krishnan.

In November, President Rajendra Prasad unveiled the National War Memorial at India Gate, in the memory of 25,000 Indian soldiers who gave their lives during the Second World War. A war memorial for those who died in the independence movement or in various wars after Independence still awaits the light of day. For those who are long gone, '*Yeh duniya agar mil bhi jaaye toh kya hai...*'

# 1958: *Suhana Safar*

*Suhana safar*
*aur yeh mausam haseen*
*Humein dar hai ki*
*hum kho na jaayen kaheen*

Lyrics: Shailendra
Music: Salil Chowdhury
Singer: Mukesh
Film: *Madhumati*

ONE of the earliest films featuring a tale of reincarnation that spawned a chain of such films for decades, *Madhumati* captivated the audience with its theme and music, setting benchmarks for quality in Hindi cinema. The names of people associated with the film speak for themselves: story and screenplay by Ritwik Ghatak, dialogue by Rajendra Singh Bedi, cinematography by Dilip Gupta, editing by Hrishikesh Mukherjee, music by Salil Chowdhury, all under the direction of Bimal Roy. Roy was well known for his earlier masterpieces, mostly serious films like *Do Bigha Zamin* (1953), *Biraj Bahu* (1954) and *Devdas* (1955). While *Devdas* had been critically acclaimed, it had not been commercially successful, putting a lot of pressure on Roy. But *Madhumati* set that record right, earning ₹4 crore and emerging as the highest earner of the year, an amount that equals ₹500 crore in current value.

The film won the National Film Award for Best Feature Film in Hindi and nine Filmfare Awards – including for Best Film, Best Director, Best Music Director, Best Female Playback Singer, Best Dialogue, Best Art Direction and Best Cinematographer – the most awards for a single film at that time. The soul of the blockbuster film was the music, enchanting and timeless, which continues to be hummed till date. Distributors, who financed the film, did not want Salil Chowdhury as the music director because he was considered unlucky; they were supported by the lead actor, Dilip Kumar, who also wanted Naushad to compose the music for the film. But Roy decided to give a chance to Chowdhury, convincing Dilip Kumar that he would replace Chowdhury if his music was not up to the mark. Chowdhury ended up signing nineteen films after the release of *Madhumati*; so much for bringing bad luck!

In her book *Bimal Roy's Madhumati: Untold Stories from Behind the Scenes*, Roy's daughter Rinki Bhattacharya gives the story of how the signature tune of the film, '*Suhana safar aur yeh mausam haseen*' came to be composed, as told to her by Salil Chowdhury's son, Sanjoy: 'Baba and Shailendra had driven up to Khandala one day. As they stood at the top of the Khandala Ghats they saw a goatherd rounding up his flock. The man was making a sharp sound which resembled "urrrrrrrrrrrr". On the spot, Baba composed the opening notation for "*Suhana safar*" including the goatherd's call.'

The song was to be originally sung by Talat Mehmood and not Mukesh, says Rinki Bhattacharya: 'It is believed that the singer originally intended for this iconic song was Talat Mehmood. Mukeshji, it seems, was going through a financial crunch. His situation prompted Talat Mehmood to suggest that the song be given to Mukesh.' That was the spirit of that era, which is also seen in Nehru's letter to the Congress Parliamentary Party on 29 April.

Nehru, who was then at the peak of his popularity and public acceptability, wrote: '... it is over eleven-and-a-half years since I became a member of the government and ten-and-a-half years since I became prime minister of India. ... These years have been very heavy with work and problems. ... The work of a prime minister allows for no respite; it is continuous and unceasing. ... There is little time for quiet thinking. I feel now that I must have a period when I can free myself from this daily burden and can think of myself as an individual citizen of India and not as prime minister. ... I have ventured to place my thoughts before my colleagues in the party frankly, and I seek their permission to act in the manner suggested. I must add that I have made my submission to the President on these lines. But the final decision must rest with our party.'

The Congress party discussed the matter and on 3 May Nehru bowed to the wishes of the party that he should give up all thought of stepping down from the position of prime minister.

Under Nehru's pressure, Sheikh Abdullah was released from prison on 8 January – he had been arrested in 1953 following his government's dismissal after he publicly advocated independence for Kashmir – but he was arrested again three months later as he continued with his separatist campaign.

Meanwhile, the communist government in Kerala had got embroiled in controversy over its education reform bill which brought protesting Christian clergy to the street. A democratically elected communist government remained a mystery to foreign observers, such as Hungarian writer George Mikes who travelled through India. 'What is a democratic Central government to do with a Communist state?' Mikes asked. 'What would the American administration do if California or Wisconsin suddenly – and I admit, somewhat unexpectedly – turned Communist? And again, how is a Communist government itself to behave with democratic overlords sitting on its neck?'

As these questions were being raised from the Left, C. Rajagopalachari, popularly known as Rajaji, was looking for alternatives on the Right. A year before he started the Swatantra Party in 1959, he published an article in May, titled 'Wanted: Independent Thinking'. He argued that 'probably the main cause for the collapse of independent thinking' in India was 'the long reign of popular favourites without any significant opposition'. However, a healthy democracy required 'an opposition that thinks differently and does not just want more of the same, a group of vigorously thinking citizens which aims at general welfare, and not one that in order to get more votes from the so-called have-nots, offers more to them than the party in power has given, an opposition that appeals to reason ...'

Meanwhile, the Central government continued with its emphasis on creating institutes of higher learning, particularly in the field of science and technology. IIT Bombay was inaugurated in July with 100 students in the first year, whose classes were held in a portion of the Silk and Art Silk Mills Research Association in Worli as the building in Powai was not ready yet. Marathwada University was inaugurated in Aurangabad in August, as was the Institute of Tibetology in Gangtok in October. In November, India also got its first explosives factory, which came up at Gomia, in what is today Jharkhand.

Finally, the Supreme Court had a building of its own, constructed in the Indo-classical style of architecture in the heart of Delhi. With a central dome 117 feet (35.66 metre) high, it has a total floor space of 18.85 lakh square feet (175,116 square metre).

On Gandhi Jayanti, the government announced that it was switching to the metric system, which had by then become the global standard.

It was also a year of many firsts for the country. Noted Gandhian Vinoba Bhave became the first-ever recipient of the Magsaysay Award, while Wilson John became the first Indian to win an individual world title when he won the World Amateur Billiards Championship. In April, the Indian Navy got its first Indian chief, Vice Admiral R.D. Katari. In a year interspersed with happy moments on a challenging landscape, it was a time for '*Suhana safar aur yeh mausam haseen*'.

# 1959: *Waqt Ne Kiya Kya Haseen Sitam*

*Waqt ne kiya*
*Kya haseen sitam*
*Tum rahe na tum*
*Hum rahe na hum*

Lyrics: Kaifi Azmi
Music: S.D. Burman
Singer: Geeta Dutt
Film: *Kaagaz Ke Phool*

THERE are very few films which are overwhelmingly rejected when they are released, but are seen as all-time classics much later. In the history of Hindi cinema, *Kaagaz Ke Phool* leads that pack of films. It was a commercial and critical disaster when released but was rediscovered as a classic in the 1980s, and is now considered to be a masterpiece of Hindi cinema. *Kaagaz Ke Phool* followed the stupendous commercial success and critical acclaim of *Pyaasa*, and Guru Dutt had devoted two years to the film. The film's failure was such a setback for Guru Dutt that he refused to lend his name as director to any more movies, and he was shattered on the personal front too.

While *Kaagaz Ke Phool* remains a classic in the portrayal of the vagaries of the film industry, its music and songs were not as much of a strong point as in other Guru Dutt films. But '*Waqt ne kiya kya haseen sitam*' is a timeless song, considered to be perhaps the best song of Geeta Dutt's career. The pain in her voice sounds genuine, as she gently glides over the notes in a rather simple tune. Kaifi Azmi, who wrote the lyrics of the song, told Nasreen Munni Kabir: 'S.D. Burman played the base tune that everyone liked. But the film had no situation for the song. As has happened on innumerable occasions in Hindi films, one had to be created at the behest of Guru Dutt.' Azmi wrote two versions of the lyrics, penning them to the metre but both were rejected. Guru Dutt then suggested using the tune in some other film, but immediately came up with the idea of a new and suitable situation, leading Azmi to quickly pen the lyrics which were to become immortal.

'*Waqt ne kiya*' also has a memorable shot where a translucent parallel beam of light shining down from the roof is used to highlight the heroine Waheeda Rehman's face. *Kaagaz Ke Phool* was the first Indian film to be shot in cinemascope and V.K. Murthy, the film's cinematographer, later recounted: 'If I were to use focus spotlights it would give a divergent and not parallel beam.' On the third day of the ten-day shoot, Murthy told 'the production people to get me two big mirrors, about 4 feet by 3 feet. I kept one mirror on the terrace and through it, I reflected the light on the one inside, which was placed on the catwalk. From the second mirror, I was able to divert the light to any angle I wanted. I used a little bit of dust and smoke.' And an all-time classic was shot.

The hit music of the year also came from S.D. Burman, but for Bimal Roy's *Sujata* which espoused the Gandhian crusade against untouchability without being preachy. The film was based on the eponymous novel by writer-journalist Subodh Ghosh, who had earlier worked with Mahatma Gandhi. But the year started with another Gandhi, Indira Gandhi, taking over as the president of the Congress party in February. She was the fourth woman president of the party, and although she had been a freedom fighter and a member of the Congress Working Committee, Nehru said: 'Nobody had mentioned it to me before, and it came rather as a surprise. I gave a good deal of thought to this matter and I came to the conclusion that I should firmly keep apart from this business and not try to influence it in any way except rather generally and broadly to say that it has its disadvantages.'

Nehru's view that 'Normally speaking it is not a good thing for my daughter to come in as the Congress President when I am the Prime Minister' of course didn't cut much ice with the party which chose Indira. It was during her time as president, and on her urging, that Nehru got the biggest blemish on his democratic credentials: sacking the communist government in Kerala over the violent protest created by the opposition to its education policy.

The year saw a major upheaval in India–China relations as after a big revolt in Tibet the Dalai Lama fled to India with thousands of his followers. He spent his first night on Indian soil at the Buddhist monastery at Tawang, before making his way to Tezpur. Within three weeks, he was taken to Delhi to meet Nehru. Although India had accepted China's rights over Tibet in a 1954 treaty, Nehru gave them asylum as refugees. They were, however, not allowed to set up a government-in-exile and were dissuaded from conducting political activities. But the Chinese were unhappy, and soon after, they opened fire on an Indian patrol party near the Kongka Pass in Ladakh, killing five Indian policemen and capturing a dozen others. There had been other clashes on the India–China border and this forced the government to review its border policy; it chose to implement a new 'forward policy' where Indian security forces would establish a series of small posts along or close to the border to assert its territorial claims.

The increasing aggressiveness of China led to a major embarrassment for Nehru when his army chief, General K.S. Thimayya, resigned after a major tiff with Nehru's friend and defence minister, V.K. Krishna Menon. Menon was insistent that the major threat came from Pakistan, not China, but what precipitated the crisis was Menon's abrasive behaviour with Thimayya and other senior officers. On 31 August, Thimayya wrote to Nehru on how 'impossible it was for me and the other two Chiefs of Staff to carry out our responsibilities under the defence minister'. The news leaked and the matter was raised in parliament. Nehru then called Thimayya to his office, and over two long sessions persuaded him to withdraw his resignation.

Notwithstanding India's tensions with China, the Congress party moved further, programmatically, to the Left when it passed a resolution in its Nagpur session that 'the future agrarian pattern should be that of cooperative joint farming'. Initially service cooperatives were to be established which would ultimately be transformed into farming cooperatives on a purely voluntary basis. In addition, there was to be a ceiling on landholdings and state trading in food grains. These decisions faced opposition both within and outside the party, some of the experiments failed, and except for land ceilings, other proposals were quietly jettisoned.

On 15 September, the president inaugurated the television service in the country, with Philips India providing the equipment to the government. The service, produced with a small transmitter and a makeshift studio in Delhi, started with two programmes a week, on Tuesday and Friday evening, each of one hour's duration.

Established with German collaboration, IIT Madras was inaugurated on 31 July, while IIT Kanpur was also established during the year.

July also saw the launch of the women's magazine *Femina*, with Irene Talyarkhan as its editor. Priced at 50 paise, its initial circulation was around 21,000 copies. It was to cross the million mark in circulation in another four decades, beside getting inextricably linked to the Miss India pageant.

American president Dwight D. Eisenhower visited India towards the end of the year, becoming the first US president to do so. American civil rights leader Martin Luther King Jr had earlier travelled to India in February.

Meanwhile, the Indian Air Force got a new crest, consisting of a Himalayan eagle in a roundel, with the state emblem on top and a scroll with *Nabha Sprisham Deeptam* as the motto. The motto, which meant touching the sky with glory, symbolized the aspirations of the airmen. With that, another linkage with the colonial British symbols was broken by independent India, where the British could perhaps lament, '*waqt ne kiya kya haseen sitam*'.

# 1960s
# Two Wars and Three PMs

## Aye Mere Pyaare Watan

Two wars, three prime ministers,
redrawing of state boundaries,
disenchantment, beginning of green revolution.

1.

2.

3.

4.

1. A patron of the arts: Jawaharlal Nehru with danseuse Mrinalini Sarabhai.

2. The beginning of India's space journey: Preparing to launch the first rocket from the Thumba Equatorial Rocket Launch Station (Thiruvananthapuram).

3. Prime Minister Lal Bahadur Shastri, Nehru's chosen successor, inaugurates a school.

4. Revisiting the 1962 Sino-India war: A poster of the film *Haqeeqat*.

# 1960: *Pyaar Kiya Toh Darna Kya*

*Pyaar kiya toh darna kya*
*Pyaar kiya koi chori nahin ki*
*Chhup chhup aahein bharna kya*
*Parda nahin jab koi khuda se*
*Bando se parda karna kya*

Lyrics: Shakeel Badayuni
Music: Naushad
Singer: Lata Mangeshkar
Film: *Mughal-e-Azam*

As a candescent Madhubala appears equal to a hundred twirling images in Sheesh Mahal, R.D. Mathur's riveting cinematography finds its place in *Mughal-e-Azam* in this year. *Mughal-e-Azam* and its songs, remain a metaphor for splendour, extravagance and a plush way of doing things.

'*Pyaar kiya toh darna kya*' is regarded as one of lyricist Shakeel Badayuni's finest. Its lines, '*Parda nahin jab koi khuda se/Bandon se parda karna kya*', uttered fearlessly by a nautch girl looking straight into the eyes of an imperial Prithviraj Kapoor playing Akbar, and forcing him to lower his gaze, is the stuff of cinematic magic.

Even as Prince Salim's love for a 'mere' dancing girl reveals the fault lines in the Mughal empire, so does India enter a decade of much inversion of rules, uncertainty and churn with 1960.

'*Pyaar kiya toh darna kya*' remains a refrain used to date, for generations born decades after the film, for a variety of forbidden loves in India. Stories about *Mughal-e-Azam* are as famous as the film itself, so it is no surprise that it was the first film picked in 2004 to get a colour makeover.

The story goes that Naushad the music director despaired over two sets of lyrics put out by Shakeel. He forced the lyricist, over an evening session that went on until the morning, to consider a folk song from UP on love not being 'chori' (theft) and reflect the same assertion and abandon in the face of authority.

The film was years in the making, with its director K. Asif having read a play on this apocryphal incident as early as 1944, which planted the idea in his head. Eventually, with K. Asif pulling no punches, the film cost more than any film till then. Each song cost almost as much as was spent on complete films until then. Folk tunes like '*Mohe panghat pe Nandlal chhed gayo re*' added more dimensions to what was already a multifaceted soundtrack, which had Bade Ghulam Ali Khan, the great classicist, singing two songs, '*Prem jogan ban ke*' and '*Shubh din aayo*.

However, '*Pyaar kiya toh darna kya*' found an eerie echo in a landmark court case which concluded this year, K.M. *Nanavati* vs *State of Maharashtra*, which resulted in the end of the jury system in India.

The second-in-command of INS *Mysore* in Bombay since 1959, a dashing and much-decorated naval officer went on to murder the lover (Prem Ahuja) of his English wife Sylvia at point-blank range in his bedroom, shortly after his wife confessed her love to him. Nanavati, in a dramatic move, walked to the nearby police station and confessed his crime.

The uproar that followed the incident resulted in an unprecedented public trial, with very few people not having an opinion on what was 'the right thing' in this scenario. The popular view almost condoned the killing. The tabloid *Blitz*, with its larger-than-life editor Russi Karanjia, made its case for condoning the murder, after much detailed and often lurid reporting on the officer and his wife's lover. When the jury declared him not guilty at the sessions court level, it was objected to in an appeal taken up in the Bombay High Court. Gyan Prakash, the author of *Mumbai Fables*, termed the Nanavati case India's first media trial, 'its own "OJ case"' (referring to the more recent trial of black athlete O.J. Simpson in the US over the murder of his ex-wife and her lover). It is believed that the way *Blitz* went on to cover and mobilize 'public' opinion demonstrated how the 'people' could be weaponized and effectively used to drum up support. The courts at the time took the position that the jury too got influenced by the position taken by people at large backing Nanavati. The jury system was abandoned thereafter.

On 5 September 1960, the Supreme Court issued an order in K.M. Nanavati's petition. The several stages of this trial were to see the emergence of Ram Jethmalani, who assisted the prosecution, as an able criminal lawyer. Eventually, after three years in prison, Nanavati was pardoned by Vijaya Lakshmi Pandit, the state governor, after the deceased Prem Ahuja's sister agreed to the idea.

Later, at least three films *Yeh Raaste Hain Pyar Ke* (1963), *Achanak* (1973) and *Rustom* (2016) were inspired by this dramatic real-life incident.

Other than this landmark case that consumed reams of newsprint, 1960 witnessed rioting in Assam against Bengalis, under the charge that employment opportunities that should belong to Assamese-speaking residents of Assam were being usurped by Bengalis who had migrated, post-Partition. Soon, things got so out of hand that Home Minister Lal Bahadur Shastri had to go to Assam, to reiterate the use of Assamese as the official language, yet allow Bengali to be used where Bengali speakers were in a majority. This was to come back and haunt India in decades to come.

The state of Bombay was split into Gujarat and Maharashtra this year on linguistic lines. Bombay though remained the financial capital of India.

The 1960s were to be about significant cultural and political simmering internationally. India too, as it appears in hindsight, was impacted. However, there was nothing much in this first year to signal this turmoil and anxious questioning after the decade of hope that the 1950s were.

This was an eventful year for Indian sports. Indian hockey suffered a setback at the Rome Olympics. For the first time since 1928, India did not win the Gold, losing to Pakistan in the final match.

In athletics, Milkha Singh's run was to achieve a near-cult status back home, in a country with little to speak of in track events. Milkha finished fourth with a timing of 45.6 seconds in the 400-metre final. This remained the national record for forty-four years.

This was the year when Guru Dutt's hit film *Chaudhvin Ka Chand* was released with its eponymous title track. This was music composer Ravi at work S.D. Burman having refused to work with Dutt after *Kagaz Ke Phool*, which had failed miserably at the box office. A love triangle, set in an old-world 'Nawabi' Lucknow, this song resonated with a significant part of India, familiar with and sentimental about the old feudal order.

# 1961: *Aye Mere Pyaare Watan*

*Aye mere pyaare watan*
*Aye mere bichhde chaman*
*Tujh pe dil qurban*

Lyrics: Prem Dhawan
Music: Salil Chowdhury
Singer: Manna Dey
Film: *Kabuliwala*

BAGGY trousers, *Pathani libas*, bearded faces are captured by the slow pan of the camera as it shifts between Afghan characters, sitting resigned and uneasy in a room in Calcutta. It pauses on the character of Balraj Sahni, as he sings, in Manna Dey's voice, of his lost homeland of Kabul. '*Aye mere pyare watan*', brings alive the pathos of Rabindranath Tagore's story, 'Kabuliwala', in a song lasting 4.58 minutes.

The story is about a dried-fruit seller having come to Calcutta to make a living, where he finds in a young girl the memories of his daughter and his home left behind. The Bengali original, which this film was based on, had music by Ravi Shankar and won the award for music at the Berlin Film Festival, without having a single song. For the Hindi remake, situations like the one with '*Aye mere pyare watan*' had to be created. Yet, this film was distinct in that it had no romantic songs that were the mainstay of films in the 1950s and '60s.

The strength of this song, apart from Salil Chowdhury's melody, is also the manner in which Manna Dey changed his style to deliver it. Madan Mohan spoke of it as being almost a whisper, conveying 'a feeling of eternal peace in spite of the undercurrent of extreme passion'. The recordist, B.N. Sharma, is reported to have asked Manna Dey if anything was wrong with his voice.

The song was written by Prem Dhawan, who went on to pen some popular patriotic songs in films like *Shaheed* and *Purab Aur Paschim*. He had an important role in the making of this memorable film. Dhawan had debuted as a songwriter in 1946, but was also a choreographer and had learnt classical music. Before that, he had participated in plenty of political action against the British, was well known as a member of the Communist Party of India and the IPTA (Indian People's Theatre Association) in Bombay.

The wonder of this song and the times was that it became such a hit, signifying Indian patriotism though it was about a set of Afghan fruit sellers remembering things back home in Kabul.

The idea of patriotism would soon get more complicated in India, with the China dimension casting its shadow. Difficult questions were cropping up over the border with China. The dispute was causing anxiety to not just Prime Minister Nehru but others within his party and outside. The summit with Zhou Enlai having failed, there were a series of white papers by the Government of India.

Speeches made in parliament this year, not just by opposition MPs like socialist Acharya Kripalani and Jana Sangh's Atal Bihari Vajpayee, but by Congress MPs too, added to Nehru's dilemma. The year could not have been an easy one for the prime minister, who was seen as someone interested in making most of the relationship with China, anxious not to escalate matters. Yet he was painted into a corner by public opinion within the country, events on the ground and a defence minister with blinkers on – Krishna Menon.

Historian Srinath Raghavan has written about a meeting of the Foreign Affairs Committee of the cabinet early this year during which Krishna

Menon suggests 'zigzagging', or in the event of the Chinese setting up posts within India, of going behind them and setting up posts, in areas 'which were claimed by China but unoccupied'. But, notes Raghavan, 'no action was initiated, presumably because of the logistical difficulties cited by the army'. Growing concerns in India over the Chinese establishing a post in Chip Chap Valley only four miles east of India's post at Daulat Beg Oldi, made the prime minister meet his military and civilian advisers on 2 November 1961 and formulate a 'forward policy' aimed at deterring 'further Chinese incursions by installing posts and ensuring patrolling'.

However, the 'forward policy' did not fully play out as Nehru had stated in parliamentary speeches, and there were problems at both ends: Nehru and Menon actually reduced the military budgets between 1960 and 1962, ignoring the military's demands of purchasing more equipment. But, army chief Gen. P.N. Thapar and chief of ground staff Gen. B.M. Kaul too did not convey the urgency of these demands adequately in their reports. Essentially, India missed sharp and focused institutional support for analysing what exactly 'limited conflict' meant, or how Chinese troops and their logistical build-up should be tackled.

Meanwhile, on the western coast, there was more military action. After more than a decade of non-violent manoeuvres asking the Portuguese to withdraw from Goa, India moved in militarily to liberate Goa on 18 December. After a day and a half of Operation Vijay, the Portuguese governor surrendered, and Goa became a part of independent India.

The year stands out for the first significant and large-scale Hindu–Muslim riot in post-Partition India. Jabalpur erupted into communal riots impacting the weavers and beedi workers amidst heavy loss of life. These riots, coming after over a decade of relative calm, were to leave deep scars. It influenced the way communal violence was orchestrated, establishing the template for a disturbing sequence of events in this decade.

*Pyaare watan* was under siege this year from much that was unfolding as the decade got off to far too eventful a start. Popular music scaled new highs with *Sahib Bibi Aur Ghulam*, a Guru Dutt film, with its dark but fascinating portrayal of a love triangle in feudal times. Its searing theme was matched by music that even today touches a chord deep within. Kishore Kumar, mostly at the urging of his brother Ashok Kumar, continued with his roles as a successful comedian and singing his songs. Music directors like Salil Chowdhury continued to push the boundaries beyond classical or folk influences: in *Half-Ticket* in '*Woh ek nigah kya mili/Tabiyat hi machal gayi*' shot on Kishore Kumar and Helen, one discerns a strong influence of Western music. In the film *Chhaya*, Talat Mehmood and Lata Mangeshkar actually sing a song inspired by a Mozart symphony.

# 1962: *Kaheen Deep Jale Kaheen Dil*

*Dushman hain hazaron yahaan jaan ke*
*Zara rakhna qadam pehchaan ke*
*Kayee roop mein hai qaatil*
*Zara dekh le aakar parwaane*

Lyricist: Shakeel Badayuni
Music: Hemant Kumar
Singer: Lata Mangeshkar
Film: *Bees Saal Baad*

'KAHEEN *deep jale kahin dil*'. This song nearly didn't happen. Lata Mangeshkar, down with asthma and sinusitis, had taken a break from professional singing and she sung it despite great fear of losing her voice.

The lilt and the haunting feeling she brought to this – perhaps also because of how fragile she felt in real life – was complemented by Shakeel's lyrics, said to simulate feelings of both 'ghostliness and longing'. Sir Arthur Conan Doyle's *The Hound of the Baskervilles* has been admirably adapted for this film and the song is a hit to this day. Hemant Kumar, with many wonderful and unusual tunes to his credit, never got the kind of press that S.D. Burman or Salil Chowdhury got, but his expertise with Rabindra Sangeet greatly helped him add depth to his music.

The lyrics speak on behalf of a woman unable to leave the marsh and suggests caution, warning of the dangers ahead: '*Dushman hain hazaron yahaan jaan ke/ Kayee roop men hai qaatil*'. The lyrics may well be seen as symbolic of the kind of trouble that Jawaharlal Nehru would have to encounter this year, despite winning his third general election in February. From within the party and outside, he was attacked and taunted for his inability to get back at China, for giving it too long a rope, and in the end, for being at war with the country's biggest neighbour.

But it was a pleasant February, with a week-long polling schedule, when independent India chose its government for the third time, and Jawaharlal Nehru returned as prime minister, the Congress having won 361 out of a total of 494 Lok Sabha seats. There had been variants of two-member constituencies in the 1952 and 1957 polls (before seats began to be reserved, a system followed to the day) but in the 1962 polls, there were no two-member constituencies. The Communist Party of India would be the second largest group in parliament, the leading opposition, but a distant second, with twenty-nine seats. It was to be the last general election fought by a united communist party.

This was the first time that indelible ink was used on the finger to identify voters who had cast their vote. This simple procedure would be adopted by other countries, much later, during the second decade of the twenty-first century.

The Akali Dal and the Dravida Munnetra Kazhagam (DMK) entered the Lok Sabha at this stage, strongly signalling that regional assertion, so soon after the linguistic states had been formed, was a fact to contend with. Despite some senior leaders turning away from it, the Congress was firmly in the saddle after this electoral victory.

But autumn in October was not as sunny as spring. India got caught up in its first big war, with China walking right into Indian positions, anxious to secure a route into Tibet via Aksai Chin. Uneasiness had crept into Sino-Indian ties on account of border disputes as also because of the relationship of the Dalai Lama with India, which was not taken kindly by the Chinese ever since they claimed Tibet. 'By 24 October, the Chinese effectively controlled the area up to their 1960 claim line on northern and central Ladakh. In North-East Frontier Agency (NEFA) they swiftly overran Indian positions along the McMahon Line'.

October was also a difficult month as there was immense opposition to Defence Minister V.K. Krishna Menon and demands for his resignation or dismissal flew in thick and fast. Eventually, Nehru had to accept his resignation. This was also a fine example of the sudden swing in political fortunes in independent India. Just one year ago, in the afterglow of the annexation of Goa, Menon had won a by-election from the North Bombay constituency very convincingly, in the face of a formidable challenge by Acharya Kripalani. But he had to take moral responsibility for what was seen as India's general lack of preparedness in the Sino-Indian war and quit the cabinet just one year on.

V.K. Krishna Menon was a staunch defender of the non-aligned policy and was hated by Western leaders for his sharp positions. Seen as an excellent wit, robust and eloquent, but criticized strongly by others for being arrogant and verbose, he is the only Indian minister to make it to a Simon and Garfunkel song, '*A Simple Desultory Philippic*' (1965).

The pressure on Prime Minister Nehru, now handling the defence portfolio, was tremendous. Even though he told the chiefs of staff, 'Our broad strategy must be governed by political factors, but detailed strategy – and tactics especially – have to be judged by military considerations', analysts say the decision to tamper with the leadership of the corps at a key juncture, in which the political leadership would have played a role, proved disastrous.

China, meanwhile, portrayed India as the aggressor and Zhou Enlai offered a three-point solution to India. But accepting that, India thought, would have meant conceding territory to China which it had acquired by force. The battle continued. Nehru's appeals to Soviet Premier Nikita Khrushchev for help went unheeded. In NEFA, China appeared ready to walk in, all the way into Assam. However, even as Nehru went on to ask President J.F. Kennedy for help, the Chinese declared a ceasefire on 21 November, saving India further embarrassment.

But the defeat had serious repercussions for India. It was seen by not just Indians, but the world for what it was. In a summit meeting with Pakistan and China, over the status of Kashmir, scheduled to start on 26 December,

Pakistan went back to its late 1948 position and Z.A. Bhutto told the Indian foreign secretary: 'You are a defeated nation, don't you see.'

Within India, the defeat damaged Jawaharlal Nehru's standing. It allowed leaders, seen as dwarfs just a year ago, to berate him for mismanagement and lack of preparedness. Nehru's faith in the fellowship amongst poorer nations was hit hard. The Bandung line appeared shaky and the support that India had extended China at international fora ever since the Chinese Revolution in 1949, along with the Panchsheel or Five Principles for Peaceful Coexistence, suddenly appeared incongruous with reality. And the fact that the Soviet Union did not overtly bat for India rubbed many the wrong way.

The Communist Party of India was wracked by deep internal divisions at this point. The death of the General Secretary Ajoy Ghosh and the emergence of S.A. Dange, who backed the Nehru government, further sharpened the divide within the party. There was a sizeable section that believed that aggression at the border was not called for and this needed resolution by speaking with the neighbour, not by armed measures. The CPI, therefore, did not appear in favour of supporting the government line. The party's silence for days after the attacks allowed suspicion to grow over their attitude. As the mood in the country slowly became one of injured pride, the communists were portrayed as not in sync with the national mood. Thousands of communists were arrested after a state of Emergency was declared on 26 October. This was the first time that Article 352 of the Constitution was used.

Parallely, the Jana Sangh, under a cloud for its association with Hindu extremists who had killed the Mahatma, used the moment to assert its 'nationalist' credentials and people like Atal Bihari Vajpayee used their oratory to good effect.

In April, incidentally, metric weights were made uniform, as they were adopted all over the country.

# 1963: *Chalo Ek Baar Phir Se*

*Chalo ek baar phir se, ajnabi ban jaayein hum dono*
*Wo afsana jise anjaam tak lana na ho mumkin*
*Use ek khoobsoorat mod de kar chhodna achchha*

Lyrics: Sahir Ludhianvi
Music: Ravi
Singer: Mahendra Kapoor
Film: *Gumrah*

B.R. Chopra, a director given to big projects pushing for social change and advocating bold themes, directed a poignant love triangle in *Gumrah*, and the song, '*Chalo ek baar phir se, ajnabi ban jaayein hum dono*', is a memorable one for many reasons.

The lyrics – accessible and dealing with fundamental human emotions of unfulfilled yet intense love – were from poet Sahir Ludhianvi's book of poems titled *Talkhiyan*. His biographer, Akshay Manwani, reveals it was first run under the title '*Khoobsurat Mod*'.

The piano, at the centre of the filming, anchors the song with three actors portraying their extremely complicated situations in a few minutes with great competence. It is enough to watch this one song to get the gist of the film. The piano was quite central to the portrayal of many such songs set in 'family' drawing-room situations, giving the director room for several tugs at emotional strings.

The character singing this on screen is Sunil Dutt. He is an artiste, in love with the character played by Mala Sinha, who is now married to a workaholic barrister Ashok Kumar. The suspicious husband, in this case, has organized this moment to be able to gauge his wife's responses. All three flit in and out of frame, each one drawing their own conclusions with each passing verse, trying to conceal their real sentiments.

While *Gumrah* stays very much within the 'Lakshman rekha' of marriage, the exploration of love outside marital boundaries without moralizing or criminalizing it clearly acknowledges the whiff of change in India, and questions being asked about societal norms. The effort is rather weak and the film in the end bats for marriage, but in this song, the lover gives full expression to his intimacy with a married woman and the beloved too acknowledges the sentiment.

This song, to date, rings as the song of many unfulfilled or incomplete stories, rendered beautifully by Mahendra Kapoor and set to tune by Ravi, who had already reached a high in 1960 with *Chaudhvin Ka Chand*.

The fact that Sahir was saying something very close to his heart and addressing a fellow poet Amrita Pritam is speculation that continues to this day. A bachelor, yet by Amrita Pritam's own admission, very close to her (she, married to someone else, after long and silent meetings with Sahir, would pick up the cigarette butts he had thrown down and smoke them). Had he already fallen for Sudha Malhotra, in 1960, and was talking to her? Or was it the suggestion that this love story be left at the beautiful turn it is at, as consummation or a public declaration is not possible, is something biographers struggle with.

The central idea of suspicion, unfulfilled love, commitment of various kinds yet a confusion and unease, reflects the mood in the nation as 1963 opened. Losing the war against China, a war that lasted less than a month, was to take its toll on India. The 1960s were already showing signs of the strain they would put on India, as the promise of the 1950s felt far away.

Less than a year after having been re-elected to power, Jawaharlal Nehru was tormented by sadness. He was shocked at the turn of events that had questioned some of the fundamental principles he had sworn by and fought for, from much before the time he spoke of India's 'tryst with destiny'.

Nehru's angst apart, 1963 is a year the socialists and the Hindu revivalists got a leg-up. What is crucial now is that Ram Manohar Lohia, the socialist giant, who found the Praja Socialist Party (PSP) far too mild in its opposition to Nehru, aligned with the Hindu revivalist Jana Sangh in a by-election. He also appealed to the Swatantra Party and the communists to unitedly oppose Nehru.

This silent recall into the political mainstream would serve to greatly rehabilitate the Jana Sangh, so far on the back foot due to its ideological parent RSS's role in the assassination of the Mahatma. Bypolls took Minoo Masani, Acharya Kriplani and Ram Manohar Lohia to the Lok Sabha.

The first-ever no-confidence motion was moved in the Lok Sabha by Acharya Kripalani in August 1963 following the debacle in the war against China. Though the government easily defeated the motion, the fiery debates that lasted for four days chipped away the aura of invincibility surrounding the Nehru government.

The so-called 'Kamaraj' Plan, which the chief minister of Tamil Nadu came up with, called upon ministers to step down to work for the party. Six Union ministers resigned as part of this plan.

The war with China served to stoke economic insecurity. To prevent a rapid depletion of foreign exchange, gold control was introduced. Finance Minister Morarji Desai banned the production of gold jewellery of more than fourteen carats. The law allowed individuals and families to only hold up to 2 kg and 4 kg of gold and silver respectively, and only in the form of jewellery. A licence was needed to open a jewellery shop or make jewellery. The Bombay Bullion Association was so stunned that it had to sell its front building at Zaveri Bazaar to pay for its members' losses.

The peacock was anointed as the national bird in January.

India also got its first woman chief minister this year, when Sucheta Kripalani assumed office in Uttar Pradesh. Married to socialist leader Acharya Kripalani, she was a freedom fighter, an alumnus of Indraprastha College and St Stephen's College and had taught at Banaras Hindu University. She had participated in the Quit India movement and was elected as an MP in 1952 and 1957 and then as an MLA in 1962.

While north India woke up to class/caste and employment issues only in 1989, the south experienced a lot of turbulence pertaining to these questions. In 1962, the state of Mysore had decreed that there were backward and more backward castes in society and backward castes would have 68 per cent of seats reserved for them. This was challenged by twenty-three petitioners in the Supreme Court. They argued that the list of backward classes was prepared only on the basis of caste and that this was unconstitutional. The court ruled that the reservation of 68 per cent was plainly inconsistent with Article 16(4) of the Constitution. In *M.R. Balaji and Others* vs *State of Mysore* it decided that a maximum of 50 per cent could be reserved for backward classes. This was modified later, but in its time, it was an important ruling.

India's Space Age too was inaugurated in 1963. Sounding rockets are one- or two-stage solid propellant rockets used for probing the upper atmospheric regions and for space research. A sounding rocket was launched from Thumba near Thiruvananthapuram – India's first-ever launch – on 21 November this year.

At the end of December, Kashmir was again in turmoil, with the disappearance of the holy relic at Hazratbal (believed to be the hair of the Prophet). Its mysterious reappearance in just a week was to signal the start of more tensions, with consequences, soon.

Painful, confusing, yet chugging along in many significant ways, 1963 in India was far away from a 'khoobsurat mod' the country may have been hoping for.

# 1964: *Hoke Majboor Mujhe Usne Bhulaaya Hoga*

*Zahar chupke se dava jaanke khayaa hoga*
*Dil ne aise bhi kuchh afsaane sunaaye honge*
*Ashq aankhon ne piye aur na bahaaye honge*

Lyrics: Kaifi Azmi
Music: Madan Mohan
Singers: Mohammed Rafi, Talat Mahmood, Manna Dey and Bhupinder
Film: *Haqeeqat*

IN a year with varied releases, *Sangam*, the Raj Kapoor magnum opus, was a big hit, musically. The music of *Woh Kaun Thi*, *Mr X*, *Dosti* and *Leader* was much discussed. But the mood of the nation, which carried over from the depression of 1962 and the tumult of 1963, was confronted head-on by Chetan Anand's appropriately named *Haqeeqat*. Its music by Madan Mohan and lyrics by Kaifi Azmi gave form to a nation's anxiety and pathos.

Particularly striking was the most unusual song, '*Hoke majboor mujhe usne bhulaaya hoga*'. It is filmed on a bunch of soldiers recalling home and hearth left behind as the war is fought and visualizing the anguish and pain their lovers undergo while trying to let go of their loves and affection for them.

Kaifi's style simply but skilfully evokes the pain of both the soldiers at the front and their loved ones left behind. Madan Mohan's music and the extremely unusual idea of having four male leads sing this at a camp over mugs in the biting and impossibly cold winter, make for a tuneful rendition of not just the soldiers remembering their beloveds:

> *Dil ne aise bhi kuchh afsaane sunaaye honge*
> *Ashq aankhon ne piye aur na bahaaye honge*
>
> (The heart would have recalled moments making even the shedding of tears impossible.)

India, though two years removed from the 1962 war, continued to reel from its aftermath, most visibly driven home by Jawaharlal Nehru's sudden ageing and loss of control over the narrative he had almost single-handedly shaped. The year began with him suffering a serious setback to his health. He fell ill while attending a Congress meeting in Orissa.

But parallel to Nehru's obvious frailty and physical decline was the Kashmir crisis. Lal Bahadur Shastri, brought in as 'minister without portfolio' to assist Nehru, played a key role in sorting out the fracas over the disappearance of the relic of the Prophet's hair (Hazratbal). Shastri admirably handled a tough situation and his proposed 'deedar' or sighting of the relic to determine its authenticity was a political face saver.

In April, the Nehru regime decided to release Sheikh Abdullah, after years of captivity, and the months of April and May saw most unusual activity and a buzz around Kashmir.

Sheikh Abdullah met C. Rajagopalachari in Madras, who, in private conversations with him, proposed 'an honourable solution' that would not have allowed either India or Pakistan to claim victory, but simultaneously ensured 'a place of honour to the people of Kashmir'. After this followed long and detailed conversations back in Delhi with Prime Minister Nehru along with a team of three: the foreign secretary, the high commissioner to Pakistan and the vice chancellor of Aligarh

Muslim University. The Rajaji formula and other proposals effectively ruled out a plebiscite and attempts were made to either get India and Pakistan to share defence and external affairs jointly while maintaining Kashmir's autonomy on other things, or of a possible confederation between India, Pakistan and Kashmir.

Sheikh Abdullah got an invite from Pakistan's president, Field Marshal Ayub Khan, to visit his country. While little is known of what he had in mind, it made Sheikh Abdullah hopeful. He met Nehru for a long time on 20 May before going to Pakistan. At this time, the innate trust that Pandit Nehru and Sheikh Abdullah had in each other is borne out by public statements about the other's intentions and politics.

Abdullah received a tumultuous welcome in Pakistan with many receptions held in his honour. While his obvious commitment to India's secularism seemed to get the goat of the Pakistani elite, it was agreed that Ayub Khan would meet Nehru in the middle of June and this was announced by Sheikh Abdullah in Pakistan on 26 May 1964.

But 27 May never saw Prime Minister Nehru wake up and, despite his desire expressed in Robert Frost's words scribbled on a notepad the night before – 'promises to keep and miles to go before I sleep' – the Nehru years effectively came to an end. All India Radio carried the news of his demise in its post-lunch broadcast.

After the swearing-in of Home Minister Gulzari Lal Nanda as interim prime minister, Congress president K. Kamaraj started consultations on who would be the best successor to Nehru. There was some discussion around Morarji Desai, but eventually, a consensus was reached on Lal Bahadur Shastri, a close colleague of Jawaharlal Nehru.

The year was to witness full-blown communal riots which exposed a template of how mob violence was orchestrated and perpetrated, causing maximum economic damage to target communities without, at the same time, resulting in any convictions or any closure. Jamshedpur, Rourkela and Calcutta, along with other parts of eastern India, saw rioting and serious trouble. Many linked this to the arrival of refugees from East Pakistan and stories that flowed of atrocities against the

Hindu minorities there. Memories of violence during Partition were rekindled as Nehru was cremated. On 11 June, in accordance with his wishes, Nehru's ashes were scattered all across India. This was two days after Shastri took oath as the prime minister and inaugurated his own short-lived but significant era. A reluctant Indira Gandhi was made minister for information and broadcasting in the Union cabinet by Prime Minister Shastri.

Another very significant event took place in the country in 1964 – the split of the Communist Party of India, till then the premier opposition in India. On 11 April, thirty-two members walked away from the CPI and formed the Communist Party of India (Marxist) (CPI[M]) citing deep ideological differences which had been emerging over the past few years. The differences centred around the direction to take to move India towards socialism, though the main issue was the attitude towards the domestic policies of the Congress. This was a debate that had taken place since Independence. The CPI consisted of the section that thought that Congress rule would eventually lead to socialism in India, while those who thought that the Congress's domestic policies were only strengthening the capitalist path in the country without eradicating landlordism split the party and formed the CPI(M).

Seeds of the green revolution too were planted this year in a village on the outskirts of Delhi in November. Fifteen farmers of village Jaunti, planted Sonora 64 wheat. They sowed the seeds of this Mexican semi-dwarf variety in some 70 acres in their village in north-western Delhi bordering Haryana. This was just over a year after scientists at the Indian Agricultural Research Institute (IARI) had imported about 100 kg seeds of Sonora 63, Sonora 64, Lerma Rojo 64-A and Mayo 64 wheat varieties and planted them in trial fields at Delhi, Ludhiana, Pantnagar, Kanpur and Indore during the 1963–64 rabi season. Encouraged by the results of the multi-location trials, it was decided to test the performance of the high-yielding strains the very next season in actual farmers' fields.

This was the year where India last displayed its supremacy in world hockey. It won the Gold at the Tokyo Olympics. The next time India would win the Gold was only in 1980, in Moscow, when several top hockey-playing countries did not participate in the games.

The naya paisa introduced in 1957 was renamed 'paisa' on 1 June 1964. Two commemorative nickel coins for Nehru, of the denominations of ₹1 and 50 paise, were also introduced this year. India also saw its first jet trainer HJT-16 make its inaugural flight in 1964.

# 1965: *Aaj Phir Jeene Ki Tamanna Hai*

*Kaanton se kheench ke yeh aanchal,*
*Tod ke bandhan baandhi payal*
*Koi na roko dil ki udaan ko*
*Dil woh chalaa aha ha ha ha*

*Aaj phir jeene ki tamanna hai*
*Aaj phir marne ka iraada hai*

Lyrics: Shailendra
Music: S.D. Burman
Singer: Lata Mangeshkar
Film: *Guide*

WAHEEDA Rehman, playing Rosie, the beautiful and talented danseuse wife of a workaholic archaeologist, sways to this tune, with Dev Anand, as Raju Guide, in the backdrop, captivating hearts and minds in 1965.

Based on the English novel of the same name, the film was way ahead of its time – and this song, in particular, spelt out the innumerable possibilities of relationships, of women, men and their roles vis-à-vis each other. The film was also unique in the sense that it was made in English too, though it had a poor opening in the US, with R.K. Narayan terming it 'Misguided

Guide'. But in Hindi, it was a musical hit, with each song being central to the narrative.

It is believed that Dev Anand and his wife Kalpana Kartik handed over a copy of the novel to writer Pearl S. Buck and film-maker Tad Danielewski. When both said wonderful things about its cinematic possibilities, Dev Anand called Narayan to acquire film rights.

Hasrat Jaipuri was initially chosen to write the songs but S.D. Burman and director Vijay 'Goldie' Anand did not like the songs Hasrat wrote. They approached Shailendra to write, who asked how much money Hasrat had received. He said they could add one lakh to that and he would be game. In 1964, no lyricist had asked for that much, but Shailendra got it and the rest is history.

Throughout the song, as Rosie rediscovers the sun and wind (contrasted with her uncaring husband's obsession with dead monuments and deep sunless digs), Raju Guide never even touches her. But their easy camaraderie and the significance of his presence in her life are brought out by some deft symbolism, his holding on to her heels on a stick, liberating her and yet protecting her whether she sways dangerously on the haystack on the horse carriage or peers down from an ancient wall of a fort, singing the line '*Aaj phir marne ka iraada hai*'. In effect, Raju's job seems to ensure that she chooses life over death.

India of 1965 had to do plenty of choosing between life and death.

The year was just the first after Nehru, with Lal Bahadur Shastri slowly assuming control. The year's Republic Day proved momentous and kicked off a new phase of strife Shastri had to manage.

Hindi was supposedly meant to be designated the official language of the Union fifteen years after the adoption of the Constitution. A lot of debate had followed on this question in the 1940s and south Indian members of the Constituent Assembly had registered their strong protest. The decision was deferred by fifteen years. But attempts to designate it the 'national language' failed miserably, as did attempts to make it the sole official language.

The south, especially Tamil Nadu, reacted badly and massive agitations erupted across the state. Ten days before Republic Day, C.N. Annadurai wrote to Shastri saying that they would be forced to observe 26 January as a 'day of mourning' should the imposition of Hindi continue, but the Centre went ahead. Attempts by the state government to control the agitation, the presence of the police and Central forces called in, were to have serious political consequences. It pushed the ruling Congress on the back foot and it proved to be a big launching pad for the Dravida Munnetra Kazhagam (DMK).

In many ways, it was reminiscent of what happened in 1937 when the Madras Presidency government led by C. Rajagopalachari had insisted on compulsory learning of Hindi and the Dravidian movement, via the Justice Party, got a major boost. The policy was revoked in 1940, but till then the agitations were sustained in almost every part of the Presidency, and this made E.V. Ramasamy (Periyar), the tallest leader of the Dravidian movement.

In 1965, when the fifteen-year time frame to make Hindi the only official language was about to expire, Tamil Nadu again led the agitations. By this time, imposition of Hindi was part of the narrative of the Aryan–Dravidian divide – the northern Aryans allegedly attempting to invade the cultural space of the southern Dravidians.

Lal Bahadur Shastri had to assure the state that English would continue as the second official language for the protests – often violent and often about self-immolations – to calm down. The agitation lasted till February, when a declaration had to be made about a change in the language policy. Prime Minister Shastri had to announce, on All India Radio on 11 February, five levels of assurances to quell the protests. Despite personally being a votary of Hindi, the intensity of the protests and the resignation of two Central ministers from Tamil Nadu forced his hand. However, after the acceptance of changes, others had things to say, especially stalwarts from western India. Essentially, the ghosts that India thought it had pacified and exorcised through the formation of linguistic states were still to be dealt with.

The second half of 1965 brought more turmoil by way of another India–Pakistan conflict.

The Indian army had lost badly to the Chinese in 1962, which created a sense of false superiority in the Pakistan army. Hoping to squeeze India with Chinese support, Pakistan had ceded land in Pakistan-Occupied Kashmir to China. As a member of various Western military alliances, Pakistan had also benefited from American aid and military equipment. Pakistan was politically stable and its economy was held up by top economists as an example for other developing countries.

Ayub Khan's belief that 'Hindu morale would not stand more than a couple of hard blows at the right time and place' was emboldened by his army's performance during the limited conflict in the Rann of Kutch in April 1965. In its award, the International Kutch Tribunal had given 350 sq. km territory to Pakistan and this put Shastri under pressure.

Meanwhile, India was still in the process of strengthening and modernizing its armed forces following the 1962 debacle and 1965 seemed like an opportune time for Pakistan to move in. Zulfikar Ali Bhutto, Ayub's young and ambitious foreign minister, had been speaking of an Algeria-like uprising in Kashmir which would finish 'the unfinished business of Partition'. Bhutto was the brain behind Operation Gibraltar, through which Pakistan aimed to stage an insurrection in J&K through massive infiltration, sabotage and subversion.

After the failure of Operation Gibraltar, Pakistan launched Operation Grand Slam to capture Jammu and isolate Srinagar from the rest of India. Shastri decided to escalate the war across the international border, taking Pakistan by surprise. Worried about the Chinese threat, India did not target East Pakistan.

Hypnotized into believing that rebellion in Kashmir supported by the Pakistan Army would lead to the overthrow of Indian rule, Ayub and his army chief, General Musa Khan, were stunned when India opened a second front.

The 1965 war ended in twenty-two days, when General J.N. Chaudhuri mistakenly assumed that the army was running out of ammunition and had suffered considerable tank losses. He advised Shastri to agree to a ceasefire even though the PM wanted to prolong the war by a few days if India could achieve a spectacular victory.

Lal Bahadur Shastri gave the memorable slogan of Jai Jawan, Jai Kisan this year, which also saw the setting up of the Border Security Force, or the BSF, on 1 December.

This year saw one of the worst mining disasters in a private mine in Dhanbad, Bihar, when more than 268 persons died as the mines caught fire after an explosion in Dhori, close to Dhanbad, on 28 May.

# 1966: *Oh Haseena Zulfon Waali*

*Oh haseena zulfon waali jaane jahan*
*Dhoondhti hain kaafir aankhen kiska nishaan*
*Mehfil mehfil aye shama phirtee ho kahaan*

Lyrics: Majrooh Sultanpuri
Music: Rahul Dev Burman
Singers: Mohammed Rafi and Asha Bhosle
Film: *Teesri Manzil*

'OH *haseena zulfon waali*' is a conversation stopper even today and for a million reasons. In 1966, it was for the film *Teesri Manzil*, a thriller. The music had a rock 'n' roll feel to it. The pacey lyrics never compromised on quality and depth but ensured that not just your feet, your heart too skipped more than a beat.

Helen, the Burma-born wonder dancer, moved to the choreography of Herman Benjamin, one of India's earliest film choreographers, who was at his best around the late 1960s. The music of this film is also special for being – in partnership with Majrooh Sultanpuri – the first mega-hit of Rahul Dev Burman (Pancham). He said that Majrooh enabled him to get his first big break as a full-time music director, and it dragged out this talented musician from under his equally stellar father S.D. Burman's shadow. His Western touch and zest was to influence Hindi film music for the next twenty years.

The song is a tease for the heroine in the film, sitting demurely, clad in a sari, in a restaurant, as the character played by Shammi Kapoor cavorts with Helen. As put by the perceptive Sharmila Tagore, who debuted in Hindi cinema around that time, figures like Helen, the dancer, and some vamps, played a very important role of being the vehicle of emotions that the necessarily more traditional heroine could not display. 'They spoke the unspeakable, conveyed longing, lust and other emotions, almost on behalf of the heroine, and very openly.' Helen does all this with great skill. Majrooh's lyrics, his *kaafir aankhen*, an indictment of Asha Parekh's ice-maiden-like character, ignoring Shammi Kapoor's character, work very well. Through Helen, Shammi asks her where all her gaze would stop as it roams '*mehfil mehfil aye shama phirtee ho kahaan*'. Helen's full-bodied answers about her quest for a lover who can satisfy her and take her spirit on, signalled the breaking of several moulds as the country entered a brand-new phase, pushed a lot by accident but also substantially by policy.

The year 1966 was marked by fast-paced developments, and with some exciting firsts. Like Reita Faria becoming the first Indian to win the Miss World. An MBBS student, Reita went on to marry a fellow doctor and settle down in the UK.

Trivia apart, the year began on a grim note for India. Prime Minister Lal Bahadur Shastri was in Tashkent with Pakistan's Ayub Khan, at a summit hosted by Soviet Premier Alexei Kosygin to find a more lasting peace between the two neighbours. Hectic negotiations and parleys led to the Tashkent Declaration signed on 10 January. India agreed to return key places like Haji Pir it had occupied during the war and to return to status quo ante as on 5 August 1965. There was an agreement on the return of prisoners, the resumption of diplomatic relations and an agreement that force would not be used to settle any future conflict. This declaration is especially important as it set aside the idea of a plebiscite over Kashmir as the way forward. It recognized the 1949 boundaries as acceptable ones.

Hours after the Tashkent Declaration, Lal Bahadur Shastri died of a heart attack in his sleep that night, to the shock of the country. His body was flown to India the next day, to be cremated on 12 January.

Indira Gandhi, the information and broadcasting minister, was sworn in as prime minister on 19 January, after she pipped the stalwart from western India, Morarji Desai, and started what was to be her long and tempestuous innings at the helm. This was also the year when veteran socialist leader Ram Manohar Lohia termed her a *goongi gudiya* (dumb doll) in parliament.

Indira Gandhi chose to go to Washington on an official visit soon after taking over as PM. Pushed by the food scarcity in India on the back of two successive drought years and with no foreign exchange to buy food in the international market, she opted for wheat support under the US Public Law 480 (called PL 480). Lyndon Johnson was effusive in welcoming Indira Gandhi but political events soon soured matters and wheat became a political football. According to Inder Malhotra: 'Infuriated by India's criticism of American bombings of Hanoi and Haiphong in the course of the Vietnam War, the irascible Texan put food shipments on such a tight leash that India literally lived from ship to mouth. With every morsel, we swallowed a little humiliation. When told that the Indians were saying exactly the same thing as the UN Secretary General and the Pope were, Johnson had retorted: "The Pope and the Secretary General do not need our wheat." Many in India started demanding that we should say no to American wheat.'

This incident and a similar event earlier during Nehru's premiership further propelled the concept of food security and self-sufficiency in food production.

The green revolution, proposed by agricultural scientist Dr Norman Borlaug during his visits to India in 1963 and 1964, had received a fresh impetus when Lal Bahadur Shastri appointed C. Subramaniam as agriculture minister. Norman Borlaug, who went on to win the Nobel Prize in 1970, had developed semi-dwarf, high-yield, disease-resistant wheat varieties when posted in Mexico. Dr M.S. Swaminathan, who has been hailed as the father of the green revolution reminisces: 'In 1966, we proposed a high-yielding-varieties programme for wheat, rice and bajra. The government approved it. It was to cover 32 million hectares. At the same time, we imported 18,000 tonnes of seeds of two varieties from Mexico because the demand from farmers was very high. What happened was called the Punjab Miracle.'

In June 1966, seven months prior to the general elections due next year, Prime Minister Indira Gandhi announced a devaluation of the rupee. The rupee, pegged to the British pound so far, fell 60 per cent in the international market. It was prompted by huge deficits, high oil bills and an end of aid from the West. Indira hoped the devaluation would make exports cheaper.

In November, several hundred Naga sadhus marched to parliament demanding a ban on cow slaughter, which took the inexperienced Indira Gandhi by surprise. The sadhus managed to make their way into the parliament complex and six persons lost their lives in the commotion that ensued after the police fired tear gas shells. The episode was serious enough for Indira to sack Home Minister Gulzari Lal Nanda, who was known to be sympathetic to the cause. More than that, it set Indira Gandhi on a political path that put her directly at odds with the sadhus and Jana Sangh, which used the occasion to launch its anti-Congress campaigns in the country. A high power committee was set up by Indira Gandhi to examine the entire issue of a law to ban caw slaughter. Headed by former chief justice A.K. Sarkar, the committee had as its members Verghese Kurien and RSS chief M.S. Golwalkar among others. The committee failed to submit any report to the government.

The Kothari Commission, appointed to look into education two years ago, came out with its 287-page report. It made some foundational suggestions to India's educational policy, like the 10+2+3 system or about teaching of languages in schools, e.g., the three-language formula, still in play in India.

In sports, this was the year when the Indian men's hockey team won the Asiad Gold for the first time in Bangkok, defeating Pakistan. In tennis, this was the first time ever that India reached the Davis Cup finals.

# 1967: *Aisa Mauqa Phir Kahaan Milega*

*Aisa mauqa phir kahaan milega*
*Hamare jaisa dil kahaan milega*
*Aao tumko dikhlaata hoon*
*Paris ki ek rangeen shaam*
*Dekho dekho dekho dekho dekho*
*An evening in Paris*

Lyrics: Shailendra
Music: Shankar–Jaikishan
Singer: Mohammed Rafi
Film: *An Evening in Paris*

A FUN romp in Europe: Shammi Kapoor with Sharmila Tagore in a double role, playing both a good and a bad girl; the hero hanging from a helicopter and the heroine water-skiing at the French Riviera in a swimsuit. The lyrics by Shailendra are basic, catchy and offer the promise of an unending good time. Sharmila Tagore's unselfconscious wearing of a swimsuit in '*Aasman se aaya farishta*', another song in this film, ensured that the film would go into the annals of Indian film history as the first one where the Hindi film heroine – not the vamp or a sidekick – dons a two-piece swimsuit.

*An Evening in Paris* is a masala wonder, which director Shakti Samanta used to the full to entertain and push boundaries. The title song (incidentally shot in Hamburg, Germany) invites the audience to the hedonistic charms of a romantic stroll on the Champs-Élysées or a visit to the Place de la Concorde. There is nothing coy in the way the film articulates desire and highlights – as in its very title in English, *An Evening in Paris* – the escapism that was to characterize the films of the era.

Escapism is what was perhaps required in large doses as independent India turned twenty in 1967. There were contentious issues which came to the fore – simmering trends in Indian politics that would crystallize decades later. But 1967 marked the first rupture in the business-as-usual politics in India: there was much political ferment in the absence of Jawaharlal Nehru during the first general election after his death.

It is significant that the Congress, now with a new prime minister at the helm, was witnessing the beginning of deep inter-party conflict. Indira Gandhi was now pitted directly against the old guard led by Deputy Prime Minister Morarji Desai, who saw premiership as his due and Indira as an usurper.

In the polls held in February, the Congress party managed to secure a majority in the fourth Lok Sabha, with 282 seats and more than 40 per cent of the votes polled, though it was seventy seats less than in the previous election. But with the communist parties weaker after the spilt, they were not the leading opposition any more. The Swatantra Party, a market-friendly, conservative party, put up an impressive show with forty-four seats. And the Bharatiya Jana Sangh also sneaked ahead. No opposition party got 10 per cent of the vote share, yet the Congress had to face severe reverses in major states. Independents and others made a strong show, suggesting a churn in Indian politics. Indira Gandhi, incidentally, picked Rae Bareli, the constituency of her late husband Feroze Gandhi, to contest for the Lok Sabha for the first time.

But 1967 is best remembered for the assembly polls where the Congress lost control of six states, which was a first, especially in Tamil Nadu and West Bengal. The loss in Tamil Nadu, after the anti-Hindi riots just two years ago, heralded the rise of parties that articulated regional aspirations better. The Dravida Munnetra Kazhagam (DMK) came to the fore, riding on consistent and rigorous campaigns on the language issue, rising unemployment and dedicated work across the state over the past few years. This had major implications in the decades to come as the Congress is yet to come to power there.

In West Bengal too, the freshly minted CPI(M) along with the Bangla Congress and a lot of smaller Left parties, such as the United Front, managed to beat back the Congress and formed the first non-Congress government in this crucial state. Ajoy Mukherjee of the Bangla Congress became the chief minister and Jyoti Basu of the CPI(M), the deputy chief minister.

In other developments, in West Bengal, the United Front–Left Front alliance engineered a debate within the Left parties over the wisdom of joining the government, in which the line advocated by Jyoti Basu won and the Left participated in power. However, events in Naxalbari in Siliguri would add a new word, Naxalism, to the lexicon of Indian politics.

The tea-garden economy here relied on exploiting the tiller-peasants working in large plantations. The Krishak Samiti, or peasants' organization, controlled by the CPI(M) and led by the radical Kanu Sanyal, fought the landlords directly. In organized militant protests which had started by March, skirmishes with the police became common and a constable was killed, leading to the police becoming more restive as the peasants took to arms and killed landlords.

It proved to be a tough call for the United Front–Left Front government in the state, which had to push back the militant farmers, and several leaders of the Naxalbari agitation had to be put in jail.

In several states of northern India – Uttar Pradesh (UP), Bihar, Madhya Pradesh (MP) and Haryana – the Congress won, but with thin majorities, which allowed the idea of the Samyukt Vidhayak Dal (SVD), or United Legislators' Party, to take root. This was a combination of the Jana Sangh, the Swatantra Party and the socialists, critically aided by breakaway Congress legislators, who came together just to grab power.

In UP, this happened under the farmer leader Charan Singh. The SVD, the start of another bold experiment in Indian politics, was a combination of the socialist streams who joined hands with the Jana Sangh (the political arm of the RSS, which was very keen to be in government after being shunned and disregarded ever since its ban over Mahatma Gandhi's assassination way back in 1948). The anti-Congress axis started the process of slow consolidation, which was not merely a move at the leadership level. The middle castes, agricultural and landed, who did not have a share in political power, asserted themselves through this route in several states. Castes like the Kurmis, Lodhs, Yadavs, Vokkaligas, Vallalas, Reddys and Kammas across states were able to experience political power directly through this experiment. The relative disarray in the Congress after the deaths of Nehru and Shastri in quick succession helped the process, as did the socialists' lack of compunction in getting together with anyone under the garb of fighting the Congress hegemony. Mulayam Singh Yadav, still a colossus on the political stage in UP, first entered electoral politics as a candidate of the Samyukt Socialist Party (SSP, led by Ram Manohar Lohia) this year.

In Bihar, the shaky coalition of six parties taking power after the polls impacted adversely the handling of the famine that followed after the serious drought of 1966. While after 1943, India had been able to avert serious famines of that scale, the Bihar situation and the inability of either the Centre or the state government to take charge had the makings of a dangerous situation for peoples' welfare. Local newspapers, *Searchlight* and the *Indian Nation*, as Paul Brass notes, went all out to report on and project the famine as one of the biggest crises in the state till then.

In Orissa too, the Congress faced an electoral rout at the hands of the Swatantra Party and a section of the landed elite.

The struggles between Indira Gandhi and the Congress party's old guard known as the Syndicate intensified in 1967. Morarji Desai was the finance minister and deputy prime minister. While K. Kamaraj completed his term as Congress president this year, he was replaced by S. Nijalingappa of the same camp, not one of Indira's choice. In a bid to outflank the Syndicate, Indira, advised by her close and now increasingly powerful bureaucrat associates, chief among them being P.N. Haksar, started her journey to the Left.

In May 1967, the Congress party passed a ten-point programme, strongly resonating her assumed socialist avatar; it spoke of the abolition of privy purses, the 'social control' of banking, ceiling on urban property, curbing of business monopolies – proposals that made the conservative Syndicate deeply uncomfortable, but which enabled Indira to chart an ideological course around which to argue her case against the old guard.

In Telangana and Srikakulam in Andhra Pradesh too there were insurgencies driven by a call to act directly against the exploitation by landlords and make a case for better conditions for the workers.

The CPI(M), formed just three years ago, was to again undergo a rupture, with leaders and cadres, who believed in physically eliminating landlords or 'class enemies' and CPI(M) members whom they classified as 'right deviationists', leaving the party to form the CPI(Marxist–Leninist).

The Naxalites seemed to draw deeply from Mao Zedong's letter to revolutionaries written on 5 January 1930: 'We shall also see that the high tide of revolution against the imperialists, the warlords and the landlords is inevitable, and will come very soon. All China is littered with dry faggots which will soon be aflame. The saying, "A single spark can start a prairie fire", is an apt description of how the current situation will develop.'

This 'prairie fire' was, of course, not to be. But Naxalbari did kindle a thought that has remained synonymous with the idea of a battle with the Indian state.

The year also saw India getting a president who was a Muslim: eminent educationist and freedom fighter Dr Zakir Husain was sworn in as the third president of the republic on 6 May.

# 1968: *Kajra Mohabbat Wala*

*Kajra mohabbat wala*
*Ankhiyon mein aisa dala*
*Kajre ne le li meri jaan*
*Hai re main teri qurban*

Lyrics: Shamsul Huda Bihari
Music: O.P. Nayyar
Singers: Shamshad Begum and Asha Bhosle
Film: *Kismat*

THE 1960s rolled along, in Hindi film music terms, with 'modern-day' (read Western) influences in the form of jiving, jazz or rock-and-roll becoming visible. Film music was happy to adapt and come out of a singularly staple 'Indian' look, but there were other trends at work too. These drew from the wellspring of India's rich traditions, while tweaking them to acquire a longevity and robustness which still make those songs memorable and among the first to be remixed.

'*Kajra mohabbat wala*' is arguably at the top of the list. It burst on the scene with words by Shamsul Huda Bihari, a talent whom modern-day lyricists remember with great nostalgia, as having crafted some of the finest poems to be set to tune, combining folk metaphors with a marked contemporary twist. This song, with O.P. Nayyar's music and the unusual Shamshad

Begum and Asha Bhosle pairing, was a big hit in its time and stayed on as a classic. If this period is marked by fidelity of the audiences to the sweet lilt of Lata Mangeshkar's voice, the more salted and dulcet variety brought in by Shamshad Begum and Asha Bhosle never really went out of style. The way this song has been filmed made their signature voices work even better.

The filming was very unusual and added to the huge appeal of this hit song. The hero, Biswajit, with false breasts, a wig and a sari pallu which, he said, 'never stayed in place' during rehearsals, does a drag-act while the heroine Babita is dressed as a Pathan. The '*adas* and *nakhras*', he added, were not tough as he had seen men enact female roles in neighbourhood plays. Yet, the radically different song, done as a stage act, had P.L. Raju's cheerful choreography, with film director Manmohan Desai also deeming it important to be on the sets for rehearsals that took a week.

While the beat of a folk tune with a beautiful reference to *kajra* or the kajal of love capturing the woman's world view was suitable for a pacier and less idyllic sensibility of 1968, India, a year after a cataclysmic change in its political map, was adjusting to the new.

The Emergency declared in India in 1962 during the Sino-Indian war was eventually revoked. It is a lesser-known fact that neither Nehru nor Shastri deemed it necessary to lift the Emergency provisions and a lot of them were used by the state to tackle internal threats like the one posed by Naxalites. It fell upon Indira Gandhi to eventually call it off in the second year of her tenure.

After the tumultuous turn in the politics of the state of Madras with the electoral success of the DMK, the Lok Sabha agreed to rename the state, with effect from January 1969, as Tamil Nadu at the instance of the ruling party in the state.

A bill for a Public Provident Fund (or PPF), seen as an essential component of employee welfare, was passed in May this year.

In science, 1968 heralded some interesting moments. Though he was a citizen of the US by then, but by birth Dr Hargobind Khorana was Indian, and his getting the Nobel prize for medicine and physiology was celebrated with much cheer in India. It was the first time after Independence that an Indian by birth had won the Nobel Prize (Rabindranath Tagore and

C.V. Raman had been awarded the Nobel earlier, but before India attained independence).

India launched its first meteorological satellite, Menaka, this year from Thumba in Kerala in December. This was also the year when Dr Profulla Kumar Sen and his team carried out the first successful heart transplant of Asia in KEM Hospital in Bombay.

This year was the second of the three-year plan holiday taken by the Planning Commission at the end of the Third Five-Year Plan. During the first three plans, which ended in 1966, resources were allocated to states without much debate or discussion. But now there was a rethinking about allocation of resources to the states, which would be based on a series of criteria less open to criticism or complaint. This was important as many states were governed by parties opposed to the Congress party ruling at the Centre.

# 1969: *Tum Pukar Lo*

*Honth pe liye hue, dil ki baat hum*
*Jaagte rahenge aur, kitni raat hum*
*Mukhtasar si baat hai,*
*Tumse pyaar hai*
*Tumhara intezar hai*
*Tum pukar lo*

Lyrics: Gulzar
Music: Hemant Kumar
Singer: Hemant Kumar
Film: *Khamoshi*

THE a remake of the 1959 Bengali film, *Deep Jwele Jai*, *Khamoshi* is believed to be Hemant Kumar's, his wife Bela's, and music arranger Manohari Singh's finest hour as music composers and singers. Gulzar's words, with mostly short lines in rich, emotion-soaked Hindustani, finds the perfect counterfoil in Hemant Kumar's Rabindra Sangeet training and quietude. A classic now '*Tum pukar lo*', its filming and context blazed a new trail.

The film takes a look at complexities around a working woman's life. A nurse at a home for the mentally unstable, played by Waheeda Rehman, struggles with work life and the two men she develops an emotional bond with. The pathos and the depth of the agony of both the patients, played by Rajesh Khanna and Dharmendra, along with Waheeda's turmoil are allowed to simmer and develop, with the songs playing an important role.

The subtlety that Asit Sen, the director, brought to the Bengali version was transposed to the Hindi one. In the Bengali version, Sen himself plays the role that Dharmendra plays in the Hindi one, keeping his back constantly to the audience, which was the case in this song too. The tune from '*Ei raat tomar aamar*' which Asit Sen wanted to use here, Hemant Kumar had already used five years ago in another song, '*Yeh nain darey darey*'. He composed something close to the spirit of '*Ei raat*' and introduced a long tuneful whistle via his arranger, the talented Manohari Singh, a polymath, saxophonist and arranger for most of S.D. Burman's film music. Kamal Bose's cinematography, lingering over frames where nothing ostensibly happens, slows down time and is able to make the most of Gulzar and Hemant Kumar's partnership of words, music and rendition.

At the end of a decade that signalled unrest and turmoil at various levels, India in 1969 too was at a cusp, being pulled in different directions. Communal riots, which the country had not seen since Partition, saw a huge spurt in the 1960s, and the absence of Nehru's reassuring, iron hand was there for all to feel. Between 1954 and 1966, the average number of communal riots per annum was 70.2. In 1967, this had risen sharply to 209, in 1968 to 346 and in 1969 this figure rose to 519.

The Ahmedabad riots of 1969 are still cited as a textbook case of communal tension, death and mayhem in an urban setting that destroyed not just old social ties and harmony, but disrupted modern equations in cities developed on class and political lines, for instance the huge working class in industrial Ahmedabad.

The blow that the Congress received in the 1967 general elections, while managing to retain power, had not left Indira Gandhi, the incumbent PM, unscathed. Her deputy, Morarji Desai, along with the Congress president S. Nijalingappa, alarmed at the dexterity with which Indira came into her own and her assumed hostility to conservative ideas of the party's old guard, ensured that the elections for the country's president became a big theatre of contest for control over India's politics.

In its choice of candidate to fill the late Zakir Husain's shoes, the party, now firmly beyond Indira Gandhi's grasp, chose an old Syndicate sympathizer, a former chief minister of Andhra Pradesh and then the Speaker of the Lok Sabha – N. Sanjiva Reddy. Indira Gandhi sensed that the party's old guard and her fierce rivals, led by the party president, were hoping to develop a powerful pole to check her moves as prime minister. No one knows how that would have shaped India, since till then the office of the president had been seen largely as a ceremonial post, certainly not meant to checkmate elected prime ministers.

Not wishing to take any chances, in the Bangalore meet of the All India Congress Committee (AICC), Indira Gandhi decided to oppose his candidature and made clear that she preferred another leader who hailed from Andhra Pradesh, the then vice-president V.V. Giri, with whom she had close personal ties. However, Sanjiva Reddy remained the official party candidate. The Bangalore AICC meeting was critical in other ways too as under the advice of her famous Kashmiri Pandit advisers (D.P. Dhar, P.N. Haksar and P.N. Dhar), she decided to firmly cast herself as a left-of-centre leader and on the side of the socialist ginger group, the Young Turks, in the party and took some other swift decisions on her return to Delhi.

She took away the finance portfolio from her arch-rival Morarji Desai, in a move that was seen as throwing down the gauntlet directly at her more entrenched rivals. Further, she went ahead and issued an ordinance nationalizing fourteen private banks in the country, in accordance with the ten-point proposal she had moved two years ago. She had argued then that for promoting equitable growth in the country, it was not enough to have 'social control' of the banks. If banks were publicly owned, they would give credit 'to millions of farmers, artisans and other self-employed persons', and not just to big business houses.

Bank nationalization was hailed by Indira Gandhi in statements to the press as the big idea that was supported by '95 per cent' of Indians and opposed only by a section of big industry whom the newspapers represented. The ordinance was challenged in the Supreme Court, which quashed the ordinance. A fresh ordinance was issued to nullify the court order.

With matters now hotting up for the presidential battle due in August, Indira Gandhi refused to bat for the party's official candidate Sanjiva Reddy. Instead, she quietly backed V.V. Giri who contested as an independent. When the old guard realized that she was waging a silent but effective campaign for Giri through younger Congressmen, Congress president Nijalingappa approached the Jana Sangh and Swatantra Party to urge them to switch support from their candidate Justice (Retd) K. Subba Rao to Sanjiva Reddy.

This was enough for Indira Gandhi to assume the moral high ground and accuse the Syndicate of betraying of party interests. Despite the party elders putting pressure on her to come out in public support of Reddy, she refused and, instead, just days before the election, called for a 'vote of conscience'. So, while Congress seniors voted for Reddy, Indira Gandhi was able to swing the majority of her partymen to vote for Giri and he won the election on the basis of second-preference votes.

This blow to the Syndicate was to be the breaking point in ties within the party and a series of letters were exchanged between Nijalingappa and Indira Gandhi, until he eventually expelled her from the party for indiscipline on 12 November. This led to rival Congress sessions being held in December as the party split into two: Congress (O), 'Organization' of the Old guard, and Congress (R), 'Requisitionist' of Indira Gandhi supporters. Nijalingappa was to go on to accuse Indira Gandhi of fostering a personality cult. Indira Gandhi, with the help of her advisers, successfully portrayed the battle as an ideological one between the pro-business old guard and her, left-of-centre, pro-poor, secular believer in socialist economics.

In parliament, 220 Lok Sabha MPs threw in their lot with Indira Gandhi. Yet it left the Congress (R) short by forty-five MPs and the party turned to independents and the Communist Party of India for support. The CPI sensed in her left turn a perfect opportunity, amidst hopes of a radical economic agenda and a firm stand against communalism.

Indian Space Research Organization (ISRO), formed this year, superseded Indian National Committee for Space Research (INCOSPAR) which had been set up seven years earlier. Dr Vikram Sarabhai was the leading scientist who emphasized the role and importance of space technology in nation building. He remained a crucial player in promoting the idea of ISRO as a priority in a largely poor country with many pressing survival needs.

# 1970s
# The Fall and Rise of Democracy

## Aane Wala Pal Jaane Wala Hai

A war that splits Pakistan into two, an oil-price shock, a nuclear test, an Emergency, and India gets its first non-Congress government.

1.

1. The liberation of Bangladesh: Pakistan Army's Lt Gen. A.A.K. Niazi surrenders to Lt Gen. J.S. Aurora in Dacca on 16 December 1971.

2. The blockbuster film *Sholay* was released in 1975 even as the country was reeling under the Emergency.

3. Democracy strikes back as Indira Gandhi is voted out in 1977.

4. Jayprakash Narayan, who symbolized the opposition to Emergency, addressing a rally in February 1977.
(Photo: IndianExpress Photo Archives)

2.

3.

4.

# 1970: *Zindagi Ka Safar Hai Yeh Kaisa Safar*

*Zindagi ka safar hai yeh kaisa safar*
*Koi samjha nahin koi jaana nahin*
*Hai yeh kaisi dagar chalte hain sab magar*
*Koi samjha nahin koi jaana nahin*

Lyricis: Indeevar
Music: Kalyanji–Anandji
Singer: Kishore Kumar
Film: *Safar*

'ZINDAGI *ka safar, hai yeh kaisa safar...*'. No respectable collection of Kishore Kumar–Rajesh Khanna songs would be complete without this one. But this ruminative song from the film *Safar* is unlike most other popular songs of the singer–actor combine. Kalyanji–Anandji composed the music for this Asit Sen film and Indeevar wrote the evocative words. Indeevar was the pen name of Shyamalal Babu Rai, who was born in Jhansi district of Uttar Pradesh in 1924. Writing under the nom de plume of Azad during the freedom struggle, he was imprisoned by the British. He gained fame in 1949 with the song '*Bade armano se rakkha hai balam teri kasam*' for the film *Malhar* and wrote many hit songs of the 1960s, '70s and the '80s. After all, how many people know that the lyrics for Nazia

Hassan's cult classics, '*Aap jaisa koi meri zindagi mein aaye* ...' and '*Laila o Laila* ...' were penned by Indeevar?

The title song of *Safar* was in keeping with the genre of sad, reflective Rajesh Khanna songs during that period. Khanna used his charm to convey the character's desperation and his conviction that just surviving somehow is not really living. It is best encapsulated in the line, '*Zindagi ko bahut pyaar hamne diya / Maut se bhi mohabbat nibhaaenge hum*'. Counted among the seventeen consecutive hit films of Rajesh Khanna between 1969 and 1971, *Safar* was a remake of the 1956 Bengali film *Chalachal*, which had also been directed by Asit Sen. It won Asit Sen the Filmfare Award for Best Director in a year which also had Dev Anand's *Prem Pujari*, Shakti Samanta's *Kati Patang* and Raj Kapoor's *Mera Naam Joker*. A common feature among them was memorable music, which continues to be popular till this day. Although *Prem Pujari* was not a commercial success, it was *Mera Naam Joker* which was an even bigger commercial disaster that put Kapoor into a financial crisis. *Mera Naam Joker*, 255-minute long with two intervals, took six years in the making and Kapoor described it as his favourite film.

*Mera Naam Joker* boasted of four lyricists, with famous Hindi poet Gopaldas Neeraj penning the very popular song '*Ae bhai zara dekh ke chalo*'. Coincidentally, Neeraj was also the lyricist for *Prem Pujari*, which had hit songs like '*Phoolon ke rang se*', '*Shokhiyon mein ghola jaye*', '*Taqat watan ki humse hai*' and '*Rangeela re tere rang mein*', the last of which remained Dev Anand's all-time Navketan favourite song. Neeraj, who was a professor of Hindi literature, unfortunately got tagged as a writer of hit songs for flop films and soon returned to the world of academia and poetry.

Rajesh Khanna's continued success and Raj Kapoor's failure bookmarked the year in which the changeover of stardom from the big three – Raj Kapoor, Dilip Kumar and Dev Anand – to Khanna actually happened. It was not just the film industry but the politics and the economy of the country too was in a similar flux. After the split of the Congress party in 1969, Indira Gandhi ruled as the prime minister without a full majority in the Lok Sabha. Her rule, with the support of the Left, gave a further impetus to socialist policies. She moved a constitutional amendment bill to abolish the privy purses of the dethroned princely families.

In return for agreeing to integrate with India and cede their powers in 1949, the princes were to be paid a privy purse, which was approximately 8.5 per cent of the annual revenue of each princely state. The amounts varied from ₹43 lakh a year to the Nizam of Hyderabad to just ₹192 a year to the ruler of Katodia (now in Gujarat). Of the 555 rulers, 398 were to get less than ₹50,000 a year. The total cost to the Indian exchequer in 1947 was ₹6 crore, which was to be progressively reduced. At the time of the abolition of privy purses in 1970, the total amount payable to all erstwhile princes was just ₹4 crore a year. This was part of a promise made by Sardar Patel in the Constituent Assembly against the wishes of many Congress party members who saw these princes as lackeys and stooges of the British colonial rulers.

In June 1967, the All India Congress Committee had passed a resolution to abolish the privy purses. The concept of privy purses and special privileges were incompatible with an 'egalitarian social order'. The Constitution (Twenty-fourth Amendment) Bill, 1970, was introduced and passed in the Lok Sabha on 2 September with 332 votes for and 154 votes against. In the Rajya Sabha, it failed by one vote to reach the required two-thirds majority, with 149 voting for and seventy-five against. Having failed in parliament, Indira Gandhi asked President V.V. Giri to derecognize the princes. This derecognition was successfully challenged by N.A. Palkhivala before the Supreme Court and Indira Gandhi had to beat a hasty retreat. But only for a year when she had the parliamentary majority to amend the Constitution.

If the abolition of privy purses was a controversial affair, the start of Operation Flood went almost unnoticed even though it would eventually make India self-sufficient in milk and dairy products. Headed by the milkman who started AMUL, Verghese Kurien, Operation Flood's objectives included an increase in milk production ('a flood of milk'), augmentation of rural incomes and reasonable prices for consumers. The agreement with the UN World Food Programme was signed by National Dairy Development Board (NDDB) in March for Phase-1 in which Operation Flood linked eighteen of India's premier milk sheds with consumers in India's four major metropolitan cities: Delhi, Bombay, Calcutta and Madras.

NDDB had been set up in 1965 at Prime Minister Lal Bahadur Shastri's behest under Kurien's leadership, by accepting Kurien's conditions that NDDB would be headquartered in Anand, Gujarat, and he would draw money from the farmers and keep the NDDB independent of government control.

In keeping with his philosophy of being independent of government control, Kurien financed Operation Flood entirely out of the money which the cooperative earned by selling 126,000 tonnes of skimmed milk powder and 42,000 tonnes of butter oil, which were initially a gift from the World Food Programme. Operation Flood struggled at first and many had doubts about its scale. 'I believe no one understood Operation Flood', said Kurien. 'No one wanted it to succeed. No one thought it would succeed because it was the most massive dairy experiment in the world. It was also the largest agricultural project ever attempted. When I conceived the scheme, I was advised not to think so big. I said no. We had to dare, we had to do things in the manner that would have an impact in a country as big as India.' By 1974, Mother Dairy had started in Delhi and the naysayers had all gone quiet. Self-sufficiency in dairy products is now taken for granted so much so that hardly anyone remembers the formal launch of white revolution in 1970.

On 27 December, Indira Gandhi announced that Lok Sabha elections would be held in March 1971, nearly a year before schedule. The announcement of these elections was the start of a journey which would slide from an exhilarating high in 1971 to an inexplicable low a few years later. A journey, as the song says, '*Koi samjha nahin, koi jaana nahin ...*'.

# 1971: *Zindagi Kaisi Hai Paheli*

*Kabhi dekho mann nahin jaage*
*Peechhe peechhe sapnon ke bhaage*
*Ik din sapnon ka raahi*
*Chala jaaye sapnon ke aage kahaan*
*Zindagi kaisi hai paheli haye*
*Kabhi toh hansaye, kabhi yeh rulaaye*

Lyrics: Yogesh
Music: Salil Chowdhury
Singer: Manna Dey
Film: *Anand*

'ZINDAGI *kaisi hai paheli*', penned in an easy Hindi by lyricist Yogesh Gaur from Lucknow, was this lyricist's first prominent break in Bombay. Till then, he was writing songs for stunt films. He went on to shine as a lyricist in Basu Chatterjee's films later in the decade but this was special. Salil Chowdhury's tune was intrinsically Indian, although it used many Western instruments as well, including the trumpet which leads the score right from the introduction.

The seaside sequence provided the apt backdrop for the thought-provoking lyrics, which encapsulated the philosophy of Anand, the lead character played by Rajesh Khanna. Khanna, in a fully buttoned lilac Khadi short kurta (his trademark guru kurta), walks on the beach, chappals in hand, surrounded by bitter-sweet evocations of life, three fishermen on a boat, children with gas balloons allowed to soar free and the waves hitting the shore and then calming down. This song was, however, not part of the film as originally envisaged by Hrishikesh Mukherjee.

Gulzar, who was the original lyricist of the film, had written the lyrics for '*Maine tere liye hi saat rang ke sapne chune*' and Yogesh had written lyrics for '*Kahin door jab din dhal jaaye*'. Salil Chowdhury asked Yogesh to write the song for another tune he had prepared, while Hrishikesh Mukherjee had already asked Gulzar to pen the lyrics. Gulzar wrote '*Jiya lage na*' and Yogesh penned '*Na ro ankhiyaan*'. There was total confusion on the sets, but Gulzar's lyrics were used during the recording. L.B. Lachman, another producer for whom Yogesh was writing songs, intervened with his friend Hrishikesh Mukherjee, asking him to compensate Yogesh with another song.

As there was no other situation for a song in the story, '*Zindagi kaisi hai paheli*' was written as a title song. When Rajesh Khanna heard the recorded version of the song, he insisted that the song be shot on him. This became the first solo sung by Manna Dey for Rajesh Khanna. Yogesh had also penned a third stanza for the song, which Manna Dey often sang in his live concerts.

'*Zindagi* ...' means many things to many people. Speaking of life, its origins and after, the song interrogates important questions with a lightness that only the best of Hindi cinema can do. Amitabh Bachchan plays the restrained doctor to the flamboyant and pensive cancer patient Rajesh Khanna, determined to live life to the fullest, in *Anand*. Much like a cheerful Rajesh Khanna and a grim Amitabh Bachchan placed in a single frame on a typical Bombay beach, this year proved to be one of contrasts and surprises for India.

In a significant break from the past, Indira Gandhi had announced the general elections a year ahead of schedule. It was an attempt to break away from the judicial restraints imposed on her minority government. The election was concluded in two weeks in February. Almost from the very beginning, it turned into a referendum on Indira Gandhi's leadership. When *Newsweek* magazine asked her what the main issues in the election were, she replied gleefully: 'I am the issue.' The National Democratic

Front, comprising the Congress (O), Bharatiya Jana Sangh, Swatantra Party, Samyukt Socialist Party and Praja Socialist Party declared its single-point objective as 'Indira Hatao (Remove Indira)'. In an inspirational response, Prime Minister Gandhi declared that it cannot be about any single individual and she was interested only in freeing her people from the scourge of poverty: '*Wo kehte hain Indira hatao; main kahti hoon garibi hatao.*' 'Garibi hatao' (remove poverty) was to become her battle cry, and laid the foundations of her prime ministership, which went on to move India into another distinct phase of her nationhood.

Contrary to media assessments of a close-run contest, Indira Gandhi's Congress (R) swept the elections, winning a two-thirds majority with 352 seats while the opposition alliance won only fifty-one seats. The Left parties won forty-eight seats. It was to be the last election for the Swatantra Party and the Jana Sangh. The Jana Sangh was to re-emerge in the next decade as the Bharatiya Janata Party.

But elections were not the only high for Indira Gandhi. The victory in the India–Pakistan war in December, which resulted in a public surrender in Dacca by Pakistani forces in East Pakistan, was perhaps the apogee of her public life. More than 90,000 Pakistani soldiers were taken prisoners of war as a new nation, Bangladesh, was created by India's decisive military victory. The American and Chinese support could not help the Pakistan Army avert the humiliation, which was brought upon by its oppression of the Bengalis. It was as much a win for the Indian Army, particularly its flamboyant chief, General S.H.F.J. Manekshaw, as for Indira Gandhi's political will and her diplomacy. It involved a fundamental shift in the cold war matrix, with India signing a treaty of friendship with the Soviet Union. This incident was to mark out the broad camp India would find itself veering towards, notwithstanding the attempts by the Janata Party government to reset it later in the decade.

The break-up of Pakistan, a state formed just twenty-four years back as a homeland for Muslims, set many ghosts to rest in India and unleashed others in the region. As historian Srinath Raghavan puts it, 'The groundswell of messianic emotions in India and Bangladesh was entirely understandable. India had not only won a decisive military victory but has seemingly exorcised the spectre of the "two-nation" theory that had haunted the subcontinent since 1947.' With this victory, following which she was hailed as Durga, Indira Gandhi finally shook off the yoke of *goongi gudiya* and Pandit-ji's *bitiya*.

Many pieces of the jigsaw puzzle that is India fell into place as it grappled with food security. It marked the peak of foodgrain production in the first phase of the green revolution. From seventy-two million tonnes in 1966, it was now 108 million tonnes, with imports declining from ten million tonnes to two million tonnes in the same period. As economists like Biplab Dasgupta put it then, it marked a 'mood of optimism' where there was a belief in the miracle seeds ending India's food crisis.

Having lost her case for bank nationalization in the courts, Indira Gandhi passed the twenty-fifth amendment to the Constitution to nationalize private banks. A big part of her left-turn package, it underpinned her anti-poverty policies and programmes.

It was the year when the census was due, and the migration, especially from the troubled former East Pakistan, was heavy. Since the 1971 census, data is being collected on the basis of place of last residence, in addition to the question on the birthplace.

Sunil Manohar Gavaskar, who was to begin shaping another Indian obsession, cricket, with his skill and perseverance, debuted in the West Indies on 6 March 1971 at Port of Spain. He was to finish the four Tests with a phenomenal average of 154.80, which included four centuries. India went on to record its first Test series win in the West Indies. Gavaskar didn't perform as well in England later in the year, where the team led by Ajit Wadekar again achieved its first Test series win.

In *Anand*, Rajesh Khanna, India's first superstar, smiled as disarmingly as ever, symbolizing India shifting into another gear with the charismatic Indira Gandhi firmly at the helm, dwarfing all others. But it was the more grim and sullen doctor Babu Moshay, Amitabh Bachhan, who was about to start his domination as the smouldering angry young man.

# 1972: *Chalo Dildaar Chalo*

*Chalo dildaar chalo*
*Chaand ke paar chalo*
*Hum hai tayaar chalo*
*Chalo dildaar chalo*
*Chaand ke paar chalo*

Lyrics: Kaif Bhopali
Music: Ghulam Mohammed
Singers: Mohammed Rafi and Lata Mangeshkar
Film: *Pakeezah*

'CHALO *dildar chalo, chaand ke paar chalo ...*' captures the elegance and poetry of romantic love of an era which was already in decline by the time the Kamal Amrohi movie was released. In an album full of mujras, this is a romantic song. Rafi is a supporting singer in the song as he sings the mukhda repeatedly, but shines with an alaap in the middle of the song. Lata finishes the song with the antara, and adds to the grand picturization across the wide expanse of sea and sky to the lovers' ride on the boat. Many years later, Saregama released *Pakeezah Rang-Barang*, a record of the songs not used in the film, and it had a fast-paced version by Lata.

The music director of this very popular and highly regarded album was Ghulam Mohammed, who was Naushad's assistant all his life though he kept doing independent films as well. Naushad did the background score and three additional songs, which were used as snatches in the background. The film had a total of eighteen songs, but only six made it to the final cut. Way beyond any mujra-based scores before or after, they are unique to Hindi film music.

But *Pakeezah* came at a time when Hindi film music had already changed to being more Western, with R.D. Burman and Kishore Kumar ruling the roost. The other films during the year were *Victoria No. 203*, *Seeta Aur Geeta*, *Jawani Diwani*, *Amar Prem*, *Dushman*, *Parichay* and *Beimaan*. Such was the situation that before *Pakeezah*'s release, the financiers wanted the music of the film changed and made 'trendy'. Amrohi's reason was that he could not betray a dead man – composer Ghulam Mohammed had passed away in 1967 – who had given him this *amaanat* of beautiful songs. 'Had he been alive, my composer would have agreed to change the music, and I would have done so too,' he told a financier.

Like all cult films, *Pakeezah* has many myths spun around it. One of the more enduring ones is that the film became a hit only after Meena Kumari's death. Meena Kumari died nine weeks after the release of the movie, by when it was already a hit. Many believe that Kamal Amrohi took fourteen years to make the film because he was a slow film-maker. He started the film in 1958, but colour cinema came into vogue in 1960 when he scrapped the black-and-white portions. A year or so later, with the widescreen Cinemascope coming into vogue abroad, Amrohi decided to once again scrap what was shot in colour as he had succeeded in acquiring a Cinemascope lens from Metro-Goldwyn-Mayer (MGM) on a royalty basis. The film was stalled from 1964 to 1968 when differences crept up between Amrohi and his wife Meena Kumari.

*Pakeezah* was a carryover from the movies of the past, and so were the events of 1972, a follow-up of what happened in 1971. Having won the Lok Sabha elections and securing a military victory against Pakistan in 1971, Indira Gandhi won the elections to thirteen state assemblies in March. It was truly Indira Gandhi's victory. As Atal Bihari Vajpayee observed, while the opposition had put up 2,700 candidates, the ruling party had in effect fielded the same candidate in every constituency: Indira Gandhi. Only the victory in West Bengal was controversial where the Congress–CPI alliance defeated the CPI(M) through mass-scale rigging of polls under police protection.

The other unfinished agenda carried over was the war which had left 93,000 Pakistanis as prisoners of war in Indian custody. Wary of making the mistake the winners of the First World War made at Versailles, India treated Pakistan as an equal, with dignity, honour and respect. Z.A. Bhutto and Indira Gandhi negotiated hard at Simla in June. India wanted a 'No war pact' but had to settle for a mutual 'renunciation of force'; instead of a treaty, it got an agreement. India did not press Bhutto on Kashmir as it would have made his position completely untenable in Pakistan. The ceasefire line in Jammu and Kashmir was designated as the Line of Control, with a verbal assurance that it would eventually become an international border. But Bhutto was to soon go back on his word, when he gave a three-hour-long speech on 14 July in the National Assembly of Pakistan. Promising his support to any freedom movement by people of Kashmir, Bhutto argued that the Simla accord was a success because Pakistan did 'not compromise on the right of self-determination of the people of Jammu and Kashmir'.

As part of the continuing political restructuring of the north-east, the government created three new states – Manipur, Meghalaya and Tripura. The princely states of Tripura and Manipur had merged with India in 1949 to become Union Territories. Meghalaya was formed as an autonomous state on 2 April 1970, after being carved out of Assam and then became a full-fledged state in January 1972.

Meanwhile, continuing with her socialist economic policies, Indira Gandhi introduced new land ceiling limits as she believed that landlessness among rural poor was the main cause of the Naxal problem and agrarian tensions. Besides reducing the landholdings per individual, stringent rules were brought in place to reduce exceptions which had helped big landowners evade the earlier ceilings. The green revolution, which had started in 1967, began showing results in terms of increased food production but it had benefited less than one-tenth of rural districts across the country. The harvest still depended largely on monsoons and a failure this year – following the Bangladesh refugee crisis the previous year – meant that India had to import foodgrains. Global food prices also rose sharply and Indira Gandhi, humiliated after the experience of getting wheat from the United States in her first tenure, chose to expend valuable foreign exchange to import foodgrains. This allowed her to pump in nearly eleven million tonnes of foodgrains into the public distribution system and prevent a humanitarian crisis. But inflation was already rearing its head; food prices rose by 24 per cent between July 1972 and June 1973.

Prime Minister Gandhi also piloted the Wildlife Protection Act through parliament, which led to the creation of wildlife sanctuaries and national parks, and strictly restricted and regulated activities in them, besides banning hunting of wildlife. A census of tigers revealed that India had barely 1,800 tigers left, which led to the launch of Project Tiger in 1973. She put a stop to hunting of the endangered houbara bustards in Rajasthan by Arabs, a practice which continues in Pakistan till date. Her concern for wildlife was driven by personal passion – she was an avid birdwatcher after her father sent her a book by the famous ornithologist, Dr Salim Ali, from Dehradun Jail – and her commitment ran deep. Even in the midst of negotiating the Simla accord with Bhutto, she wrote a letter to the Bihar chief minister in response to a plea by the legislature about the release of the rich Madanpur forests for a development project. She asked the then chief minister to halt the diversion of the forest.

The year marked twenty-five years of India's independence, which was commemorated by a special midnight sitting of the Lok Sabha. India had made a lot of progress since 1947 but there was always the argument that this progress was not enough. India was producing fifty-six million kilowatts of power compared to 6.6 million in 1950. But even the most conservative estimates put the count of India's poor at around 200 million. Even though the percentage of literates had gone up, there were more illiterates in 1972 than there were in 1947. A mere 4 per cent of women in rural Bihar were literate compared to over 60 per cent in Kerala. In the silver jubilee year of Independence, India's southernmost state had established itself as the most progressive and egalitarian state in the country. It was a state, bestowed with natural beauty, you would have wanted to take your beloved to, perhaps humming '*Chalo dildaar chalo, chaand ke paar chalo ...*'

# 1973: *Chura Liya Hai Tumne Jo Dil Ko*

*Chura liya hai tumne jo dil ko*
*Nazar nahin churana sanam*
*Badal ke meri tum zindagani*
*Kahin badal na jaana sanam*

Lyricist: Majrooh Sultanpuri
Music: R.D. Burman
Singesr: Asha Bhosle and Mohammed Rafi
Film: *Yaadon ki Baraat*

'CHURA *liya hai tumne jo dil ko ...*' is an R.D. Burman classic which hasn't dated with time at all. The sounds are Western, especially the opening guitar and the instrumental interludes, but the song is absolutely Indian. One would expect an iconic classic R.D. Burman song to be sung by Kishore Kumar but it is Mohammed Rafi who partners Asha Bhosle here. In fact, as with many of the songs in the 1970s, Rafi is a supporting singer here in which Asha creates sheer magic with her voice.

Nasir Hussain's films have always been known for lilting tunes and super-hit music, and *Yaadon Ki Baraat* was no exception. His filming of the songs, the set designs, the wigs, the looks and the dresses of the actors were meant to capture the zeitgeist of the times. The picturization of the song with Zeenat Aman at her glamorous best – hardly anyone remembers her co-star Vijay Arora – adds to the charm and longevity of the song, making it stand out in an era full of similar peppy, Western numbers.

*Yaadon Ki Baraat* was written by Salim–Javed, with the script based on the lost-and-found formula which went on to become a staple of Hindi cinema. It was a multi-starrer but the only real star in the film, besides the music, was Dharmendra.

If *Yaadon Ki Baraat* was all fun and frolic, *Garm Hava*, which was also released during the year, was a movie which explored the festering wounds of Partition and Muslim identity in India. Based on Urdu writer Ismat Chughtai's short story, which was adapted by Shama Zaidi and Kaifi Azmi, M.S. Sathyu's directorial debut depicts how the events of Partition in 1947 and Mahatma Gandhi's assassination in 1948 affects a Muslim family in Agra because of their unwillingness to migrate to Pakistan like many other members of their community.

In 1973, the film had to grapple with the Central Board of Film Certification (CBFC) for a year before getting the certificate. 'They had doubts that the film could create tension in the society. Political leaders like Bal Thackeray and Lal Krishna Advani attacked the film. Advani wrote a review without watching the film. Later, when he became the information and broadcasting minister, he apologized for writing on hearsay,' Sathyu recalled in 2014 when a digitally restored version of the film was released. This film boasts of what is considered to be one of the finest performances by Balraj Sahni, who passed away a day after finishing the dubbing for the movie. Sahni played the lead character of Salim Mirza who is plagued by self-doubt: Should he have left in 1947 itself? Where is home – and what does it mean to be a Muslim in India?

It is noteworthy that a movie dealing with Indian Muslim identity and Pakistan could be perceived as communally sensitive when India had just won the Bangladesh war of independence, laying to rest the two-nation theory. Indira Gandhi was at the peak of her powers but even though she had seen the film at Sathyu's request and approved it for screening, the movie did not get an early release. The year 1973 was a tough one for her economically with inflation shooting above 20 per cent as global crude prices rose by more than 200 per cent in April. The nationalization of the energy sector did not help as even Indira Gandhi was forced to make a much-publicized show of using a horse-drawn buggy to travel from her residence to the parliament.

But a huge import bill for petroleum, foodgrains and fertilizers forced the government to bring a law to regulate and conserve foreign exchange, the Foreign Exchange Regulation Act or FERA. Section 29 of FERA made it mandatory for foreign companies operating in India with a parent holding of over 40 per cent to dilute their holdings. They were given two years to do so. Coke and IBM refused, while many others like Colgate agreed. None of this, however, helped the government tide over a balance of payments (BoP) crisis, and India had to borrow from the IMF, including under a special dispensation for oil.

Despite all the economic troubles, Indira Gandhi's emergence as a popular national leader – perhaps the only leader – had led Sheikh Abdullah and Naga rebels to enter into protracted negotiations with her government. In December, she travelled to Kohima to mark the tenth anniversary of the formation of Nagaland as a state. She asked the Naga underground to 'come out and shoulder the responsibilities of building up Nagaland' which led to assembly elections three months later.

But the one thing which was to have long-lasting impact on India's political structure happened on 24 April. Chief Justice S.M. Sikri and twelve judges of the Supreme Court assembled to deliver the most important judgment in its history. The case of *Kesavananda Bharati* vs *State of Kerala* had been heard for sixty-eight days; the hard work and scholarship that had gone into the preparation of this case were breathtaking. The then Attorney General had made a comparative chart analysing the provisions of the Constitutions of seventy-one different countries.

By a narrow majority of 7:6, the court ruled that there are certain principles within the framework of the Constitution of India which are inviolable and hence cannot be amended by parliament. These principles were commonly termed as the Basic Structure of the Constitution. This basic structure doctrine, as future events showed, saved Indian democracy, and *Kesavananda Bharati* will always occupy a hallowed place in our constitutional history. In the glorification of the basic structure theory, it is important to bear in mind its infirm roots and how predilections and prejudices of judges, chance and accidental circumstances have played a greater part rather than any logic or conscious formulation of it.

But the actual verdict involved a lot of drama. Eleven separate judgments were delivered, which agreed on some points and differed on others, by nine judges – Chief Justice S.M. Sikri, Justices J.M. Shelat, K.S. Hegde, A.N. Grover, B. Jaganmohan Reddy, D.G. Palekar, H.R. Khanna, A.K. Mukherjee and Y.V. Chandrachud. Six judges – Chief Justice S.M. Sikri and Justices J.M. Shelat, K.S. Hegde, P. Jaganmohan Reddy, A.N. Grover and S. Mukherjea – were of the opinion that parliament's power was limited because of implied and inherent limitations in the Constitution, including those in fundamental rights. Six other judges – Justices A.N. Ray, D.G. Palekar, K.K. Mathew, S.N. Dwivedi, M.H. Beg, and Y.V. Chandrachud – were of the opinion that there were no limitations at all on parliament's power to amend the Constitution. But one judge, Justice H.R. Khanna, took neither side. He held that parliament had the full power of amending the Constitution; but because it had the power only 'to amend', it must leave 'the basic structure or framework of the Constitution' intact. It was a hopelessly divided verdict after all the labour and arguments of five months. No majority, no minority, nobody could say what the verdict was.

How was it then said that the court by a majority held that parliament had no power to amend the basic structure of the Constitution? Immediately after the eleven judges finished reading their judgments, Chief Justice Sikri, in whose opinion parliament's power was limited by inherent and implied limitations, passed on a hastily prepared paper called a 'View of the Majority' for signatures by the thirteen judges on the bench. One of the conclusions in the 'View of the Majority' was that 'Parliament did not have the power to amend the basic structure or framework of the Constitution'. This was lifted from one of the conclusions in the judgment of Justice H.R. Khanna. Nine judges signed the statement in court. Four others refused to sign it. The Chief Justice retired the next day.

Coming to know of the judgments in advance, the government disregarded the seniority of three judges who had been part of the majority – Justices J.M. Shelat, K.S. Hegde and A.N. Grover – for the appointment of the next CJI, and appointed Justice A.N. Ray the next day.

At a dinner hosted by the SC gazetted staff on 25 April in honour of the retiring Chief Justice of India, he told Ray, 'You will rue the day you accepted the chief justiceship'. His conduct as the CJI, when he tried to review the Kesavananda Bharati judgment without an appeal being made and the judgment in the habeas corpus case on illegal detention, was to lose him the respect of the legal fraternity.

# 1974: *Kai Baar Yun Hi Dekha Hai*

*Kai baar yun hi dekha hai*
*Yeh jo mann ki seema rekha hai,*
*Mann todane lagtaa hai*
*Anjaanee pyaas ke peechhe,*
*Anjaanee aas ke peechhe,*
*Mann daudane lagtaa hai*

Lyrics: Yogesh
Music: Salil Chowdhury
Singer: Mukesh
Film: *Rajnigandha*

'*KAI baar yun hi dekha hai, yeh jo mann ki seema rekha hai …*' is a rare song in Hindi cinema for a couple of reasons. It was perhaps the only occasion Mukesh was not singing for a hero on screen, and the song captures the emotional dilemma of the heroine but a male playback singer provides the voice to her predicament. The song, which won Mukesh the National Award, was to be originally sung by Lata Mangeshkar. She had asked for ₹3,000 as remuneration but the producers thought that was too much for a small-budget film. They thus went with Mukesh, who agreed to render the song for only ₹1,000. Written by Yogesh, who was Salil Chowdhury's preferred lyricist after Shailendra's demise, the song from *Rajnigandha* was based on a Bangla song by Salil Chowdhury, '*Ami cholte cholte theme gechhi*'.

Directed by Basu Chatterjee, *Rajnigandha* was based on Hindi writer Mannu Bhandari's short story, 'Yehi Sach Hai' and featured two newcomers – Vidya Sinha and Amol Palekar. The film's central character, Deepa, played by Vidya Sinha, was ahead of her times in exploring her conflicting emotions about the two men in her life. '*Kai baar yun hi dekha hai* ...' was shot in a taxi, with little action by or expression from the characters, but the interlude provides the sense of urgency and turmoil. The lyricist Yogesh Gaur had to delve deep into the script to come up with the song. He crafted the song, particularly the most critical line '*Yeh jo mann ki seema rekha hai, mann todne lagta hai*' on a dialogue in the film, 'Jo saamne hai, wohi sach hai'.

*Rajnigandha* also created a market for a genre of low-budget popular films, without established stars, made with a different sensibility from the more mainstream aesthetic of crudity, anger and violence. These were the 1970s' version of the multiplex films, meant for an urban middle-class audience, neither falling into the art cinema category nor into the commercial blockbuster slot.

This was the year when art cinema became popular with Shyam Benegal's debut film, *Ankur*, which also was the first release of Shabana Azmi. Besides earning a lot of critical acclaim, *Ankur* was also a commercial success, earning more than ₹1 crore despite being produced in ₹5 lakh. But the biggest commercial success of the year was *Roti, Kapda aur Makaan*, a Manoj Kumar multi-starrer which reflected the dominant discontent of the times, about the lack of jobs. Its title was based on a political slogan used by Pakistani prime minister Z.A. Bhutto in his public speeches but resonated with the socialist phase of Indira Gandhi's politics starting from the late 1960s. In a show of political correctness, the film has Indira Gandhi's speech against hoarders in the end.

Hoarding was a big crisis as inflation, particularly food inflation, shot through the roof following the global oil crisis and the balance of payments crisis. This was independent India's worst inflationary episode, from November 1973 to December 1974, when inflation never dropped below 20 per cent and was above 30 per cent for four consecutive months starting June. In September, inflation reached 34.6 per cent, a figure never reached since, but dropped to 25.4 per cent by the year-end before plummeting below zero in 1975. A group of 140 economists had submitted a memorandum on a policy to contain inflation to Prime Minister Gandhi in February.

The government reversed the nationalization of wholesale grain trade but the other measures included curbs on wages, salaries and allowances. Harsh internal security laws were invoked to crack down on smugglers, hoarders and black marketeers. As secretary, economic affairs, Manmohan Singh was part of the group in the finance ministry that devised the measures to control inflation. He said that 'Mrs Gandhi was able to take the risks' and there was no worry among the government about hurting investment and growth, while attaining price stability.

As is often the case in any democracy, an economic crisis was accompanied by a political crisis. It all started from Gujarat. The students of L.D. Engineering College in Ahmedabad protested against increased mess charges, leading to statewide protests by students against food inflation. This was the beginning of the movement which brought cataclysmic changes in the country. A Navnirman Samiti was formed by the student organizations of various opposition political parties to spearhead the movement. The state government was headed by Chimanbhai Patel, who had the support of 140 members in the House of 168. Beset by allegations of huge corruption, particularly of making money by allowing the price of groundnut oil – the most popular cooking oil in the state – to rise, the chief minister was called Chiman chor by the agitating students. The government resigned in February and president's rule was imposed. But Jayaprakash Narayan or JP, a much-respected freedom fighter who became a Gandhian after Gandhi's assassination, visited Ahmedabad and asked the students to continue their protests till the state assembly was dissolved. This resulted in fresh violence leading to ninety-five deaths. On 11 March, Morarji Desai went on to an indefinite fast and the Central government succumbed, dissolving the assembly on 15 March.

The success of the Navnirman movement inspired student wings of political parties – the Bharatiya Jana Sangh (BJS), the SSP, the CPI and the Congress (O) – to organize themselves in Bihar to protest the misdeeds and corruption of the Congress government. They led protests around the slogan, '*Poora ration poora kaam, nahin toh hoga chakka jaam.*' In February 1974, the AISF, the student wing of the CPI broke away on ideological grounds and the rest of the student organizations formed the Chhatra Sangharsh Samiti (CSS). On 18 March, the CSS marched to the state assembly demanding its dissolution. They clashed with the police, leading to three deaths, and trouble spread across the state. On a request from the students, JP stepped in to lead the movement. The Bihar movement now became the JP movement as students were exhorted to boycott classes. By April, street protests had intensified. On 5 June, at a public rally at Gandhi Maidan, JP gave the call of Sampoorna Kranti or Total Revolution. The country was at that time paralysed by a railway strike led by George Fernandes.

JP, who was an old family friend of the Nehru–Gandhis, and Indira Gandhi entered into negotiations, which broke down within six weeks. By August, JP had returned to Bihar to convert it into a nationwide movement. Some of his old associates warned JP that the local leadership of the movement was passing on to the Jana Sangh and the protests were un-Gandhian and undemocratic in an independent India. A final round of talks between Indira Gandhi and JP on 1 November resulted in failure, after JP refused to accept the compromise formula of dismissing the Bihar government if he didn't insist on dissolution of other state assemblies. By year-end, the politics was polarized and many were hailing the JP movement as the second freedom movement.

Amidst all the political turmoil, India conducted the nuclear test at Pokhran on 18 May, christening it a Peaceful Nuclear Explosion (PNE). Prime Minister Gandhi had given the go-ahead to the scientists at the Bhabha Atomic Research Centre (BARC) to manufacture the nuclear device they had designed and prepare it for a test. To preserve secrecy, very few records of any kind were kept either on the development process or the decision making involved in its development and testing. It was codenamed 'Smiling Buddha', in all probability at the suggestion of P.N. Dhar in the Prime Minister's Office.

The quasi-independent state of Sikkim was acquired by Indira Gandhi after a popular vote saw the pro-India party, stoked by New Delhi, win all but one seat in the elections. But these two achievements provided only temporary relief to Indira Gandhi as her opponents grappled with questions of constitutional norms while intensifying their protests.

# 1975: *Tere Bina Zindagi Se Koyi Shikwa Toh Nahin*

*Kaash aisa ho tere qadmo se*
*Chun ke manzil chale aur kahin door kahin*
*Tum gar saath ho, manzilon ki kami toh nahin*
*Tere bina zindagi se koyi, shikwa toh nahin*

Lyrics: Gulzar
Music: R.D. Burman
Singers: Kishore Kumar and Lata Mangeshkar
Film: *Aandhi*

'TERE *bina zindagi se koi shikwa toh nahin* ...' is a signature song of the R.D. Burman–Gulzar collaboration, the kind of music which topped the charts not only in the 1970s but held its own even in the 1980s. More importantly, these songs continue to be extremely popular today, bearing the test of time. In fact, '*Tere bina zindagi se* ...' from Gulzar-directed *Aandhi* boasts of one of the largest number of YouTube hits for any old song. Gulzar wrote the song after he heard R.D. compose the Bangla song, '*Jete jete pathe holo deri* ...' with Bangla songwriter Gouri Prasanna Majumdar. This song is another Lata–Kishore duct, but sung in the background, to capture the internal romantic turmoil of the middle-aged couple. Filled with a couple of sharp musical interludes, the song is also interspersed with a dialogue between Suchitra Sen and Sanjeev Kumar. The camera sticks to the facial expressions of the characters, with the ruins of the Martand temple at Anantnag providing the metaphorical backdrop of their emotional state.

Gulzar narrates an anecdote about the scene in the song where Sen's eyes are glistening, but she can't shed a tear. 'Mrs Sen asked me to play the stanza that goes, "*Tum jo keh do toh aaj ki raat chaand doobega nahin*"... She listened with her eyes shut while Haribhai (Sanjeev Kumar) pressed his little finger against the corner of his eyes. Then, with a flick of her hand, she indicated that the music be stopped. Haribhai gestured that the two-in-one playing the song be taken away. Both of them were ready for the take. They looked at each other as if to live the whole life's longing in the span of that one line, "*Raat ko rok lo, raat ki baat hai, aur zindagi baaki toh nahin* ..."'

Iconic films like *Sholay*, *Deewaar* and *Jai Santoshi Maa* were released this year but *Aandhi* held its own, helped in good measure by the big political controversy surrounding the movie. The political drama came to be publicized as being based on the life of the then prime minister, Indira Gandhi, and her relationship with her estranged husband, Feroze Gandhi. While a poster in south India declared, 'See your prime minister on screen', another advertisement in a Delhi daily called the film 'the story of a great woman political leader in post-Independence India'. Gulzar though clarified that Sen's look was inspired by Congress politician Tarkeshwari Sinha and Indira Gandhi.

Surprisingly, the film was released without any hassle but it was banned after it had run for twenty weeks. The ban triggered by the Gujarat assembly election campaign where opposition candidates started showing scenes of Sen's character smoking and occasionally drinking to malign Indira Gandhi. Gulzar solved the problem by inserting a scene of the heroine standing in front of the photograph of Indira Gandhi and calling the prime minister her ideal. Like Sen's character, Indira Gandhi was an ideal for many an Indian but things were going downhill rather quickly. On the midnight of 25 June, she imposed the infamous Emergency.

The declaration of Emergency came as a surprise to everyone, including the members of her cabinet who were asked to endorse the decision retrospectively at a dawn meeting. In the early hours of 26 June, hundreds of prominent leaders of the JP movement were arrested, mainly in the northern states, under the draconian Maintenance of Internal Security Act (MISA). Normal political processes were suspended, immense powers conferred on the executive, and fundamental rights and civil liberties guaranteed under Article 19 of the Constitution were suspended. The news was suppressed by cutting off power supply to Bahadurshah Zafar Marg from where most of the national dailies were published. *The Statesman* and the *Hindustan Times* were, however, able to carry the news in their editions as their presses were located in Connaught Place, New Delhi. This was, however, only a beginning. In December, the government brought in an ordinance which provided for strict censorship, and in many cases, pre-censorship on newspapers, magazines and other publications. It also abolished the Press Council of India, an independent body working for the freedom of the press.

The seeds of Emergency were sown two weeks before it was announced, when Justice Jagmohan Lal Sinha of Allahabad High Court declared Indira Gandhi's election null and void over two of the twelve charges of corrupt electoral practices. The Uttar Pradesh government had made a high rostrum for her, and her election agent was still in government service when the campaign began. Justice Sinha stayed the order for twenty days to allow an appeal in the Supreme Court. On 23 June, the vacation bench of the Supreme Court issued a conditional stay on the order: the prime minister could attend parliament but could not vote till the final disposal of her appeal. On 25 June, S.S. Ray, the chief minister of West Bengal and a renowned barrister, helped prepare an ordinance for Emergency which the president signed at midnight.

A few days after the imposition of Emergency, organizations such as the RSS, the Jamaat-i-Islami, Ananda Marg and their affiliated groups were banned, and their leading cadre arrested. The arrests continued through the nineteen-month Emergency, during which a total of 110,000 persons were arrested under MISA and Defence of India Rules (DIR). However, most of the arrested were released after a few days or months. JP was released on 12 November on health grounds. Other opposition leaders like Asoka Mehta, Atal Bihari Vajpayee and Charan Singh were set free in 1976.

The parliament met on 21 July to approve the Emergency, where all the members of the opposition voted against the proposal. 'This action is totally within our constitutional framework and it was undertaken in order not to destroy the Constitution but to preserve the Constitution, to preserve and safeguard our democracy,' Indira Gandhi told the Lok Sabha while defending the imposition of Emergency.

The government then introduced the thirty-eighth amendment to the Constitution which barred the proclamation of the Emergency from being challenged in the courts. Amendments to the Representation of People's Act were passed to invalidate the Supreme Court judgment in Indira Gandhi's case and to prevent any further legal challenge. Civil liberties were denied and strikes and protests crushed with a heavy hand. The government was seen as determined to act strongly against those 'who were working against the nation'.

In the initial months, there was a popular acceptance of the Emergency, with a noticeable improvement in social discipline and public order. There was an immediate improvement in government departments and public services, with trains running as per schedule. Especially popular was the anti-smuggling drive under which nearly 2,000 smugglers, including top names like Haji Mastan and Yusuf Patel, were put behind bars. Such was the initial acceptance that Vinoba Bhave described the Emergency as 'Anushasan Parva' or the Era of Discipline.

But the biggest improvement was in the economy, helped in good measure by the best monsoon in five years. Foodgrain and edible oil production rose by 21 per cent, industrial production rose by 6 per cent, and exports went up by 21 per cent. GDP grew by an impressive 8.5 per cent while inflation came down, with food prices declining by 20 per cent. All the top businessmen, including J.R.D. Tata, came out strongly in support of the Emergency. This was acknowledged by *Time* magazine in its October issue, which said: 'The Prime Minister has won widespread support for seizing a rare opportunity to ram through a score of social reforms.' That was a one-sided view, for Indians may have been going through their lives but their lives had no meaning without democracy.

# 1976: *Kabhi Kabhi Mere Dil Mein Khayal Aata Hai*

*Kabhi kabhi mere dil mein khayal aata hai*
*Ki jaise tu mujhe chaahegi umr bhar yun hi*
*Uthegi meri taraf pyaar ki nazar yun hi*
*Main jaanta hoon ki tu ghair hai magar yun hi*

Lyrics: Sahir Ludhianvi
Music: Khayyam
Singer: Mukesh
Film: *Kabhi Kabhie*

'KABHI *kabhi mere dil mein khayal aata hai ...*' immediately transports the listener to the bygone era of romantic love, where the whole world is only seen in soft focus. Mukesh's soulful voice, Khayyam's melodious tune, Amitabh and Raakhee together, and cinematography which captures the salubrious climes of Kashmir were all outstanding. But the song is a timeless classic mainly because of Sahir's lyrics. The song was a simpler version of the original Urdu poem by the same title from his collection *Talkhiyan*, which was published in 1960. Besides using chaste Urdu, the original poem was darker and more sombre in capturing the separation of the poet from his beloved. A stanza from the original poem is recited by Amitabh in his own voice, later in the movie, to convey his state of painful separation from his ex-lover, played by Raakhee. That was a fitting tribute to Urdu poetry in a film which was itself inspired by Sahir's original poem.

The music for *Kabhi Kabhie* – the extra 'e' was added for numerological reasons – won Khayyam the Filmfare Award, and the song brought the same laurel for Mukesh and Sahir. Khayyam had in fact originally created the tune for an unreleased film made in 1950 by Chetan Anand. The song, recorded by Geeta Dutt and Sudha Malhotra, was never released. Like the tune of the song, *Kabhi Kabhie* was also a throwback to more pleasant times of romance and complicated relationships. *Zanjeer*, *Deewaar* and *Sholay* had established Amitabh as the angry young man, and this movie cast him in a romantic role although he is sulking, bitter and angry for a large part of the film. The film stood out among all the other hit films this year which were typical masala films: *Dus Nambari*, *Nagin* and *Fakira*. The average quality of films which ruled the box office reflected the state of the country which was by now feeling the full force of the Emergency.

In its early months, despite the fear it aroused, the Emergency had a comparatively mild character as far as repressive regimes went. India under Indira was certainly authoritarian but it was not totalitarian. Indira Gandhi had neither the party machinery of storm-troopers nor a coherent ideology or a majoritarian social base but only the run-down bureaucracy to ensure the implementation of her orders. American scholar Granville Austin noted that 'ugly as the Emergency was, New Delhi in 1976 was not Berlin under Hitler'. People had accepted the Emergency initially without much resistance because they saw it is a short-term expedient to meet a specific situation and not as an alternative form of government or as a substitute for democracy.

But the Constitution was amended and general elections, due in February, were postponed twice, once in February and then in November. In November, the term of the Lok Sabha was extended up to 18 March 1978. The forty-second amendment to the Constitution, a twenty-page document giving unprecedented power to parliament, providing legislature further immunity from judicial scrutiny and giving the Centre greater power over the states, was signed by the president on 18 December.

As the public perception of the Emergency started changing, Indira Gandhi started losing legitimacy and opposition leaders started finding listeners on the ground. Further, concentration, subversion and misuse of power, along with the increasing eclipse of institutions, was worsened by the rise of the prime minister's younger son, Sanjay Gandhi, as an extra-constitutional authority. Although he held no official position either in the government or in the party, he had access to government files, cabinet papers and participated in decision making of the government, passing verbal orders. He operated through select cabinet ministers like Bansi Lal, pliant junior ministers such as Om Mehta and Pranab Mukherjee, and handpicked bureaucrats like Navin Chawla. Such was his say in decision making that he sat with the defence minister, Bansi Lal, to interview the two rear admirals in line to be selected as the navy chief. Popular playback singer Kishore Kumar's songs were banned from AIR and Doordarshan on 4 May (the ban continued till the end of the Emergency) for his refusal to perform at a Congress rally in Mumbai.

By April, Sanjay had emerged as a parallel authority, seen as the second most powerful person in the country after his mother. He was extensively covered in the media, given elaborate welcomes by chief ministers and the party organized large rallies for him. A cult of Sanjay was built around the thirty-year-old through the Youth Congress, which provided him with a following, cadre and organization personally loyal to him. During the year, the Youth Congress claimed to have recruited five million members. The rise of the Youth Congress was accepted by Indira Gandhi herself at the Guwahati session of the party in November when she declared that the Youth Congress had 'stolen our thunder'. He was hailed by the press too, with Khushwant Singh stating: 'Sanjay Gandhi has added a new dimension to political leadership: he has no truck with shady characters or sycophants; he is a teetotaler, he lives a simple life ... his words are not hot air but charged with action.'

In July, Sanjay put forward his own five-point programme that rivalled and eclipsed Prime Minister Gandhi's twenty-point programme. His points were: dowry abolition, family planning, planting of trees, promotion of literacy and ending caste distinction. Among these, family planning and urban beautification, involving slum clearance, were implemented as crash programmes, in an authoritarian and coercive manner. This ham-handed behaviour led to some of the worst excesses of the Emergency, particularly in north India. Forcible sterilization, or nasbandi, created and spread a fear psychosis among the people, leading to the unpopularity of the regime. The emergence of Sanjay as an extra-constitutional authority further convinced the people that temporary authoritarianism was being transformed into a long-term dictatorship by a handful of people.

Meanwhile, the RSS leadership continued with its efforts to buy peace with the government and get the ban on the RSS removed. Balasaheb Deoras, the RSS chief, had already written to Indira Gandhi in 1975 from Yerwada prison, praising her Independence Day speech and congratulated her on the successful election appeal in the Supreme Court. Asserting that the RSS had no connection with the JP movement, he asked her to utilize the 'power of the Sangh for the upliftment of our country'. In January and February, he wrote at length to Vinoba Bhave, asking him to intercede with Prime Minister Gandhi on RSS's behalf so that it could contribute to the country's progress under her leadership. But she did not relent, reading the RSS offer as a tactical move to avoid government repression.

By the end of the year, Indira Gandhi had realized the enormity of the misuse of the family planning programme. In November and December she tried to stall the campaign, dissociate herself from it and blame its excesses on overzealous bureaucrats. She stopped the enactment of the bill on compulsory national sterilization for those having two or more children and asked the state governments to desist from using coercive methods. By then, it was already too late though she would not have realized it as the opposition was looking for a compromise with her. Barring George Fernandes and Madhu Limaye, the firebrand socialist leaders, most others were keen on seeking a negotiated political compromise with the government.

In mid-December, DMK leader K. Karunanidhi convened a meeting of opposition leaders to initiate talks with Indira Gandhi without laying down any prior conditions and with a view to normalizing the political situation. But these efforts did not go far as JP, the undisputed leader of the opposition movement, did not approve of these efforts and Indira Gandhi was unwilling to conciliate the seemingly powerless opposition leaders. Had she accepted the offer from the opposition, or had Sanjay Gandhi not emerged as this extra-constitutional power centre, India's political trajectory would have been different.

# 1977: *Anhoni Ko Honi Kar Dein*

*Sapan salone le ke aayi hai yeh raat saloni*
*Ek jagah jab jama ho teeno Amar Akbar Anthony*
*Amar Akbar Anthony*
*Anhoni ko honi kar dein, honi ko anhoni*

Lyrics: Anand Bakshi
Music: Laxmikant–Pyarelal
Singers: Kishore Kumar, Mahendra Kapoor and Shailendra Singh
Film: *Amar Akbar Anthony*

'ANHONI *ko honi kar dein, honi ko anhoni, Ek jagah jab jama ho teeno, Amar, Akbar, Anthony* ...' does not boast of outstanding poetry, great music or a wonderful composition. But the title song from Manmohan Desai's monster hit *Amar Akbar Anthony* is more than the sum of its parts. It is a song typical of the times and the genre, where the climax in the villain's den always needed an extravagant number with the heroes in disguise. The song is followed by a fight, which ends with the bad guys either dying or being put behind bars. But what makes '*Anhoni ko honi kar de* ...' different from other such numbers is the fun element in the song, integral to the over-the-top surrealism which Manmohan Desai specialized in. That the three heroes are shown to be from three different religions – Hinduism, Islam and Christianity – also makes the song unique in Indian cinema.

The song was in keeping with the spirit of the film, a fast-paced multi-starrer extravaganza with a fantastical, convoluted plot about three brothers who get separated and lost in childhood. In an involved tale of secularism, the three men are brought up in three different religions and fall in love with a girl of their practising religion. The outlandish plots needed 'lapses in logic and leaps of faith required of the audiences', as Amitabh Bachchan told Sidharth Bhatia for the book *Amar Akbar Anthony: Masala, Madness and Manmohan Desai* (HarperCollins). Most lessons about religious pluralism and secular harmony in the film are in-your-face, such as the three brothers practising different religions, unknowingly donating blood to a blind woman, who is their mother. It symbolizes the three religions coming together to serve India, the motherland. The children were separated on 15 August from under the statue of Mahatma Gandhi, and their reunion in the end completes the nationalistic allegory. The song also reaffirms the message that the three religions are 'pillars of the nation' and when they work together, they can beat any evil – in this case, their common villain.

The most successful film of the year, *Amar Akbar Anthony* was one of the first set of commercial Indian films to be broadcast by BBC television during prime time. The film competed with three other Manmohan Desai films released that year: *Parvarish*, *Dharam-Veer* and *Chacha Bhatija*. With each of these films – equally outlandish – going on to become jubilee hits, the year established Desai as the new king of Hindi cinema.

On 18 January, Indira Gandhi announced elections to the Lok Sabha, much to the surprise of the nation, even though the previous November's constitutional amendment made the elections unnecessary for another year. Opposition leaders, still behind bars, were released and two days later, the Emergency 'relaxed' to allow 'normal' political activity. There have been endless speculations about the reasons for Indira Gandhi's sudden change of heart. They include her confidence of winning the poll, her desire to prevent any further dent to her reputation internationally, a desire to be seen as democratic and accountable to the people, and pressure from people close to her like P.N. Dhar and B.K. Nehru who wanted her to call elections.

No one knows her precise motivations but perhaps it was a combination of factors that drove Indira Gandhi to renew her 'mandate'.

The elections, held between 16 and 20 March, led to a massive defeat for the Congress party. The party was wiped out in UP and Bihar, and lost badly in all states except Andhra Pradesh, Karnataka, Assam and Manipur, to finish with 153 out of the 542 seats for which elections were held. Indira Gandhi herself lost to Raj Narain in Rae Bareli and Sanjay lost in Amethi, along with thirty-four ministers in the Central government. Indira Gandhi accepted the defeat graciously, saying that the collective judgement of the people must be respected. On 21 March, a day before her government resigned from office, the acting president, B.D. Jatti – Fakhruddin Ali Ahmed had died of a heart attack in his bathtub on 11 February – revoked the Emergency on the government's recommendation.

The party that came to power was the newly formed Janata Party, which won 270 seats, while its ally, the Congress for Democracy (CFD), won twenty-nine seats. While the authoritarian rule contributed to Indira Gandhi's defeat, a united political opposition was critical to her defeat. There had been a lot of chatter about opposition unity since previous autumn but they came together so rapidly and effectively that it took Indira Gandhi, and perhaps the opposition leaders themselves, by surprise. The day after the announcement of the elections, JP declared: 'If the opposition parties merge into one single party, I am prepared to render full support during the elections; otherwise I prefer to keep myself away from the election campaign.'

On 23 January, Bharatiya Lok Dal, Bharatiya Jana Sangh, Congress (O), Samyukta Socialist Party and the tiny 'rebel' Congress came together as the Janata Party, with Morarji Desai as the chairman and Charan Singh as the deputy chairman. The CPI(M) did not officially join the Janata coalition, but announced its support for the party which was led by JP. When Indira Gandhi made her surprise announcement to hold elections in March 1977, the entire opposition looked up to JP. He was persuaded to come to Delhi from Patna.

On 2 February, the Janata Party was bolstered by the formation of CFD by the veteran Congress leader Jagjivan Ram who broke away from the Congress party. Ram, who was joined by two former chief ministers, H.N. Bahuguna of UP and Nandini Satpathy of Orissa, had been party to all the decisions during the Emergency as a senior cabinet minister. In fact, he had moved the resolution approving the Emergency in the Lok Sabha.

The first non-Congress government in independent India's history was sworn in on 24 March, with Morarji Desai taking oath as prime minister. Desai had put his hat in the ring to be the prime minister after Nehru's and Shastri's death but had lost out in the Congress parliamentary party. Even now, Desai's selection was not easy as both Charan Singh and Jagjivan Ram had prime ministerial aspirations. JP chose Desai, placating the other two contenders by giving them senior cabinet posts, although neither was happy about it. Even the selection of ministers led to a lot of heartburn among the various constituents of the Janata Party. At dawn, the newly elected Lok Sabha members of the ruling combine took a pledge at Raj Ghat to give the best to the weakest, to promote national unity and harmony, and to uphold the rights of the people.

Neelam Sanjiva Reddy was elected as the Speaker but gave way to K.S. Hegde in July when Reddy became the president. On 27 March, the government revoked the state of external Emergency proclaimed in 1971 for the Bangladesh war. But the challenge of repairing the Constitution was not easy: the ruling party did not have a majority in the Rajya Sabha, where Congress had 154 of the 244 seats. Within two weeks of coming to power, the government moved the forty-third amendment to the Constitution, containing only seven clauses, to partially repair the damage done by the forty-second amendment. Premature, the bill got lost in other government activities as the ruling party sought a way to bring enough Congress MPs on board in the Rajya Sabha.

In late October, the government sent forty-seven proposals for restoring the pre-Emergency Constitution. The Congress party passed twelve of them, and accepted the rest with modifications. Based on these discussions, the forty-third constitutional amendment bill was introduced in the Lok Sabha on 16 December. It was passed on 20 December, 318 to 1. The Rajya Sabha passed it on 23 December with not even a single nay vote. The bill was then sent to state assemblies for ratification.

Meanwhile, the government had repealed the press censorship laws but was not keen on doing away with preventive detention without trial under the MISA. A bill introduced in the Lok Sabha on 23 December to repeal MISA actually incorporated those clauses in the CrPC, causing uproar in the House. The bill was eventually withdrawn in March 1978. Alongside, the government decided to ask the nine Congress state governments, which were elected in 1972, to resign and seek fresh elections, failing which the Centre would dismiss them under Article 356. The state governments took it to the Supreme Court which upheld the Centre's stance, whereby these state government were dismissed on 30 April. The June elections in the states led to Congress's defeat in the states.

But what created the greatest public spectacle were the attempts to bring Indira Gandhi to justice for her deeds during the Emergency. Charan Singh justified a trial on the 'Nuremberg Model', as did the CPI(M) leader E.M.S. Namboodiripad. A commission of inquiry under retired chief justice J.C. Shah was formed in April. On 3 October, acting on the orders of Charan Singh, the CBI arrested Indira Gandhi over allegations of corruption. She came out smiling for the arrest, was kept in New Delhi Police Lines overnight, and when presented before a magistrate next morning, was released when the prosecution counsel admitted: 'We have no evidence at present.' Indira Gandhi capitalized upon the fiasco, moving politically within a year, from the impossible to the possible, from *anhoni* to *honi*.

# 1978: *Hum Bewafa Hargiz Na The*

*Hum bewafa hargiz na the*
*Par hum wafa kar na sake*
*Humko mili uski sazaa*
*Hum jo khata kar na sake*

Lyrics: Anand Bakshi
Music: R.D. Burman
Singer: Kishore Kumar
Film: *Shalimar*

'HUM *bewafa hargiz na the ...*' is another unforgettable, super-hit song – from a forgettable film that flopped – which has become a timeless classic. If the film *Shalimar* is still remembered today, it is mainly because of this song. Set to a somewhat typical Western melodious rhythm by R.D. Burman, the song is lifted out of its ordinary by the full-throated voice of Kishore Kumar. The lyrics by Anand Bakshi are nothing to write home about but Kishore's pitch, tone and tenor of delivery lend the words greater gravitas.

What also makes the song unusual is the hook provided by the '*jhinga lala hoo*' chorus that accompanies the song almost throughout its length. Liberally peppered with humming, bizarre sounds like *hurr hurr*, and nonsensical phrases such as *abu gachu kaba chabu kusu baka*, the song shows tribal men and women dressed in colourful but outlandish costumes and headgear engaged in some primitive ritual of sorts. Such has been the impact of the song that 'jhinga lala hoo' has entered the urban dictionary as a term denoting a happy, carefree state of mind.

The song is the only saving grace in a movie which did not lack in ambition, conception and production. Krishna Shah was a Gujarat-born producer and director in Hollywood who came to India in 1978, announcing that he wanted to make an international movie. Shah got a cache of Hollywood stars such as Rex Harrison, Sylvia Miles, both admittedly past their prime, and John Saxon (of *Enter the Dragon* fame). Shah wanted to sign up Amitabh Bachchan for the film but was allegedly kept waiting by the actor. He got angry, left and promptly signed Dharmendra. *Shalimar* was one of the most written-about films of its time, spawning books and commercial merchandise. The film was, in fact, shot separately in English and Hindi – each each sequence picturized first in English and then in Hindi – over a relatively short period of twelve weeks. The English version was called *Raiders of the Sacred Stone*, but it failed at the box office. The Hindi version too, despite the hype, eventually turned out to be a dud. Something similar was meanwhile happening to the Janata Party government at the Centre.

Having come to power on an anti-Indira platform, the Janata Party government was unable to punish the former prime minister. It only had the fiasco of an arrest in October 1977 to show for its intents, and Indira Gandhi capitalized on it to make her political comeback. Having refused to earlier appear before the Shah Commission on the grounds that its appointment was politically motivated, she appeared before it on 11 January. Claiming that making a statement would 'amount to a violation of my oath of secrecy', she refused to take an oath and to testify before it. But, for thirty minutes, she read out a statement justifying her actions about the Emergency. Justice Shah called it a 'political speech', and ordered a complaint filed before a magistrate against her for failing to testify. The issue was considered for the next ten months by the legal system.

In December, the Delhi High Court ruled that Indira Gandhi had not refused to take an oath before Shah because she merely said 'No' to a question, 'Are you willing to take an oath?'. This allowed her to claim in 1979 that the Shah Commission and other committees 'have found practically nothing against her'. That is far from the truth, as the commission's reports provide a host of documentation about the events of the Emergency and the denial of democracy during the period. The three volumes of the Shah Commission report are not officially available till date; even the copies sent to Indian embassies abroad were reportedly withdrawn by the Congress government when it returned to power in 1980.

Meanwhile, on 3 May, Sanjay Gandhi was sent to the Tihar Jail by the Supreme Court after his bail in the *Kissa Kursi Ka* case was cancelled to prevent him from tampering with witnesses in the future. The court agreed that Sanjay had abused his liberty by trying to suborn witnesses. Submitted to the censor board in April 1975, *Kissa Kursi Ka* was a political satire produced by Amrit Nahata, who was elected as an MP on the Janata Party ticket in 1977. As it spoofed Sanjay Gandhi's auto-manufacturing plans and his closest supporters, the film was banned. Shah Commission had held Sanjay guilty of burning the prints. Sanjay was prosecuted along with others and was sentenced to two years of rigorous imprisonment. Though he was given bail pending appeal, the Supreme Court cancelled his bail and Sanjay had to spend a month in Tihar Jail. The then information and broadcasting minister V.C. Shukla was also jailed for two years, in a verdict that was later overturned.

By June, the cabinet was confronted with another crisis as it was divided over the matter of prosecuting Indira Gandhi in special courts established particularly for that purpose. It pitched Morarji Desai against his home minister Charan Singh. Desai said that he didn't agree with communist leader E.M.S. Namboodiripad's demand for Nuremberg-like trials, Charan Singh argued that if the government could not tackle an individual, the people would lose their faith in its ability to deal with the country's problems. Charan Singh issued a statement that people saw the government as 'a bunch of impotent men' which led Desai to ask him to resign forthwith. Charan Singh withdrew his resignation two weeks later.

Indira Gandhi's political comeback plan was, however, already on track. In November, she was re-elected to the Lok Sabha from Chikmagalur in Karnataka, defeating a formidable united opposition candidate, Virendra Patil. Coined by Devraj Urs, the slogan '*Ek Sherni, Sau Langur, Chikmagalur, Chikmagalur*' captured the imagination of the electorate barely eighteen months after she was thrown out of power. But her stay in parliament was brief. The privileges committee cited her for breach of privilege on grounds of obstruction, intimidation, harassment and institution of false cases against officers preparing answers to the questions, in parliament in 1974 on Maruti car factory and Sanjay's involvement in it. Her punishment was 'left to the wisdom of the House', and on 19 December, by a vote of 279 to 138 – with thirty-seven abstentions – the Lok Sabha adopted the motion to expel her and to sentence her to jail until the prorogation of parliament, a week later. The Election Commission later ruled that she had lost her seat in the Lok Sabha by being expelled. Indira Gandhi vowed to recontest from Chikmagalur, which she successfully did to return to parliament in 1979.

The belied promise and hope of the Janata Party were reflected in the proceedings of the commission of inquiry looking into the alleged medical negligence of JP by the PGI doctors in Chandigarh during the Emergency. After treatment for a short while in Jaslok Hospital following his release from prison in 1975, JP was flown to Seattle, USA, where he remained under the treatment of the world-famous nephrologist, Dr Christopher Blagg. The US doctor was asked to report as to when exactly JP's kidneys were damaged. On 23 April, Dr Philipose Koshy had been appointed by the government to look into the 'nature and adequacy of the medical treatment' given to JP while in prison. After his sudden resignation, the government replaced him with Dr K. Nagappa Alva, who also resigned subsequently. The Janata Party government's failure to expedite the inquiry and the two resignations further highlighted the ruling party's indifferent attitude towards the founder of the party.

By the end of the year, the implosion of Janata Party seemed an inevitability as it bungled and mishandled all attempts to punish Indira

Gandhi and her associates for the events of the Emergency. The cabinet was not united on matters of policy, government investigations were ill-conducted and its prosecutions poorly prepared. The ham-handed actions instead gave Indira Gandhi the halo of a martyr on which to build her political comeback, leaving little space for the Janata Party government to push a constructive programme of its own. The image of vengeful ineptness hastened the downfall of a government that signalled a break from the past. Letting down the people may not have been its intention but as the song said, '*Hum bewafa hargiz na the, par hum wafa kar na sake ...*'

# 1979: *Aane Wala Pal Jaane Wala Hai*

*Ek baar waqt se lamha gira kahin*
*Wahan dastan mili lamha kahin nahin*
*Thoda sa hasaake thoda sa rulaake*
*Pal yeh bhi jaanewala hai*

Lyrics: Gulzar
Music: R.D. Burman
Singer: Kishore Kumar
Film: *Golmaal*

'AANE *wala pal jaane wala hai* ...' is another gem in the Gulzar–R.D. Burman treasure trove. An exceptional Kishore Kumar delivery provides the liveliness that made the song stand out from other creations of the duo. The breezy song benefits from the gravitas provided by Gulzar's meaningful lyrics. Directed by Hrishikesh Mukherjee, *Golmaal*, a laugh riot, is based on the Bengali story 'Kana Machhi' (Blindman's Buff). And like almost all of the film-maker's comedy, *Golmaal* too is not loud at any point, its humour subtle and intelligent.

Over the years, it has gained a cult status, with remakes in various languages besides being remade in Hindi itself. Any list of top ten comedy films in Hindi cinema would be incomplete without *Golmaal*, which stars Utpal Dutt, Dina Pathak, Bindiya Goswami and Amol Palekar. Mukherjee initially wanted to cast Rekha as the heroine but thought that the role was not powerful enough for her. As in most of his films, Amol Palekar plays a typical middle-class person but with the twist of a double role which leads to comic situations arising out of his interactions with veteran actor Utpal Dutt. Dutt was a lifelong Marxist and an active supporter of the Communist Party of India (Marxist). His leftist 'Little Theatre' was a phenomenon in contemporary Bengali theatre, for which he was detained and jailed for some months in 1965.

Dutt won a Filmfare Award for Best Comic Actor, while Palekar got one for the Best Actor. Palekar, in fact, beat Amitabh Bachhan in *Muqaddar Ka Sikandar* to win the award. Gulzar won the Award for Best Lyrics for '*Aane wala pal jaane wala hai*'.

The song exemplified the changing political situation in the country, with the ruling Janata Party coming apart at the seams. In December 1978, Charan Singh, after having been thrown out of the cabinet six months earlier, demonstrated his power by bringing 200,000 farmers to Delhi for a rally. The show of strength forced Morarji Desai to recall Charan Singh to the cabinet in February as finance minister and deputy prime minister. Jagjivan Ram was also appointed another deputy prime minister.

But at the crux of the troubles in the Janata Party was the issue of dual membership of the members of the former Jana Sangh. The socialist group of the party wanted these members to dissociate from the RSS, which the erstwhile Jana Sangh members refused, arguing that the RSS was a cultural organization. They even ignored Jayaprakash Narayan, who publicly advised them to merge the RSS with the other student and youth organizations of the Janata Party or to open its doors to men and women of all religions.

That the RSS members of the Janata Party ignored JP was not a surprise for he was now a broken man. On 23 March, at 1.10 p.m., All India Radio interrupted its regular programme to tell the nation that Jayaprakash Narayan had died. News agencies flashed the message across the country, and within minutes, Jaslok Hospital was under siege as reporters, photographers and thousands of people tried to break through the security cordon. President Sanjiva Reddy air-dashed to

Bombay. At 1.15 p.m., the Speaker of the Lok Sabha, K.S. Hegde, who had been informed of JP's 'death' by Prime Minister Morarji Desai, broke the news to the House. After the traditional two-minute silence, the House adjourned.

The government's macabre gaffe was exposed almost immediately. Barely half an hour after the Lok Sabha's adjournment, came the news flash of JP's 'resurrection'. Ironically, it was the Janata Party president, Chandra Shekhar, who came over the hospital loudspeakers to announce in a broken voice that JP was very much alive, though his condition was still critical. This was the most insensitive blunder of the Janata Party government, which owed its very existence, not to say its coming to power, to JP. He died in Patna on 8 October, three days before his seventy-seventh birthday.

Well before JP died, the government he had literally brought to life had come to an end. In July, the socialists chose to sit in a separate group in parliament and Morarji Desai lost his majority. On 15 July, he wrote two letters to President Neelam Sanjiva Reddy, one of his resignation as the prime minister and another advising the president to give him an opportunity to form an alternative government. President Reddy instead invited the official leader of the opposition, Y.B. Chavan of the other faction of the Congress, who failed to rustle up enough support. Charan Singh was next invited and on 28 July, he formed a minority government with the outside support of Indira Gandhi's Congress (I).

As expected, Indira Gandhi withdrew her support from Charan Singh's government, and on 20 August, he resigned as prime minister. He became the first and only prime minister so far to not face the Lok Sabha, and along with his resignation, he advised the president to dissolve the House and hold fresh elections. Meanwhile, Jagjivan Ram had taken over as the leader of the Janata Parliamentary Party from Desai, and wrote to the president that he be allowed to form a government. He argued that Charan Singh lacked the legitimacy to advise dissolution, but the president – in a much-debated and controversial move – rejected his claim and dissolved the Lok Sabha on 22 August. Charan Singh continued as caretaker prime minister till the elections in the first week of January 1980.

Earlier in May, the government had been able to pass a bill to establish special courts to try Indira Gandhi for pre-Emergency as well as Emergency offences. By the end of the month, two special courts had been appointed and the cases against Indira Gandhi and others were tried but there were no convictions. Although the Supreme Court upheld the Special Courts Act in December, the Delhi High Court ruled the Special Court No. 2 illegal in January 1980. Special courts ceased to function on 31 March 1980, and the cases pending in them and in other courts resulting from the Shah Commission report were all dropped.

Although the Janata Party government is seen as a failure because of its internal bickering and unsavoury end, it achieved two important things. It saved the Constitution and representative democracy by piloting the forty-fourth amendment. It also established the Mandal Commission, to provide social justice for Other Backward Classes, which was to forever change Indian social, political and governance discourse in a decade. The B.G. Verghese working group, which was meant to free the public broadcasters from government control, was far less successful. Charan Singh's Union budget as finance minister increased outlays for farmers and for rural India, while India also saw the first Muslim as a service chief during this period: Air Chief Marshal I.H. Latif took over as the head of the Indian Air Force (IAF) in September 1978.

With the demise of the Janata Party experiment, Morarji Desai retired from politics at the age of eighty-three. He had tried to become the PM, both after Nehru's and Shastri's death, but was foiled by the Congress party's satraps. He eventually succeeded, but his government's failure to complete its term and govern responsibly did not leave him with much credit. Within two years, it was truly a case of '*aane wala pal jaane wala hai ...*'

# 1980s
# Hard Drive in Tough Times

## Tum Itna Jo Muskura Rahe Ho

The disco decade. Kashmir and Punjab burn, a prime minister is assassinated, anti-Sikh riots scar India. India gets its youngest prime minister who makes a date with modern times: computers and telecommunications.

1. India's glorious win at Lord's: Kapil Dev lifts the Prudential World Cup in June 1983.

2. Rajiv Gandhi by the body of Prime Minister Indira Gandhi who was brutally killed by her bodyguards. Rajiv succeeded her as prime minister.
(Photo: Photo Division)

3. Smoke belching out of a gurdwara in the Golden Temple complex in Amritsar, which was hit during Operation Blackthunder in 1987.
(Photo: Pravin Jain)

4. Jugalbandi: Violinist and conductor Yehudi Menuhin hugging sitar maestro Ravi Shankar.
(Photo: Pravin Jain)

5. Former president Giani Zail Singh on his morning walk. An aide is reading out the day's newspaper to him.
(Photo: Pravin Jain)

# 1980: *Aap Jaisa Koi Meri Zindagi Mein Aaye*

*Main insaan hoon, farishta nahin*
*Dar hai behak, na jaaun kahin*
*Tanha dil na sambhlega pyaar bina yeh tadpega*
*Aapsa kahaan hai dil aapko hi paaye*
*To baat ban jaaye*

Lyrics: Indeevar
Music: Biddu
Singer: Nazia Hassan
Film: *Qurbani*

'AAP *jaisa koi meri zindagi mein aaye ...*' was not only a super-hit song but it was also a path-breaking one in many ways. It introduced a new composer, Biddu, who did just this one song in Feroze Khan's *Qurbani*. The rest of the music was composed by Kalyanji–Anandji, and was an equally big hit. Along with a new composer came a new singer, fifteen-year-old Pakistani-British Nazia Hassan, who took India by storm. In fact, Nazia was chosen because Biddu wanted the song to be recorded in London, and didn't wish to use any playback singer from India. *Qurbani*'s heroine, Zeenat Aman, on whom the song was filmed, knew the Hassan family and referred her to Feroze Khan. In an impromptu audition at Hassan's house, Nazia sang a verse from '*Dance little lady*' as Biddu strummed along.

Biddu could barely comprehend Indeevar's lyrics but based the tune on a song he had written for Tina Charles. The Latin-based rhythm was composed as a catchy melody in an hour. When the song was recorded, Nazia's voice sounded 'lonely' and Biddu thought, she was 'losing it' in the layered sounds. He then made Nazia sing along with her first take, matching every single nuance, which led to a thickening of her voice and a natural feel. There were a couple of other tricks. A whistle-like effect at the end of the line '*Baat ban jaaye*' was created by Biddu playing a syndrum, while the guitar was modulated to make it sound like the sitar. The outcome was perfect and the song was a craze even before the release of the movie. Nazia became the first Pakistani and the youngest recipient of the Filmfare Award for the song.

'*Aap jaisa koi*' was India's first experience of truly international sound in music. It brought the word disco to India which soon became a rage. Biddu and Nazia collaborated on the hit songs of the film *Star* and the album '*Disco Deewane*'. She was diagnosed with cancer soon after and died very young. Bappi Lahiri went for an overkill of the disco music, but that was far in the future. Hits like *Karz* and *Dostana* also boasted of some great music in the year but Ramesh Sippy's expensive, multi-starrer follow-up to *Sholay*, called *Shaan*, sank without a trace. That was some coincidence because Indira Gandhi's decline with the Emergency started in 1975, the year *Sholay* was released and was a blockbuster. In 1980, she had already come back to power as *Shaan* flopped miserably.

Parliamentary elections were held during 3–6 January, and the results brought 353 seats for the Congress (I), bettering Indira Gandhi's emphatic victory in 1971. The Janata Party, or whatever was left of it, was reduced to thirty-one seats and the two communist parties to fifty-seven. Indira Gandhi won from Rae Bareli by a margin of over two lakh votes, while Sanjay Gandhi avenged his defeat in the neighbouring Amethi constituency. Indira Gandhi was, once again, the unchallenged leader in the Congress party and government. In her first address to the nation on 14 January, she said that 'our commitment to democracy, socialism and secularism is a matter of faith'.

Following in the footsteps of the Janata Party, which had dismissed the Congress governments in the states in 1977, Indira Gandhi dismissed governments of nine states ruled by the opposition parties and placed them under president's rule. Ironically, the legal challenge to her order was dismissed on the basis of the arguments proffered by Janata Party in the Rajasthan case three years back. Elections to the nine state legislatures were held during 28–31 May and Congress (I) won two-thirds majority in five and a majority in three of them. The only exception was Tamil Nadu where Tamil parties maintained their ascendancy. In Uttar Pradesh, the Congress Legislature Party suggested to the party's central leadership that Sanjay take over as the chief minister of the state. It was believed that Sanjay had engineered the affair, perhaps as a stepping stone to bigger things. But Indira Gandhi declined, telling a UP Youth Congress delegation that it was 'out of the question'. Sanjay continued to be the national general secretary of the party.

Sanjay's ambitions and whatever plans his mother had for him came to an abrupt end on 23 June, when he was killed in an aeroplane crash. The accident followed warnings that he had been piloting the light aeroplane recklessly for several weeks. 'Sanjay's going has affected me profoundly,' Indira Gandhi wrote to her American friend, Dorothy Norman. Her condolence message said that '[He] had come to symbolize the heroic spirit, promising new direction, reaching out to the future... .' An All India Congress Committee resolution praised Sanjay in extravagant terms, although many speculated whether Sanjay would have eventually sidelined his mother and taken over the reins of power himself. Rajiv Gandhi, her elder son, much against his will and the wishes of his Italian-born wife Sonia, entered politics to help his mother.

The disarray in the ranks of the opposition continued. Jagjivan Ram resigned from the Janata Party in late February and the Jana Sangh faction left the party in early April to reconstitute itself as the Bharatiya Janata Party. This happened after the Janata Parliamentary Board decided on 12 March that no party functionary or legislator could take part in the day-to-day activities of the RSS.

The Minerva Mills case in the Supreme Court, argued by Nani Palkhivala, had once again reopened the question of Basic Structure of the Constitution during the Charan Singh government. The orders, however, were delivered on 9 May and upheld, much to the discomfort of the government, that the Basic Structure of the Constitution could not be amended by parliament. While the bench was deliberating during January, Justice P.N. Bhagwati – who later became the Chief Justice of India – wrote a 'Dear Indiraji' letter to the newly re-elected prime minister. Not only did he congratulate her, he asked her for necessary 'structural and jurisdictional changes', praising her 'iron will ... uncanny insight and dynamic vision, great administrative capacity and ... heart which is identified with the misery of the poor and the weak'. Seen in the light of Indira Gandhi's earlier tenure, this raised fears about the independence of the judiciary under her.

The internal security situation in the north-eastern states, particularly Assam, was assuming worrying proportions. In June, rioting between tribals and non-tribals left 300 dead and many thousand homeless in Tripura as it was brought under president's rule. The political situation in Punjab was starting to assume dangerous proportions, with the Akalis playing hardball with the Centre.

Meanwhile, the economy had started looking up, with inflation slowly coming down from the high double-digit figures of the Charan Singh era. The GDP growth rate also picked up to 7.2 per cent, although on a base of a negative growth of 6.2 per cent caused by a severe drought and increasing global price of oil. Many economists were to later see 1980 as the juncture when the Indian economy started to pick up. Prime Minister Gandhi was to tell the National Development Council in February 1981 that 'In socialist countries, there is now not only greater but visible emphasis on giving up controls and rigid regulations in favour of ... individual incentives and market forces'.

Amidst all this, India won the Gold in hockey at the Moscow Olympics, which was boycotted by the West due to the Soviet invasion of Afghanistan. That was the last time India won the Olympic Gold in hockey.

# 1981: *Dekha Ek Khwaab Toh Yeh Silsile Hue*

*Dekha ek khwaab toh yeh silsile hue*
*Door tak nigahon mein hain gul khile hue*
*Yeh gila hai aapki nigahon se*
*Phool bhi ho darmiyaan toh faasle hue*

Lyrics: Javed Akhtar
Music: Shiv–Hari
Singers: Kishore Kumar and Lata Mangeshkar
Film: *Silsila*

SHOT against the background of Dutch tulips, this romantic duet from Yash Chopra's *Silisila* remains one of the best-shot songs in Hindi cinema. The song marked the debut of Javed Akhtar as a lyricist. Though Javed belonged to an illustrious family of Urdu poets, he made his name in Hindi cinema as a script and dialogue writer. Partnering Salim Khan, the duo introduced the 'angry young man' to Hindi cinema and went on to write some of the biggest super-hits in Hindi cinema, including *Sholay* and *Deewaar*.

'I started to write my own poetry in 1978, but it was not published. There were some people who knew about my writing and they heard my poems. And one of them was Mr Yash Chopra, the famous producer and director. And one day he came to me and said that he wanted me to write songs for his film,' Javed told a German magazine about how the offer to pen the lyrics for *Silsila* came up. But, Javed recounted, 'I was quite surprised because I was not inclined to do that or that somebody would ask me to write film songs. I don't know why. But then he insisted. I was not interested. But he made me some offers. And then when I wrote some songs I enjoyed it. So that's the story of how my career as songwriter started.'

Besides marking the debut of Javed as a lyricist, it was also the first independent film for composers Shiv–Hari, comprising the two famous classical musicians, Shivkumar Sharma and Hariprasad Chaurasia. They had been offered the music of *Kaala Patthar* by Yash Chopra in 1979, after he fell out with the music composer Rajesh Roshan, but they had refused because Rajesh's father was their friend.

The combination of cinematography in beautiful surroundings, fresh music and poetic lyrics was powerful but what raised eyebrows was the coming together of Amitabh Bachchan and Rekha.

According to gossip film tabloids of the time, Amitabh, who was married to Jaya, was romantically involved with Rekha. Yash Chopra explained the casting in an interview on his eightieth birthday, 'Smita was going to play the role that was ultimately played by Jaya Bhaduri. I was not very convinced with the casting. I always wanted Rekha and Jaya Bhaduri. Amitabh was shooting for his film *Kaalia* in Kashmir. I went to meet him. He likes to read the bound script. He read the script and asked me, "Are you sure you have made the right casting?" I told Amitabh that I wanted Jaya and Rekha in the film. He paused for a moment and then said, "Bombay *jaake unko mil lete hai*" (Let's go to Bombay and meet them). The very next day we took a flight and during the whole journey we didn't even speak a word. I met Jaya and Rekha and both of them agreed to do the film.'

Even though the tale of infidelity and extramarital romance didn't do well at the box office, primarily because the casting coup created the kind of hype the film's content failed to live upto, *Silsila* set the template for Yash Chopra's 'king of romance' phase. Good locales, beautifully shot songs, brilliant music and lyrics, and heroines dancing in the rain. The story and the script of the movie which were strong points of Yash Chopra movies before *Silsila* took a back seat. *Silsila*'s lead pair also had two mega musical hits of their own. Rekha starred in Muzaffar Ali's *Umrao Jaan*, one of the last films on the bygone Awadhi culture. It boasted of outstanding music and marked the transformation of Rekha into a serious actor. Amitabh also had another mega musical hit, *Yaraana*, which created waves because he wore a suit with electric lights in a song shot in Calcutta's Netaji Subhas Stadium.

As Amitabh reached the peak of his career, where a cine magazine called him Number 1 to 10 in Hindi cinema, his old childhood friend and reluctant politician, Rajiv Gandhi, was steadily climbing his way up the political ladder. Having taken over as the national president of the Youth Congress, Rajiv contested from his late brother Sanjay's parliamentary seat of Amethi in February 1981 and swept the election by securing 84 per cent of votes cast.

This was the year Rajiv got to showcase his managerial skills as the head of the Asian Games Special Organizing Committee tasked to hold the Games in 1982. Although New Delhi was anointed as the host in 1976 when Indira Gandhi was the prime minister, Charan Singh's government had decided not to hold the Games on account of the expenditure involved. Indira Gandhi gave the green signal by reversing her predecessor's decision in April 1980, and to deal with the multiplicity of authorities in the capital Rajiv was given the charge of monitoring all activities concerning the event. Rajiv and the two Aruns (Arun Nehru and Arun Singh) were part of the committee which was based in Pragati Maidan. In less than two years, eighteen sporting venues, including eight new ones, were to be constructed or renovated for the Delhi Asiad.

The situation in Punjab had meanwhile taken a turn for the worse. Akali leader Sant Harcharan Singh Longowal had lodged himself in the Golden Temple, from where he was announcing various street protests. But a simultaneous politics of assassination was being undertaken by Jarnail Singh Bhindranwale in the name of Khalistan. He was suspected to be behind the murder of the Nirankari leader Baba Gurcharan Singh in Delhi in April 1980 but no action was initiated against him. In September 1981, Lala Jagat Narain, an ex-minister of Punjab, member of parliament, chief editor and proprietor of Jallandhar's *Hind Samachar* group of papers who had vigorously critiqued Sikh extremism was killed 4 kilometres outside Ludhiana.

An arrest warrant was issued against Bhindranwale and the police went to a gurudwara in Haryana to pick him up. By then he had moved to the safety of his seminary in Punjab, and the Union home minister Zail Singh dissuaded Chief Minister Darbara Singh from pursuing him there. Bhindranwale sent word that he was willing to surrender, but only at a time of his choosing and only to Sikh police officers who sported beards. Amazingly, the state government agreed and Bhindranwale courted arrest outside his seminary amidst much fanfare as his supporters chanted slogans and pelted stones at the police. The scenes were repeated in many other places, which led to police firing resulting in the death of a dozen people. Three weeks later, Bhindranwale was released for lack of evidence. It marked a turning point in his career as he turned from a murder suspect into a hero who had challenged and defeated the Indian government.

Meanwhile, the formation of the Bharatiya Janata Party (BJP) coincided with a wave of communal violence in north and west India, which continued in 1981: in Bihar Sharif in April–May, in Vadodara in September and Godhra in October. There was widespread loss of lives and property, and rioting had to be quelled by use of the armed forces. But the decision of an entire village of Harijans in Tamil Nadu to convert to Islam provoked outrage among the Sangh Parivar. Nearly 1,000 residents of Meenakshipuram became Muslims and renamed their village Rehmatnagar. Cries of 'Hinduism in danger' and 'Gulf money' being used for conversions were raised but there was no introspection about upper-caste oppression in Hinduism which had led to this event.

Amidst this turbulence, Indira Gandhi continued to warn of forces opposing India's progress and criticized the opposition parties' rejection of her appeal to build a strong and self-reliant India. She still did not realize that the seeds of massive trouble in various parts of the country were rapidly being sown. The 'khwab' the song from Silsila was articulating was soon to turn into a nightmare.

# 1982: *Tum Itna Jo Muskura Rahe Ho*

*Aankhon mein nami, hansi labon par*
*Kya haal hai kya dikha rahe ho*
*Kya gham hai jisko chhupa rahe ho*
*Tum itna jo muskura rahe ho*

Lyrics: Kaifi Azmi
Music: Jagjit–Chitra
Singer: Jagjit Singh
Film: *Arth*

'TUM *itna jo muskura rahe ho/ Kya gham hai jisko chhupa rahe ho ...*' is the signature song of Mahesh Bhatt's *Arth*, which has met the ultimate test of a classic: longevity. It remains as current, fresh and popular as it was when the film was released; although there was a huge delay between the making of the film and its release as no distributor wanted to touch a seemingly 'experimental' film. The songs stood out not only as a part of the film – Mahesh says that taking away the songs will take away a big chunk of the film – but even as stand-alone numbers which were repeatedly sung by Jagjit Singh at his live concerts all over the globe. Jagjit, who had also composed the music of the film, kept the orchestration minimal, in keeping with the overall mood of the film. As the character which features in all the songs in the film, played by Raj Kiran, is a guitarist, the songs were also built around guitar chords.

Adding tremendous value to the soulful music were the lyrics penned by Kaifi Azmi, father of the heroine of the film, Shabana Azmi. Kaifi, a communist, had gained fame as a poet and songwriter, but he pulled off one of his great feats in Chetan Anand's *Heer Ranjha* released in 1970. Considered to be his ultimate work, the entire dialogue of this film was in verse. Kaifi was known to enrich the calibre of the tune and take the story further by encapsulating the quintessence of the character's sentiments, and *Arth* was no exception.

The theme of *Arth* – a married man involved in a relationship outside his marriage – has been explored both before and after the film with varying degrees of success. But what set *Arth* apart was the layered, complex characterization of the three principal protagonists, the husband, the wife and the other woman. The film was made from the viewpoint of the deserted wife, but the result was still a raw, hard-hitting and moving film. The lyrics of '*Tum itna jo muskura rahe ho* ...' captured the sensitivity, the dilemma and the internal conflict of the deserted wife, without making her into an '*abla naari*'.

Always closely linked with *Arth*'s music is the music of another film released in 1982, Raman Kumar's *Saath Saath*. The linkage is perhaps because all the songs of *Saath Saath* were also sung by Jagjit, although the lyrics were written by Javed Akhtar and the music was composed by Kuldeep Singh. Other films which boasted of hit music this year were Sagar Sarhadi's *Bazaar*, Prakash Mehra's *Namak Halaal* and Raj Sippy's *Satte Pe Satta*, but it was B. Subhash's low-budget *Disco Dancer* which proved to be the surprise super-hit with its disco music composed by Bappi Lahiri. With lyrics by Anjaan, flashy costumes and signature Mithun moves, the film's title song '*I am a Disco Dancer* ...' became a rage. While flashy and flamboyant disco music had started with *Qurbani*, *Disco Dancer* marked its real arrival which was to soon eclipse the melody and lyrics of an earlier era. That Jagjit Singh faded out from Hindi film music after *Arth* while Bappi Lahiri ruled the roost for over a decade tells us which stream of popular music was on the wane and which one on the rise.

If *Disco Dancer* brought flashy and flamboyant music, the 1982 Asiad brought colour to the homes as the state broadcaster, Doordarshan, started colour broadcast in India. India performed well at the Games to finish fifth in the medals tally, although it lost by a humiliating score line of 7–1 to arch-rival Pakistan in the hockey finals. But the glory for the government lay more in organizing the games successfully at a short notice than on account of the performance on the sports field.

Rajiv Gandhi and his team had built five new stadiums and seven new flyovers in two years, 290 km of roads were widened, fifty intersections redesigned and two new hotels created from scratch: Kanishka and Ashok Yatri Niwas. At a time when getting a phone connection was a rare privilege, Delhi got 12,000 new phone lines, power distribution was upgraded and Delhiites began getting an extra fifteen million gallons of water daily with the Ganga–Yamuna Link. Government officials were so paranoid that they even stopped the 'export' of bread from Delhi to other states. As 1972 and 1976 Olympic Games organizer Sepp Blatter wrote about the 1982 Asiad, 'There is very little I could say towards their improvement.'

While the prime minister's son had proved his mettle with the Asiad, Indira Gandhi's widowed daughter-in-law, Maneka Gandhi, created a public scene as she moved out of the prime minister's residence. Accompanied by her three-year-old son, Varun Feroze, Maneka claimed that she 'was thrown out of the house, for what I do not know'. She became part of an organization called the Sanjay Vichar Manch, and started campaigning for election from her late husband's Amethi parliamentary seat. In the 1984 Lok Sabha elections, she contested against her brother-in-law Rajiv and lost badly. Her political career was to flourish, but much later and in different circumstances.

The year had begun on a tough note for the city of Bombay, where an indefinite strike by textile workers began on 18 January. The action, led by a medical doctor, Datta Samant, emerged from the rejection of his demand for an increase in the minimum wage of textile workers from ₹670 to ₹940 per month. More than 20,000 workers participated in the strike which lasted for almost two years. The strike had much larger social consequences as the striking workers clashed with blacklegs seeking to break the strike. Policemen also tried to form a union of their own and protested on the streets. The Border Security Force had to be called in to disarm and arrest the protesting policemen.

The start of the Bombay textile strike coincided with the Festival of India organized in the United Kingdom for eight months. Indira Gandhi attended the opening and the closing ceremonies, and was treated as the star of the show. Her international image, which had taken a beating during the Emergency, was now being redeemed.

Meanwhile, back home, Andhra Pradesh had been a bastion for Indira Gandhi but her tendency to impose chief ministers from Delhi was causing resentment. Rajiv's behaviour at the airport in February with the chief minister, T. Anjaiah, left the latter teary-eyed. The Telugu media went to town with the insult to Andhra pride and in March, local matinee idol N.T. Rama Rao (NTR) formed a regional party, the Telugu Desam Party, for 'the honour and self-respect of the 60 million Telugu speaking people'. Wearing saffron, NTR travelled across the state in a van remodelled to look like a chariot. Local Telugu daily *Eenadu* put its weight behind him, and NTR swept to a two-thirds majority in the assembly elections held in January 1983.

Things were going from bad to worse in Punjab as Sant Longowal issued an authenticated version of the Anandpur Sahib Resolution, which said that the Akali Dal would 'also try that the Indian Constitution becomes more federal in the real sense and all states are equally represented at the Centre'. In Kashmir, Sheikh Abdullah passed away in September and was replaced by his son Farooq Abdullah as the chief minister of the state. The All Assam Students Union (AASU) was becoming more strident in its anti-foreigners agitation in the state, even calling for a 'direct action' which it later withdrew. Things were in a ferment in the states, even though Indira Gandhi remained the tallest leader in the country, with her son in place to succeed her. The success of the Asiad and the Festival of India could only tell us of the warts that were being concealed ... '*Tum itna jo muskura rahe ho, kya gham hai jo chhupa rahe ho* ...'

# 1983: *Aye Zindagi Gale Laga Le*

*Aye zindagi gale laga le*
*Hum ne bhi*
*Tere har ik gham ko gale se lagaya hai*

Lyrics: Gulzar
Music: Ilaiyaraaja
Singer: Suresh Wadkar
Film: *Sadma*

THE remake of the Tamil film, *Moondram Pirai*, *Sadma*, to this day, touches those recesses in the heart where our cinema usually does not attempt to venture. The Tamil film also featured the same lead pair, Kamal Haasan and Sridevi, the same director, Balu Mahendra, and the same music director, Ilaiyaraaja. But the words that tie Ilaiyaraaja's fabulous score in Hindi are written by Gulzar. '*Aye zindagi gale laga le* ...' went on to become a cult classic in Hindi; it was also a very popular song in a slightly different tune in the Tamil version, '*Poongatru puthithanathu*'.

Suresh Wadkar's silken voice and enthusiastic rendering brought a freshness and pathos to the song which comes at one of the emotional high points of the movie. It shows Sridevi's character, who has regressed in age due to an accident, discovering the joy of growing up under the tender love and care of Kamal Haasan. The movie is, however, famous for its climax when Sridevi's character has recovered fully and forgotten about Haasan, as he tries to come to terms with the separation, almost going maniacal with emotions. Sridevi's role was initially offered to Dimple Kapadia, but she could not accept the role due to other commitments. Sridevi went on to deliver what is considered her career-defining performance and bagged a Filmfare Award for it.

*Sadma* was Ilaiyaraaja's first foray into Hindi cinema, and A.R. Rahman worked as his assistant in the film. Haasan won the National Award in the Tamil original. While the Hindi version flopped at the box office, it came to be regarded as a classic nevertheless, made memorable by Kamal Haasan and Sridevi's best performances. If this film from south India didn't do that well, there were other Hindi films being made in Madras which were rocking the box office. Films like *Himmatwala, Mawaali* and *Justice Chaudhury*, featuring Jeetendra and Sridevi, were much crasser in their storyline, music and acting but broke all records. Their song picturization, with PT-like choreography, multiple dancers and props, was to become a trademark in Hindi films for the next twenty-five years.

The popularity of these B-grade 'Madras' films also marked a period of rapid social transition, as families started moving away from watching films in theatres. Television and VCRs – rented for a day – became the alternative source of entertainment and film viewing for families in middle-town India.

Meanwhile, India made a mark at the unlikeliest of places, the Academy awards ceremony where Richard Attenborough's *Gandhi* won eight Oscars. Bhanu Athaiya became the first Indian to win an Oscar, for costume design for *Gandhi*. Attenborough, who had struggled for more than twenty years trying to secure finances for his film, said in his acceptance speech: 'It is not me or Ben Kingsley who is honoured. You have honoured Mahatma Gandhi and his plea to all of us to bring peace.'

But peace was far removed from the state of Punjab where Sikh militancy under Bhindranwale took an ugly turn. Till September 1983, killings by militants were confined to Nirankaris, petty government officials and Sikhs who disagreed with Bhindranwale. A new dimension was added, when he started targeting Hindus, giving the unrest a communal colour. He also organized the looting of local banks, jewellery shops and home guard armouries, and random bomb blasts. April saw the killing of A.S. Atwal, a DIG of Punjab Police, as he was coming out of the Golden Temple after offering prayers.

The state administration and police were demoralized, and Indira Gandhi seemed hesitant to take a bold stand against militancy. Bhindranwale moved into the safety of the Akal Takht inside the Golden Temple in December, making it his headquarters and armoury. He smuggled in light machine guns and other sophisticated arms into the temple, erected pillboxes in and around the Akal Takht.

The press was bullied and the local citizenry terrorized as Bhindranwale gave a call for separation from the Indian state through an armed struggle, emphasizing the sovereignty of the Sikhs. The nation had not faced a more serious challenge since Independence, and the Indian state's eventual response led to all sides paying a heavy price.

Besides Punjab, Indira Gandhi was also facing political challenges in various states. NTR had swept the polls in Andhra Pradesh, while the Janata Party's Ramakrishna Hegde became the chief minister of neighbouring Karnataka. The Left Front returned to power in Tripura, with Nripen Chakravarty being sworn in again as the chief minister of the north-eastern state. The Congress party, however, formed governments in Himachal Pradesh and Assam, although through farcical elections in Assam and the accompanying massacre of 2,000-odd immigrants in one night at Nellie in Nagaon district over their voting rights.

New Delhi hosted the first ever Commonwealth Heads of Government Meeting (CHOGM) in November, after it had hosted the SAARC (South Asian Association for Regional Cooperation) conference in August. These followed perhaps the biggest multinational summit hosted by India in Delhi in March – the Non-Aligned Summit with ninety-nine of the 101 member countries attending. When the summit opened on 7 March, the delegates were greeted with pictures of the murdered and mutilated children of the 'Nellie massacre' on the cover of a leading Indian news magazine. But when Fidel Castro handed the chairpersonship of the movement to 'sister' Indira, pictures of the hug in which he held her dominated the media across the world. Natwar Singh, who was then the Secretary General of NAM (Non-Aligned Movement), noted in his book that during the summit, Castro requested a viewing of Attenborough's *Gandhi*, which was apparently not available in Cuba because of the US embargo.

The high point of the year was the surprise win of the Indian cricket team in the Prudential World Cup at Lord's in June. When Kapil Dev led against West Indies in India's opening match of the 1983 World Cup, the bookmakers' odds on India were 66:1. India won that opening game to everyone's surprise and barely survived a scare from Zimbabwe at Turnbridge Wells; reduced to 17 for 5, before Kapil Dev rescued the team with a brilliant 175. Starting as unfancied underdogs with London bookies offering 50:1 odds against them in the finals, the Indian eleven steered a triumphant if somewhat erratic course to a nail-biting cliff-hanger of a final against the seemingly invincible West Indies, champions in one-day cricket and winners of the previous two World Cups. Indira Gandhi declared a public holiday after she heard former Indian cricketer Farokh Engineer tell Brian Johnston on BBC's Test Match Special towards the closing stages of the final that Indira Gandhi would declare a public holiday the next day.

Engineer later recounted: 'I told him that I had absolutely no doubt that she would [declare a holiday]. It is a great occasion for Indian cricket, a great occasion for India. And within five minutes we got a phone call at our BBC headquarters [in London] from the [Indian] Central Cabinet and the phone call was relayed on to the commentators' box at Lord's cricket ground that Mrs Gandhi has in fact heard your comments and declared a public holiday. It was frightening to sort of hear that, but it was a great occasion, a momentous occasion for Indian cricket.' Undoubtedly, 1983 was the year that changed the face of Indian cricket. Its popularity rose, more money came into the sport and India became the unofficial powerhouse of world cricket. It would not be unfair to say that the seeds of the Indian Premier League (IPL) were sown on that warm June day in London by Kapil Dev and his team.

It was a good year for India's space programme as well. The second Rohini RS-D2 satellite was placed in near-earth orbit by a four-stage rocket and India's unique three-in-one satellite INSAT-1B was launched from Cape Canaveral in August. In July, the first unit of the indigenously built nuclear power station was commissioned at Kalpakkam near Madras, while India-born S. Chandrasekhar brought more glory for the country when he shared the Nobel Prize in physics for his work on the structure and evolution of stars. It gave a cause to celebrate, of embracing life – *Aye zindagi gale laga le.*

# 1984: *Mann Kyun Behka*

*Baat kahte bane kya adhi raat ko*
*Aankh kholegi baat adhi raat ko*
*Hamne pi chaandni adhi raat ko*
*Chand ankhon mein aya adhi raat ko*

Lyrics: Vasant Deo
Music: Laxmikant–Pyarelal
Singers: Lata Mangeshkar and Asha Bhosle
Film: *Utsav*

DIRECTED by Girish Karnad and produced by Shashi Kapoor, *Utsav*, based on an ancient Sanskrit play, *Mrichchhakatika*, is in itself a great metaphor for 1984. It incubated the old in a new, colourful medium, with an honest portrayal of human nature and its many forms.

The song, '*Mann kyun behka*' pays a tribute to the quiet sensuality of older times and not just the second century BC in which the film is set. With two bejewelled and beautiful women, Rekha and Anuradha Patel, recounting half-told stories of a night which does not sleep, the film is about a night full of promise and of consummation, of a creeper (*bela*) of delicate fragrance and deep erotic undertones.

Lata Mangeshkar peppers the song with the right amount of sweetness and Asha Bhosle's more complex and saline tone makes it more interesting. Laxmikant–Pyarelal, who composed the music for the film, used instruments imagined from the past and little of the mechanized instrumentation which was catching the fancy of composers and music directors at the time. However, the song would not have been what it turned out to be but for Vasant Deo's elegant Hindi lyrics (he went on to win the Filmfare Award for this song next year and translate the Vedic shlokas into Hindi for Benegal's *Bharat Ek Khoj*). Deo could transform the mood and challenge the imagination of viewers in ways where they wanted to listen to the song repeatedly, and alone.

While this song was the most compelling piece of music emerging from Bombay's film industry in 1984, it bore little resemblance to events in the country. The song can be seen to stand out as an instance of the great contrast (or refuge) that art can offer in times of deep tumult. Others, though, can say it is the perfect anthem for the year.

The year ended with India getting its 'strongest-ever majority' government at the Centre – the Congress party let by Rajiv Gandhi won 401 seats, beating Jawaharlal Nehru's record of 371 seats in 1957. The main opposition was Telugu Desam Party with just twenty-eight seats and the BJP had two.

But the word 'stability' would be the last in mind for those who lived through 1984. To invoke the Motihari-born British writer George Orwell's book of the same name is not an exaggeration. To throw in Charles Dickens in the mix too, it was 'the best of times, it was the worst of times'.

The year began with India getting its first cosmonaut. Rakesh Sharma floated into outer space, in the Soviet Soyuz T-11 spacecraft, on a manned Indo-Soviet space flight which spent eleven days there. When asked by Prime Minister Indira Gandhi about how India looked from way above, he famously remarked, '*Saare jahan se achchha*'.

The Everest was scaled without oxygen for the first time by Phu Dorjee, and Bachendri Pal became the first Indian woman to climb the highest peak on the planet. She was on her first Everest mission.

But scaling peaks and battling gravity was one thing, the tumult of those below, another. Communal riots in Bhiwandi in Maharashtra cost 167 lives. There was much drama as three state governments were dismissed this year:

Sikkim, Jammu and Kashmir, and Andhra Pradesh. The dismissal of N.T. Rama Rao's ministry though did not go as expected for the Centre, and political activity around it forced his reinstatement. Events happening far away from Kashmir had a disturbing impact in the Valley. R.H. Mhatre, an officer in the Indian high commission in London was kidnapped and killed by British militants belonging to the Jammu and Kashmir Liberation Front (JKLF). In the same month of February, Maqbool Butt, the founder of the JKLF, was executed after his mercy petition was rejected by the president.

But the real trouble point, which dominated 1984, was Punjab. It was to prove the biggest challenge to the writ of the Indian state after Jammu and Kashmir, with militants calling for Khalistan ensuring that there was terror activity almost on a daily basis. The Akali Dal refused to call off its non-cooperation. Areas in most of Amritsar, Gurdaspur and Kapurthala had been declared as 'disturbed areas' and president's rule was extended for another six months in March. Extraordinary powers were vested in the military and state police to search all citizens in the state.

On 2 June, the army was called in to assist the police to quell terror. Militants gunned down twenty-one people in the state and curfew was imposed in the state capital, Chandigarh. Firing at the security forces is said to have started from inside the Golden Temple. The army then moved into the temple on 6 June, in what came to be termed 'Operation Blue Star', to flush out militants, and a violent battle took place. The army lost ninety men. The bodies of Jarnail Singh Bhindranwale and Amrik Singh, the head of the All India Sikh Students Federation (AISSF), were recovered from inside the Golden Temple on 7 June. There was retaliatory violence all over India, though the Sikh troops who had deserted the army after Operation Blue Star surrendered on 11 June. The army was eventually moved out of Golden Temple in September, after president's rule was extended for another six months. The Golden Temple was handed back to five Sikh head priests and the Shiromani Gurdwara Prabandhak Committee (SGPC) on 29 September.

Operation Blue Star unleashed a series of events that is yet to find closure. Two planes of Indian Airlines were hijacked by Sikh militants in

July and August 1984, though all passengers were released safely. It was a portent of grimmer weeks to follow.

To 'avenge' Operation Blue Star, two Sikh bodyguards, Beant Singh and Satwant Singh, gunned down Prime Minister Indira Gandhi at her residence in the early hours of 31 October. Indira Gandhi had just finished a television interview and was not wearing her bulletproof gear, when she had bullets pumped into her. It was to be India's first assassination of a sitting prime minister. Indira Gandhi had received intelligence about Sikhs close to her office, but had turned down the plea to change guards. Her death on 31 October led to a pogrom against Sikhs, especially in the capital, where over 2,000 Sikhs were killed.

Responding to rumours that sweets were distributed by some Sikhs when they heard of Indira's death, mobs attacked Sikhs, easily identifiable by their turban, and mayhem ensued in the capital. It was clear that the local Congress party did little to stop the carnage and that in fact some local MPs were actively involved in leading mobs who killed and looted Sikhs. Gurdwaras were vandalized.

On 3 November, Indira Gandhi was cremated after her son, MP from Amethi and general secretary of the Congress, Rajiv Gandhi, was sworn in as prime minister by President Zail Singh.

There was no end to the horror that 1984 was to spell for India even as the calendar ran out of steam. The noxious gas methyl isocynate leaked from the Union Carbide factory in Bhopal in the dead of night on 2 December, snuffing out the life of 410 persons immediately. It proved to be the world's worst industrial disaster to date, affecting the lives of expectant mothers, unborn children and the health of about 6.5 lakh persons. The government settled for a compensation of $470 million, after demanding more than six times the amount initially.

Satyajit Ray received the Dadasaheb Phalke Award for Lifetime Achievement this year. But in the field of popular culture, 1984 would be remembered as the year that gave birth to India's first TV soap, *Hum Log* which not only essayed the life of its amorphous, small middle class but also helped build it. *Yeh Jo Hai Zindagi*, a comedy show, also started this year. *Mashoor Mahal*, a game show, was broadcast from October. Television became both the teller of stories and started its life in a new avatar that changed life and communications. The rate of growth of colour TV sets crossed 47 per cent and TV was replacing the radio in even small towns and villages of India.

Glimmerings of the new communications or 'media' dawn were there for all to see – growing from the very much state-run TV, eight years before the Cable TV era was to take it to another level.

# 1985: *Zihal-e-Miskin*

*Zihal-e-miskin makun ba-ranjish*
*Bahaal-e-hijra bechara dil hai*

Lyrics: Gulzar
Music: Laxmikant–Pyarelal
Singers: Lata Mangeshkar and Shabbir Kumar
Film: *Ghulami*

SUFI poet, musician and scholar Amir Khusro wrote '*Zihal-e-miskin makun taghaful*' in the thirteenth century. His poem, performed by many qawwals to this day, is unique as it alternates between the use of Persian and Brij Bhasha in different lines. Poet Gulzar took inspiration from Khusro's masterpiece and used Persian for the opening stanza of the song. Loosely translated, it means, 'Why look at my poor heart with enmity when it is already suffering the pain of separation?'

The song was composed by Laxmikant–Pyarelal, the duo that ruled the charts and awards in the 1980s. *Ghulami*, directed by J.P. Dutta, had an ensemble cast and was a rare mainstream Hindi film to portray caste and class struggle on screen. It portrayed a society in which the upper-caste feudal lords ruled over the poor, lower-caste people ruthlessly with the active assistance of the law-and-order machinery. In a heart-wrenching scene, a young groom is shot dead as he does not belong to an upper caste.

His father, a police constable, keeps reminding the landlords and the police about the law but is ignored. The scene in this 1985 film remains relevant in India, decades later.

True to his image, Prime Minister Rajiv Gandhi decided to break from the past and give the first dose of hope in his first budget. The budget, presented by Finance Minister Vishwanath Pratap Singh, was widely hailed by Indian industry and international observers alike. Famous budget analyst Nani Palkhivala, known for his general criticism of Union budgets, year after year, called it the best ever. The three big departures announced by Rajiv's government were simplified taxation including the end of estate tax (or death duties), liberalization of import guidelines for industry and amendment of the Monopolies and Restrictive Trade Practices (MRTP) Act (which raised the asset limit above which firms were subject to MRTP regulation from ₹20 crore to ₹100 crore even though industry groups like the Federation of Indian Chambers of Commerce and Industry [FICCI] wanted it raised to ₹50 crore). These were significantly different positions from what Indira's government had been forced to take through the 1960s and '70s. The *Wall Street Journal* had 'Rajiv Reagan' as a header in its analysis of India's budget.

While *Ghulami* broached an important issue in 1985, it was veteran film-maker Raj Kapoor's *Ram Teri Ganga Maili* which was the big draw that year. Music composer Ravindra Jain, who had earlier been noticed for his music for Rajshri Films' productions, worked with Raj Kapoor for the first time in this film and went on to win the Filmfare Award for Best Music for the year. He was also the lyricist for all except two songs in this film. The year also saw R.D. Burman make waves for his compositions in Ramesh Sippy's *Saagar*, which had Rishi Kapoor, Dimple Kapadia and Kamal Haasan in lead roles. Haasan was nominated for both the Filmfare Best Actor and Best Supporting Actor categories for his performance in the film and went on to win the Best Actor trophy.

For Rajiv Gandhi's government, 1985 was an eventful year as it faced one challenge after another throughout. While it was praised for trying to bring in a new outlook to Indian economic policymaking, it was facing major political challenges. Some were the legacy of events of the previous year while some were newly minted. On 23 June 1985, Air India flight 182 (Toronto-Montreal-London-Delhi) was blown up by a bomb at an altitude of 31,000 feet, killing 329 people on board. This bombing was done by a group of Khalistani terrorists in retaliation for Operation Blue Star conducted by the Indira Gandhi government in the previous year.

Punjab was in a state of turmoil through the year and the threat of terrorism loomed large as the state went to polls towards the end of the year. Political parties like the Congress and Akali Dal contested the polls, with their candidates making arrangements for protection against potential violent attacks. News reports from the period indicate that Punjab was polarized on communal lines, a result of Khalistani separatism in the state.

The other big political challenge that singed the Rajiv government was a consequence of the court verdict in the Shah Bano case, which continues to cast its shadow over Indian politics till date. Shah Bano and her five children were thrown out by her husband. He later divorced her. Shah Bano's petitions for payment of maintenance were accepted by the lower court and was upheld by the high court, which directed her former husband to pay her maintenance of ₹25 per month. A five-judge bench of the Supreme Court also ruled in her favour. Sections of the Muslim community saw this as interference in their personal laws and protested. The Rajiv Gandhi government was caught off guard and was worried about its implications in the polls. Leaders in the party held that it needed to overturn the apex court's judgment by an Act of parliament.

After Prime Minister Indira Gandhi's assassination by her own bodyguards in 1984, the government decided to set up the Special Protection Group (SPG) which would be entrusted with the security of the prime minister of India. The SPG came into being on 8 April 1985. The year also saw the establishment of the Indira Gandhi National Open University (IGNOU), to provide higher educational opportunities to all, especially the disadvantaged sections. It was set up with a budget of ₹2 crore.

The year 1985 was not without its share of smiles, though. The Indian One-Day cricket team, which had wrested the World Cup from West Indies in 1983, reaffirmed its position in the shorter form of the game by winning the World Series Championship (WSC) in Australia, beating Pakistan in the finals. The WSC was beamed live to Indian homes on television and it became famous for the visuals of the Indian cricket team riding in an Audi car, which was the prize won by all-rounder Ravi Shastri as the 'Man of the Series' in the tournament.

The year also saw businessman Dhirubhai Ambani making waves in Bombay. He had been around for twenty-five years and had revolutionized the stock market in the country by attracting a large number of small investors to Reliance. In an interview to T.N. Ninan, published by *India Today* magazine in 1985, Ambani spoke about his journey thus far and what he envisioned in the future. When asked about his ability to manage the external environment favourably, Ambani answered that he will salute anyone in the government. He was positive but guarded about the future. When asked whether he had set himself any goal, like making Reliance the largest company in the country, he replied that he would not like to say what he wants before he did it.

Ambani's frank views about business in the year the Indian government decided to loosen the regulatory shackles on Indian industry could have been summarized by another song released in 1985:

*Duniya maane bura toh goli maaro*
*Mar ke jeena hai koi jeena yaaro!*

# 1986: *Chitthi Aayi Hai Aayi Hai*

*Bade dinon ke baad, hum bewatanon ko yaad*
*Watan ki mitti aayi hai,*
*Chitthi aayi hai aayi hai, chitthi aayi hai*

Lyrics: Anand Bakshi
Music: Laxmikant–Pyarelal
Singer: Pankaj Udhas
Film: *Naam*

LONG before non-resident Indians (NRIs) became the flavour of the season for the Hindi film industry, a relatively little-known singer (in India) sang a song that tugged at the heartstrings and reminded those abroad about the country they'd left behind. Pankaj Udhas wasn't well known in India back then but was popular in the NRI circuit. It was this popularity that the producer of the film *Naam*, Rajendra Kumar, wished to encash with this song. Based on Anand Bakshi's lyrics, the song was composed by Laxmikant–Pyarelal. Udhas was known to sing ghazals and '*Chitthi aayi hai*' wasn't one. It moved people to tears, both in India and abroad, and became the song which Udhas came to be known by. He also performed the song on-screen in this film, which made him easily recognizable.

*Naam*, directed by Mahesh Bhatt, was a film produced by Rajendra Kumar to salvage his son Kumar Gaurav's acting career. With a tight script, written by Salim Khan, a super-hit song like '*Chitthi aayi hai*' and good performances, *Naam* was a success but helped the career of another star son, Sanjay Dutt, more than it helped Kumar Gaurav.

The year 1986 was another strange one for Hindi films. After Amitabh Bachchan's departure for politics, the industry was not sure what was going to work at the box office. New stars had not replaced Bachchan in the audience's minds just yet and the void showed. The most successful film of the year was Subhash Ghai's *Karma*, which had veteran star Dilip Kumar in the lead with Anil Kapoor, Jackie Shroff, Naseeruddin Shah, Nutan and Anupam Kher adding to the cast. *Karma* also had a song which became wildly popular this year: '*Dil diya hai, jaan bhi denge, aye watan tere liye*'. This was also a collaboration between Laxmikant–Pyarelal's music and Anand Bakshi's lyrics. *Karma* represented the mood in the country well. It portrayed the struggle of patriotic people against those who were trying to break the nation through violent means. On-screen, unnamed anti-national powers were given a face in the form of Dr Dang, portrayed by Anupam Kher.

The situation wasn't rosy in politics either, with the Rajiv Gandhi government under pressure from Muslim conservatives to do something about the Supreme Court's Shah Bano ruling towards the end of 1985. With pressure being put on him by partymen, Rajiv decided to overturn the court's ruling by an Act of parliament. Thanks to the huge majority the ruling party had in the Lok Sabha, the Muslim Women (Protection of Rights on Divorce) Act, 1986, was passed by parliament. The Act limited the liability of a Muslim husband to pay maintenance to his former wife to the period of *Iddat* only (till ninety days after divorce). With this action the government was able to assuage the conservatives in the Muslim community but it ended up strengthening another challenge to itself, as Hindu conservatives used this move to portray the government as partial to the Muslims.

In Punjab, the state government was unable to control Khalistani militancy and the state was getting polarized on communal lines. Shah Bano and Khalistani separatism gave wind to Hindutva groups who had started to become assertive during the period. Shah Bano allowed them to paint the Rajiv government as partial to Muslim interests while Khalistani separatism and targeted killings in Punjab allowed them to paint a picture of Hindu victimhood. These groups had been trying to drum up support for a Ram temple in Ayodhya at what they considered the birthplace of Lord Ram. This was in place of the Babri Masjid that stood at the spot and it had been locked as per court's orders with a Hindu priest allowed to perform puja at the spot once a year.

For the larger RSS family, the Sangh parivar, the Shah Bano controversy came at an opportune time. Already facing heat from Muslim conservatives, the Rajiv Gandhi government now faced heat from Hindutva groups as well. The increasingly militant Hindutva groups got a shot in the arm in February when the district court in Faizabad ordered the disputed site to be unlocked and allowed the public to pray at the spot. This seemingly small concession was to prove expensive in the future.

In Punjab, it wasn't just polarization which was causing havoc. Polarization was the result of an even deeper problem – Khalistani separatism. Operation Blue Star, the subsequent assassination of Prime Minister Indira Gandhi and the anti-Sikh pogrom that followed in Delhi and elsewhere didn't put an end to the menace of separatism. Separatists continued to stoke fires and Punjab continued to burn. A government had been formed by the Akali Dal under Chief Minister Surjit Singh Barnala in the second half of the previous year but it was hardly in control of the affairs in the state. Dozens were killed in different incidents by Khalistani terrorists at various places.

In February, Khalistani hotheads even seized control of the Golden Temple in Amritsar. The tricolour was burned, a saffron flag with 'Khalistan' emblazoned on top was hoisted, a new 'hit list' was released and extremist slogans were raised that reminded people of the days of Jarnail Singh Bhindranwale. The militants had a hit list of people they wanted to kill in retaliation for Operation Blue Star conducted in 1984. Number four on the list was the then chief of army staff, Gen. Arun Shridhar Vaidya. He had retired and taken residence in Pune. On 10 August 1986, terrorists shot him dead, pumping eight or nine bullets as he was driving home from the market.

Even as the Rajiv government battled these political challenges, it continued to push its economic agenda ahead. While the first budget presented by his government in 1985 was hailed as a landmark budget, the one in 1986 pushed their reform agenda even further. The big change in this budget was the introduction of Modified Value Added Tax (MODVAT). It allowed set-off of duty paid on raw materials against duty paid on the final products. This was done to reduce the cascading effect of taxes on the final prices of products. This started a reform of the indirect tax regime in the country which culminated in the rollout of the Goods and Services Tax in the country in 2017.

While India was struggling with separatism in Punjab, it was succeeding elsewhere in the country. In Mizoram, India was able to bring lasting peace to the state as the Mizo National Front (MNF), led by Laldenga, signed the Mizo Accord with the Indian government in June 1986. A former havildar in the Indian Army, Laldenga had started the MNF in 1961 and led the separatist movement. The government was eventually able to convince him to sign the accord and join the political process in the state. He became the interim chief minister of Mizoram after signing the accord, with the incumbent chief minister Lal Thanhawla stepping down to become the deputy CM. MNF went on to win the elections in Mizoram in 1986 and Laldenga became the elected chief minister.

In the world of sports, the year 1986 belonged to a twenty-two-year-old athlete from Kerala – P.T. Usha, the Payyoli Express. After the heartbreak at the Los Angeles Olympics in 1984, when she finished fourth in the 400-metre final, Usha literally struck gold in the tenth Asian Games at Seoul in South Korea. She won the silver medal in the 100-metre sprint and won four gold medals in the 200-metre, 400-metre, 400-metre hurdles and 4x400-metre events. She was awarded the Golden Shoe award for best athlete at the Seoul Games.

In cricket, India was part of only the second tied Test match in the history of the game. In the first match of the three-Test series played in Madras between India and Australia, the result was a tie.

As India battled with rising sectarian challenges in 1986, Anand Bakshi's words tried to counsel good sense with:

*Hindu Muslim Sikh Isaai, humwatan humnaam hain*
*Jo kare inko juda, mazhab nahin ilzaam hai*
*Hum jiyenge aur marenge, aye watan tere liye.*

# 1987: *Mera Kuchh Saaman*

*Sawan ke kucch bheege bheege pal rakhe hain*
*Aur mere khat mein lipati raat padi hai*
*Wo raat bujha do, mera wo saaman lauta do*

Lyrics: Gulzar
Music: Rahul Dev Burman
Singer: Asha Bhosle
Film: *Ijaazat*

WHEN film-maker and lyricist Gulzar asked his old friend R.D. Burman to compose a song on *Mera kuchh saaman*, he brushed him aside and in a frustrating tone asked him whether he would ask him to compose a song on some newspaper headline next. This was an old battle between old friends Gulzar and Pancham (as RD was known) who had worked together on many occasions before *Ijaazat*. Gulzar's verse was hard to compose thanks to its complex metre, and Pancham was struggling with this one when Asha Bhosle started humming the lyrics. Pancham latched on to that tune and composed '*Mera kuchh saaman*'.

In the film, the song is based on a letter between lovers in which the woman asks the man to return her things, things which are actually memories of times spent together. Like most Gulzar–RD collaborations this too had a gentle tone with a classical base. Asha gave her voice to the song and went on to win her second National Award for her rendition. The song is interspersed with santoor interludes by Ulhas Bapat, which add to the song's texture and quality. The light orchestra allows Asha's voice and Gulzar's poetry to shine in this song, which is considered a Hindi film music classic and is still as popular as it was in 1987.

*Ijaazat*, starring Naseeruddin Shah, Rekha and Anuradha Patel in the lead roles, had four songs, all of which are testament to the same Gulzar–Pancham chemistry that has given us some memorable songs. '*Chhoti si kahaani se*', '*Katra katra milti hai*' and '*Khaali haath shaam aayi hai*' along with '*Mera kuchh saaman*' make it one of the best Hindi film soundtracks from the 1980s.

The other big musical success of the year was a Hindi science fiction film directed by Shekhar Kapur where the lead character's charm lay in his being invisible. *Mr India*, produced by Boney Kapoor and starring his younger brother Anil Kapoor, is rated one of Hindi cinema's must-see films and continues to remain a popular entertainer even now. The film is famous for its taut script (the last film written by the Salim–Javed duo), excellent music and excellent performances by the actors, especially Amrish Puri in a career-defining role as the arch-villain Mogambo whose dialogue '*Mogambo khush hua*' is as popular as Gabbar Singh's dialogues in *Sholay* (1975). The film had music by Laxmikant–Pyarelal who, with their peppy orchestration, showed once again why they were the most popular composers in this period. They were in great form with some popular songs like '*Kaate nahin kat-te*', '*Hawa hawaai*' and '*Zindagi ki yahi reet hai*'.

'*Kaate nahin kat-te*', a sensuous song sung by Kishore Kumar and Alisha Chinai, became famous for its on-screen depiction with Sridevi dancing seductively with an invisible paramour. *Mr India* had a science fiction theme but it was in many ways similar to *Karma* of the previous year. These films spoke about powerful individual villains who were spreading anarchy in the country to try and subjugate it. In *Karma* it was Dr Deng and in *Mr India* it was Mogambo. Both films depicted the upheaval that the country was facing with communalism on the upswing and violent separatism wreaking havoc in Punjab. The blame was put at the doorstep of unknown 'foreign forces' in both the films but the upheaval was correctly reflected.

In the middle of this upheaval, revolutionary changes were happening, but quietly. This was the computer revolution. Sam Pitroda set up the Centre for Development of Telematics (C-DOT) under Indira Gandhi in 1984 to develop digital switches for India's telecom network. When Rajiv became prime minister, he decided to push the country towards extensive use of computers to power it towards the twenty-first century. In 1984, the government decided to allow Indian companies to tie up with foreign companies and liberalized the import of computer chips and other vital components. Computer prices, which used to be around ₹1.2 lakh earlier, dropped to ₹40,000 and eventually to ₹25,000.

As Rajiv pushed for more and more use of computers in government offices and banks, there was widespread political opposition, and resistance from employee unions as well. Despite the political opposition, the computer bug had bitten the country and by 1987, there were one lakh of these machines in India. The start was slow but firm, with even the private sector adopting their use for various activities. In 1984, the Reserve Bank of India (RBI) had envisaged computerization of 8,900 bank branches all over the country. Bank workers feared a loss of jobs and protested against it and the plan was scaled down to 5,700 branches. By the end of 1987, they had installed Advanced Ledger Posting Machines (ALPMs) in 3,500 of these branches.

Rail travellers in the four metro cities were welcomed with computerized ticket reservation system, which was a mini-revolution in itself that involved two years of complex programming work to develop. It was also the first time that the government decided to connect all the districts in the country with state capitals and New Delhi through a nationwide information network, called NICNET, at a cost of ₹140 crore. These steps were the foundation stones of an information technology revolution which the country witnessed in the subsequent decade.

Even as computers were establishing their presence in India, promising a prosperous future, the present carried with it the spectre of war; a prospective fourth war with Pakistan. This was when 340,000 Indian and Pakistani troops were facing each other along the international border from the desert in Rajasthan to the mountains in Kashmir. This was the result of Operation Brasstacks, a military exercise launched by the Indian Army under its chief Gen. Krishnaswamy Sundarji towards the end of 1986, that concluded in 1987. Operation Brasstacks was said to be the biggest mobilization of an army since the Second World War.

The Indian Army maintained that the 'core objective of Operation Brasstacks was to test new concepts of mechanization, mobility and air support devised by [the] Indian Army'. Generals in Pakistan saw it differently, however, and assumed that it was a plan to invade Pakistan. They responded by mobilizing their forces and by mid-January 1987 the two armies were within each other's firing range. The situation de-escalated in March 1987 when both countries reached an agreement to withdraw troops, first in the Kashmir area and later in the desert area.

The border with Pakistan was not the only place where the Indian Army was called into action. For the first time, the army was to take part in an Out of Area (OOA) action in Sri Lanka. While it had been part of operations abroad as part of the UN peacekeeping forces, this was the first time that the Indian Army saw action in a foreign country on its own. It was the result of an accord between the Indian and Sri Lankan governments to secure peace in the island country in the Indian Ocean. The Indian Peacekeeping Forces (IPKF) landed in Sri Lanka in mid-1987 at the request of the Sri Lankan president, J.R. Jayewardene, to disarm all the militia groups that operated in the country's northern province. This included the LTTE, the Liberation Tigers of Tamil Eelam. The confidence with which the Indian forces joined action in Sri Lanka can be seen in what the chief of staff of the Indian Army, Gen. K. Sundarji, told the press in Colombo when the action began. When asked how long it would take to finish the LTTE in Sri Lanka, his answer was 'one week'. Eventually the IPKF ended up spending thirty brutal months in the island nation. One of the toughest battles it fought was Operation Pawan, launched to take control of Jaffna from the Tamil Tigers (LTTE). In what turned out to be a military disaster, the operation lasted three full weeks and the army lost 214 soldiers in that period. Seventy of these men died in the first two days of the battle at Palali.

The Indian Army could have taken heart from these lines by Javed Akhtar for a song in Mr *India*:

> *Zindagi ki yahi reet hai*
> *Haar ke baad hi jeet hai.*

# 1988: *Papa Kehte Hain Bada Naam Karega*

*Magar yeh to*
*Koi na jaane*
*Ki meri manzil*
*Hai kahaan*
*Papa kehte hain bada naam karega*

Lyrics: Majrooh Sultanpuri
Music: Anand–Milind
Singer: Udit Narayan
Film: *Qayamat Se Qayamat Tak*

WHEN a twenty-three-year-old Aamir Khan enacted this song as a student graduating from college in 1988, he was only trying to convey the anxieties of a young man, still unsure about his future. But this song, that made him a household name all over India, could very well have been about the anxieties of the Hindi film industry in the late 1980s.

The 1980s are often termed as the worst decade for Hindi films and film music. It is not because the box office was not kind enough to the film industry in this decade but because of a completely different reason. It was a time when one man eclipsed every aspect of Hindi cinema. As the 1980s progressed, the Hindi film industry went from being very sure to being very anxious about the future. Eventually, direction came from unexpected quarters.

The Bachchan era of Hindi films was at its peak at the dawn of the 1980s. The 'angry young man' was all that mattered and for all practical purposes Amitabh was the film industry and the film industry was Amitabh. And then like a bolt from the blue, a childhood friend of Amitabh's asked him to leave it all and run for public office. As Amitabh Bachchan opted to become a member of parliament in 1984, beating Hemvati Nandan Bahuguna, the film industry suddenly found the wind had gone out of its sails. This shock marked the beginning of the end of the Amitabh era in Hindi films. Amitabh never really went away completely as his films kept releasing through this phase, but an anxious film industry was not sure what direction it wanted to take. Audiences were not responding to the kind of formulaic films that were being made. A new formula was needed.

In 1988, hoardings appeared in Bombay, asking a question: 'Who is Aamir Khan?' It was followed by another hoarding sometime later that added a line under it, that said: 'Ask the girl next door.'

This teaser campaign ended with the final billboard asking people to watch Aamir Khan in *Qayamat Se Qayamat Tak* (*QSQT*). The film's music marked the beginning of the return of gentle, romantic melodies to Hindi cinema as well. *QSQT* was a film that probably launched more careers than any other Hindi film has ever done. It propelled Aamir Khan and Juhi Chawla to stardom. The music was composed by Anand–Milind whose linear melodies were reminiscent of the Shankar–Jaikishan songs in Raj Kapoor films – hummable, gentle melodies. Hindi film music had not yet recovered from the loss of Kishore Kumar, who had died in 1987, and it struggled with Rafi or Kishore clones. *QSQT* gave Hindi films the voice of Udit Narayan. Alka Yagnik also became famous with this soundtrack and then topped the year with the biggest chartbuster of 1988, '*Ek do teen*' from *Tezaab*, composed by Laxmikant–Pyarelal.

*QSQT* had only two experienced hands on the team. One was its producer Nasir Hussain, who was famous for delivering musical hits, and the other was the lyricist Majrooh Sultanpuri, who had been at it for decades. Majrooh wrote '*Papa kehte hain ...*' for Anand–Milind in *QSQT* in 1988 and had written '*Laagi choote na*' for the film *Kali Topi Lal Rumal* in 1959, one of the most famous songs composed by Chitragupta, Anand and Milind's father.

While Hindi cinema was watching with hope the arrival of another star on the scene, India was also experiencing the same in politics. Vishwanath Pratap Singh, who had quit the Congress party in 1987 to launch Jan Morcha, contested from Allahabad, a seat Amitabh vacated. India got another Mr Clean just as the original Mr Clean Rajiv Gandhi's image was getting sullied. His career seemed to echo another song from *QSQT*, '*Akele hain toh kya gham hai*' (So, we're alone. Where's the cause for sadness?). Later in the year, on the birth anniversary of Jayaprakash Narayan, 11 October, Jan Morcha, Janata Party factions, Lok Dal and Congress (S) merged to form the Janata Dal.

On Sunday, 31 July 1988 at 9. 00 a.m., the seventy-eighth and final episode of Ramanand Sagar's television epic, *Ramayan*, was broadcast on Doordarshan. *Ramayan* had held the nation spellbound as it narrated the story of Lord Ram of Ayodhya. *Ramayan* was over, but it had helped create a television audience across the country. This audience did not have to wait too long before the 9 a.m. slot on Sunday was taken over by another mythological TV show, which had an even bigger scale. This was veteran film-maker B.R. Chopra's *Mahabharat*. The first episode was broadcast on 2 October 1988. The screenplay and dialogues were written by Rahi Masoom Raza. In what could be called a precursor to how issues divide our society in present times, Raza faced the wrath of Hindu fundamentalists who were unhappy with a Muslim writing the screenplay for a television show based on a Hindu epic. In an interview to *India Today* in January 1990, Raza said that he was both amazed and hurt by the threats. 'Am I not an Indian?' he asked. *Mahabharat* captured public imagination like no other Indian TV show had or has since.

While Indians were crooning '*Papa kehte hain*' and watching *Mahabharat*, India was asserting its supremacy in its neighbourhood. In November 1988, rebels tried to overthrow the Maldivian government led by President Maumoon Abdul Gayoom. As the mercenaries attempted a coup d'etat, the president hid in a safe house. With little real information available, the Indian Army launched a counter to secure the president and the Government of Maldives in Male. Prime Minister Rajiv Gandhi let his team in Delhi know that the neighbourhood was India's area of influence and he intended to keep it that way. The assault was swift and the results were positive. Called to intervene on a very short notice, India helped a friendly government in the neighbourhood in a way that sent a strong message to the world. India's swift response surprised the world. *Time* magazine was soon to run a cover story titled 'Superpower Rising' that spoke about how India was taking its place as a military heavyweight.

The year 1988 was a year of many starts. The Indian government set up a non-statutory body to govern the securities market in the country. It came to be known as Securities and Exchange Board of India, (SEBI). The year 1988 was also the first time in thirty-four years that an Indian prime minister landed in Beijing on an official visit to China. The visit led to an increased expansion of bilateral exchanges between India and China, which had undertaken economic liberalization in 1978 and was in the middle of the second phase of these reforms.

While one Vishwanath was making news in politics, his namesake was making waves in the world of sports. Vishwanathan Anand, eighteen years old, became India's first and the world's fourth teenaged chess grandmaster.

What direction would India take as 1988 bid goodbye? As Majrooh wrote and Udit Narayan sang:

*Meri nazar se*
*Dekho toh yaaro*
*Ki meri manzil*
*Hai kahaan*

# 1989: *Dil Deewana Bin Sajna Ke*

*Dil deewana bin sajna ke*
*Maane na*
*Yeh pagla hai, Samjhaane se*
*Samjhe na*

Lyrics: Asad Bhopali
Music: Raam Laxman
Singers: S.P. Balasubrahmanyam and Lata Mangeshkar
Film: *Maine Pyar Kiya*

IF *QSQT* changed the direction Hindi cinema took, *Maine Pyar Kiya*, released in 1989, guaranteed this shift to romantic films as it became the biggest success of the year. *Maine Pyar Kiya* had music by Raam Laxman. Raam Laxman is actually Laxman alone, as the other half of the duo, Raam, passed away in 1976. Laxman's real name is Vijay Patil.

*Maine Pyar Kiya* was produced by Rajshri Productions who had been famous for their low-budget, family-drama films that starred lesser-known actors. This one, directed by a debutant director who belonged to the family that owned Rajshri Productions, Sooraj Barjatya, was no different as it starred a little-known actor in the lead role. His name was Salman Khan. It had nine romantic songs that gave expression to a budding romance in the voices of Lata Mangeshkar and a singing superstar from the south Indian film industry, S.P. Balasubrahmanyam, also known as SPB. He had earlier sung Hindi songs for some of Kamal Haasan's films and now his voice got associated with Salman Khan.

The lyrics for this song were written by Asad Bhopali, a lyricist who had been in the industry for four decades but enjoyed little success. With *Maine Pyar Kiya*, he struck gold but as luck would have it, he had to retire as he suffered a paralytic attack. His family moved him to Bhopal, where he passed away in 1990 after he had been awarded the Filmfare Award for Best Lyrics (for '*Kabutar ja ja ja*' from *Maine Pyar Kiya*), an award he couldn't collect.

The year 1989 was a tumultuous one for India. It was the year when the Republic of India had to go for general elections. V.P. Singh and the Janata Dal had already launched an offensive against the Rajiv Gandhi government on the issue of corruption, thanks to the Bofors scandal. The year also saw the RSS and its sister organization Vishwa Hindu Parishad's (VHP) Ram Janmabhoomi campaign, which had begun in 1984, reach a crescendo. The Raijv Gandhi government was already facing allegations of Muslim appeasement thanks to the Shah Bano issue and as pressure from Hindu fundamentalists mounted, it capitulated. The Ram Janmabhoomi movement saw the beatific smiling depiction of Lord Ram being replaced by a more aggressive, angry avatar in posters and paintings.

The campaign was notable for the slogans it used to inflame passions across India. They ranged from '*Saugandh Ram ki khaate hain hum mandir vaheen banaayenge*' (We swear by Ram we will build the temple at the same site) to '*Bachcha-bachcha Ram ka, Janmabhoomi ke kaam ka*' (Every child belongs to Ram and for Ram Janmabhoomi) and eventually morphed into direct appeals to Hinduism as they shouted '*Jis Hindu ka khoon na khaule, khoon nahin vo paani hai; Janmabhoomi ke kaam na aaye, vo bekaar jawaani hai*' (That Hindu whose blood does not boil has water in his veins, youth that does not serve Ram Janmabhoomi is youth lived in vain).

The Union government gave permission to complete the foundation-laying ceremony for the Ram temple at the disputed site of Babri Masjid in Ayodhya, in the Faizabad district of UP. The *shilanyas* was completed on 10 November 1989.

As India saw communal violence break out in areas which had not seen it earlier, including in rural India, the then Union home minister, Buta Singh, strangely said, 'International forces are active in this violence. We are the largest democracy in the world. This is our test.' One of the worst incidents of communal rioting in independent India's history till then took place in Bhagalpur in Bihar where a Ramshila (bricks with Ram etched on them) procession was organized by the VHP on 24 October 1989. The procession rekindled old communal rivalries and for nearly two months, Bhagalpur and close to 250 villages around it were caught in the worst form of communal violence that claimed more than 1,000 lives. As per the then superintendent of police, some members of the procession had shouted, '*Hindi, Hindu, Hindustan. Mullah bhago Pakistan*' (Hindi and Hindus for India, Muslims, get lost to Pakistan).

In November 1989, India voted to elect the ninth Lok Sabha. The verdict came out to be a hung House. The Congress (I) led by Rajiv Gandhi was reduced from 414 MPs to 197 MPs. The National Front alliance with Janata Dal as the main constituent had projected V.P. Singh as a clean contender against Rajiv Gandhi. It won 143 seats in the house of 545. The BJP, which had been reduced to just two MPs in 1984, returned with a rich haul of eighty-five Lok Sabha MPs as its vote share went up to 11.36 per cent. On 2 December 1989, V.P. Singh, who had been fired from the cabinet the previous year, became the seventh prime minister of India. His government was formed with the support of the BJP and the Left Front parties including the CPI and CPI (M).

The V.P. Singh government faced its first big crisis just six days later. On 8 December 1989, twenty-three-year-old Rubaiya Sayeed, an intern at Lal Ded Memorial Women's Hospital in Srinagar, was kidnapped as she was returning home. She was kidnapped by members of the Jammu and Kashmir Liberation Front (JKLF), a militant group that wanted Kashmir to be 'liberated' from India. The kidnappers demanded the release of five militants from prison in exchange for Rubaiya's release. They had picked their target carefully. Rubaiya was the daughter of the newly sworn-in home minister of the Union government, Mufti Mohammad Sayeed. The J&K government led by Mufti Sayeed's political rival, Dr Farooq Abdullah, did not want to accept the demands of the kidnappers but the V.P. Singh government disagreed. The five militants, including Mushtaq Ahmed Zargar, were released. Rubaiya was reunited with her family after five days of being kidnapped. The militants had scored a major victory over the Indian state. The released militants were led in a 'victory' procession by thousands of young men around the Rajouri Kadal area in Srinagar.

On 16 November 1989, in Karachi, Pakistan, a shy, sixteen-year-old boy from Bombay stepped out to bat for the first time in his career. This was the second day of the first Test match between India and Pakistan in the series. Sachin Tendulkar scored just 15 runs on debut but he could have been humming Asad Bhopali's words:

*Aur bhi kucch hain dil ke iraade*
*Kya kehna*

# 1990s
# Old Battles, New Direction

## Dekha Hai Pehli Baar

Open sesame: Economic liberalization;
castc and religious polarization; panchayati raj

1. Prime ministers of India in the 1990s (L to R): I.K. Gujral, H.D. Deve Gowda, P.V. Narasimha Rao and Chandra Shekhar.

2. The man who did not become the PM: Left stalwart and West Bengal chief minister Jyoti Basu.

3. A peace move that was scuttled by the Kargil war: Prime Minister A.B. Vajpayee with Prime Minister Nawaz Sharif of Pakistan at Lahore in February 1999.

4. Sonia and Priyanka Gandhi at Shakti Sthal (where Indira Gandhi was cremated) as Madhavrao Scindia watches from a distance.

5. Lalu Prasad Yadav, the chief minister of Bihar, the man who stopped L.K. Advani's Rath Yatra.

(Photos: Pravin Jain)

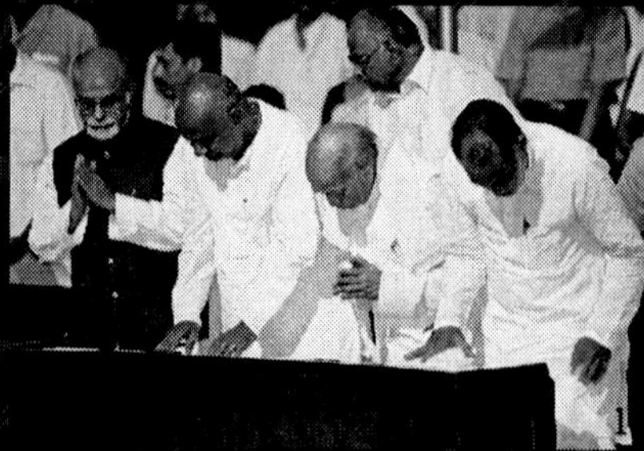

1

2.

3.

4.

5.

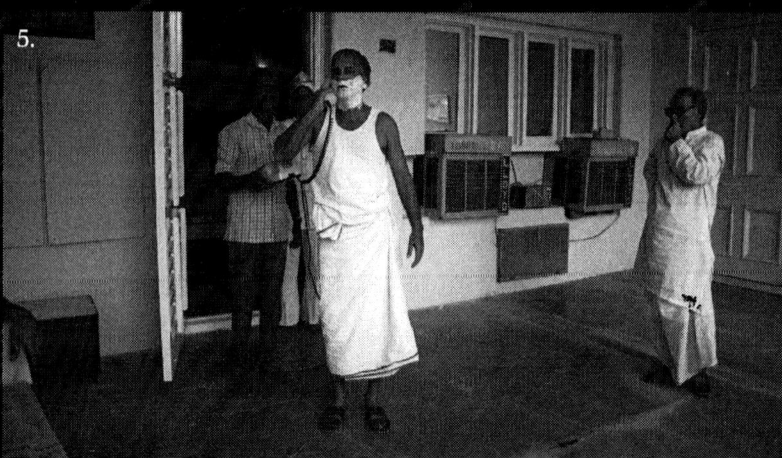

# 1990: *Agneepath, Agneepath, Agneepath*

*Yeh mahaan drishya hai*
*Chal raha manushya hai*
*Ashru swed rakt se*
*Lathpath lathpath lathpath*

Poet: Harivansh Rai Bachchan
Recited by: Amitabh Bachchan
Film: *Agneepath*

HARIVANSH Rai Bachchan was a famous Hindi poet who also taught English at Allahabad University early in his career and worked in the Ministry of External Affairs as an officer on special duty later in his life. His poem 'Agneepath' became the leitmotif for his son Amitabh Bachchan's film of the same name that was released in the year 1990. The poem is about a human being's struggle through life and exhorts us to battle all the challenges till we achieve our goals. The film was an Indian take on the Al Pacino-starrer *Scarface* that was released in 1983. It was also an ode to Amitabh as an angry young man who was not so young any more. Bachchan Senior's poem became the thread which held the protagonist's journey for revenge in this film.

While Amitabh was trying to rekindle his old charm at the box office, real success was still elusive as *Agneepath* failed to click. The old formula was not working but the new one of a good musical romance was as successful in 1990 as it was in the previous two years. This time, the film was *Aashiqui*. Its soundtrack became a rage and propelled the film to box-office success. *Aashiqui* marked the beginning of many successful careers in the Hindi film industry – Kumar Sanu, Anuradha Paudwal, Nadeem–Shravan and the film's producer, Gulshan Kumar, who had made a splash in the Hindi film industry in 1985 when he offered ₹5 lakh for the audio rights of the Amitabh Bachchan-starrer *Mard*. He had been around for some time but found real success with *Aashiqui*.

Gulshan Kumar had started life at his family's juice shop in Delhi and then started his independent business of selling cheap, pirated audio cassettes. The enterprising Kumar kept going from strength to strength and moved up the value chain. From selling audio cassettes to producing devotional music to producing films and film music, Kumar had made his brand T-Series a name to reckon with. *Aashiqui* was the second film he had produced. It announced T-Series's arrival as a player in the Indian film and film music industry.

While *Qayamat Se Qayamat Tak* propelled Udit Narayan and Alka Yagnik to success, *Aashiqui* did the same for Kumar Sanu and Anuradha Paudwal, both of whom went on to establish themselves as top playback singers for many years after *Aashiqui*. The album was such a success that it was the music alone which made *Aashiqui* a box-office success despite it being a below-average film with poor acting by its lead pair of Rahul Roy and Anu Aggarwal. *Aashiqui* was also the beginning of another important film association. This was between Nadeem–Shravan and Gulshan Kumar's T-Series. *Aashiqui* sold more than one crore audio cassettes, making a profit of ₹1 crore for Super Cassettes Industries.

For India, the year 1990 was no less than a path of fire that Bachchan's poem had been about. Just a month after the release of five militants by the V.P. Singh government in Kashmir, the separatist movement took an even more sinister turn. This time the victims were the minorities in the Kashmir Valley, the Pandits. The separatist movement had taken on a religious colour and it saw the non-Muslim Pandits, who had lived in Kashmir for ages, as fifth columnists. Eminent Pandit personalities living in the Kashmir Valley were killed and in January 1990, the Hizbul Mujahideen published a press release asking Hindus to leave the Valley. As the valley rose in a religious ferment, loudspeakers from mosques blared slogans in the local language. The messages delivered were '*Ralive, tsaliv ya galive*' (Convert to Islam, leave the place or perish) or '*Yahaan kya chalega? Nizam-e-Mustafa. La sharqiya la garbiya, Islamia, Islamia*' (What will work here? The rule of Mustafa. No eastern, no western, only Islamic, only Islamic). On 19 January 1990, amidst fears of death, the exodus of the Kashmiri Pandits began. They left the Valley in the middle of the night to escape to the safety of Jammu or beyond. The constitutional Republic of India had suffered a massive defeat.

As Kashmir was in the middle of an insurrection, the secular, constitutional Republic of India was facing an *Agneepath* elsewhere too. One reason for this was the implementation of the Mandal Commission report by the V.P. Singh government. The commission had recommended a quota of 27 per cent for Other Backward Classes (OBC) in government jobs and educational institutions, which would take the total quota to 49.5 per cent including the pre-existing quotas for Scheduled Castes and Scheduled Tribes. This was done to redress discrimination, and used eleven indicators to decide backwardness. What became contentious was that the marker for OBC status was decided primarily based on caste. The V.P. Singh government gave its nod to this report in August 1990 and India was thrown into chaos.

A survey conducted by MARG in September 1990 revealed that the move faced strong opposition from not only the upper castes but also the Scheduled Castes and Tribes who felt that the intermediate castes were their immediate oppressors. If the move was made for electoral benefit, it was unlikely to help, the survey revealed, as the Janata Dal was likely to lose votes rather than gain. Reservations for OBCs had existed for much longer in the southern states, so the move had a more significant effect on the Hindi heartland where Janata Dal was stronger. Roads, transport, schools, colleges and businesses were shut down in a wave of protests.

Rajiv Goswami, a student leader from Delhi University, set himself on fire to protest the implementation of the Mandal Commission report. He survived but suffered long-term implications of this act. He died at the age of thirty-three in a hospital in Delhi.

As India was reeling under the effect of protests against the Mandal Commission report, the Sangh Parivar was making its move to counter a split in its consolidated Hindu votebank due to the reservation move. In September 1990, the president of the Bharatiya Janata Party and leader of the Ram Janmabhoomi movement, Lal Krishna Advani, decided to launch a 'Rath Yatra' from Somnath in Gujarat to Ayodhya in Uttar Pradesh to make the people aware of the issue of a Ram temple in place of the Babri Masjid. While Ram temple was the rallying cry, the yatra was an assertion of a more militant form of political Hinduism, known as Hindutva. The slogan that was shouted was '*Garv se kaho hum Hindu hain*' (Say with pride, we are Hindus). Advani argued that other political parties practised pseudo-secularism under the garb of secularism with the sole purpose of appeasing minorities, especially Muslims, and this practice was unfair to the Hindus.

The yatra left a trail of violence and communal riots in its wake. In its effort for Hindu unity, Advani's yatra left India deeply divided, polarized and scarred. The chariot of fire commanded by 'General' Advani was stopped on 23 October 1990 at Samastipur in Bihar when the Lalu Prasad Yadav government arrested Advani. In response, the BJP withdrew support from the V.P. Singh government, which lost the vote of confidence in the Lok Sabha 142 to 346. Within eleven months as prime minister, the anti-corruption crusader V.P. Singh had been slayed by the troops of the Ram Janmabhoomi movement. He was succeeded as prime minister by Chandra Shekhar who was supported from outside by the Congress (I) led by Rajiv Gandhi.

Even as India was facing political turmoil, a bigger challenge came from outside India as oil prices more than doubled from $17 a barrel to $36 a barrel because of the Gulf War. India's oil import bill went up substantially and Indian exports declined as their main market, the USSR, was in the middle of its own crisis. At the end of the year, India faced the double whammy of increasing fiscal and current account deficits. An economic time bomb was ticking.

As 1990 came to a close, with all the challenges – internal and external – it weathered, the Republic of India might have drawn solace from Bachchan's poem:

*Tu na thakega kabhi*
*Tu na thamega kabhi*
*Tu na mudega kabhi*
*Kar shapath, kar shapath, kar shapath*
*Agneepath, agneepath, agneepath*

# 1991: *Dekha Hai Pehli Baar*

*Dekha hai pehli baar*
*Saajan ki aankhon mein pyaar*
*Dilbar tujhe milne ko*
*Kab se hun mein beqaraar*
*Ab jaake aaya mere, bechain dil ko qaraar*

Lyricist: Sameer
Music: Nadeem–Shravan
Singers: S.P. Balasubrahmanyam and Alka Yagnik
Film: *Saajan*

'DEKHA *hai pehli baar*' may not be the most well regarded of songs, lyrics or musical arrangement so many years on, but as the song burst on to the scene in 1991, it became one of the most memorable hits of the year. Salman Khan and Madhuri Dixit dancing to simple lyrics and the unique signature music of the hit composer duo Nadeem–Shravan went on to propel the film *Saajan* into a blockbuster.

Lyricist Sameer was to hit many jackpots in this phase and what he wrote seemed to work wonders at the box office for the films. Sameer, born Shitala Pandey in Benares, was the son of another renowned lyricist, Anjaan. The early 1990s, at least, were years when whatever he wrote turned into gold. He went on to hold the Guinness world record for penning the maximum number of songs ever. An easy mix of simple Urdu and Hindi, his lyrics worked to help Hindi film watchers slowly transition back to tuneful songs and romantic *dhuns*. While the poetic quality was not a patch on Saahir or Shailendra, it created space for meaningful lyrics, not just banal wordplay or prisoners of the synthesizer rhythm they were mostly accompanied by in the 1980s.

The year 1991 is a landmark one and a break in many ways that escaped attention at the time. '*Dekha hai pehli baar*' certainly applied to the first time that war found live coverage and was beamed via satellite on TV to music playing in the background. In January 1991, when the US-led coalition attacked Iraq (Operation Desert Storm), discotheques in five-star hotels in Delhi turned into viewing galleries for CNN, the 24-hour US network that brought war home. This was no attempt to speak of the horrors of the devastation, but this spoke of the comfort of home viewing and the possibilities of cable and satellite TV, which was to kick-start many more fundamental revolutions in India – media-related, of course, but several to do with societal norms. It was to go on to influence the 1990s in ways quite unprecedented.

The rapid crumbling of the Soviet Union too began to send shock waves all around and especially in this region. India's close economic and military ties with the USSR, the most ambitious experiment of the twentieth century, left it uniquely vulnerable.

The year started on a shaky note with India's economic reserves crashing. The fundamental concern now was how to shore up the economy.

The Ballia MP, Chandra Shekhar, who led a breakaway faction of the Janata Dal, had become the prime minister after V.P. Singh's resignation in November 1990 when the former had managed to secure the support of the Congress party led by Rajiv Gandhi. Chandra Shekhar, who led a small party, was almost totally dependent on the Congress for survival. This was a dramatic end to the V.P. Singh government, which had stayed in power for eleven months, with support from both the Right and Left flanks of the Indian polity, a variant of the 1967 Samyukt Vidhayak Dals, rooted in deep anti-Congressism. So, Rajiv Gandhi, quickly learning to play politics in parliament, managed to get a big socialist icon, Chandra Shekhar, to agree to taking Congress support was a mini-coup in terms of his own personal and political growth. Rajiv Gandhi, it was thought post-Bofors, was primed for his second innings to help shape and be shaped by India.

A sudden withdrawal of support to Chandra Shekhar's government in March, ostensibly because two Haryana policemen were spying upon Rajiv Gandhi's house, threw the country into another election. This was something the Congress wanted as it seemed set to recover lost ground and again make a bid to run the country, having lost face and the poll comprehensively in 1989.

It was a hectic campaign and a long election season.

But the excitement this year was far from over. In the heat of the campaign, at Sriperumbudur, 50 km from Madras, at a night election rally, Rajiv Gandhi met India's first woman suicide bomber, a Sri Lankan Tamil, Dhanu, who detonated a belt that was to kill her and the former prime minister of India in seconds. Loose security, the hurly-burly of a campaign and meticulous planning by the LTTE, determined to get its prime target, stunned the nation.

Forty-six-year-old Rajiv, going the way he did, left the nation shell-shocked; the campaigning was suspended and electioneering resumed only later in parts of the country.

The Congress managed to come back as the single-largest party in parliament barely two years after it had exited office under the most odious charges of 'corruption', back-room defence deals and a technocrat-dependent PM seen to have lost his way and got overwhelmed by his own popularity.

Rajiv Gandhi's wife, Italian-born Sonia Gandhi, was offered the top job before her husband's body was consigned to flames, but she refused and instead suggested that the former chief minister of Andhra Pradesh and former Central minister, P.V. Narasimha Rao, take charge. Having seen himself as unfit to contest the 1991 poll, it was a dramatic turn of fortune for Rao. His ascent in the party marked not just the Congress's first attempt at running a minority government, but was characterized by a deliberate and impassioned attempt at breaking out of so many accepted, set practices, starting with economic policies.

A soft-spoken economist and unassuming former governor of the RBI, Manmohan Singh, was handpicked by Rao (after I.G. Patel of the London School of Economics refused the job) to head the finance ministry and signal what became popularly known as the liberalization and globalization phase of the Indian economy. The fundamental problem at the time was a foreign-exchange crisis which came to a head when the Rao government took over, and reserves dropped to $5.8 billion. It appeared as if India might default on its foreign-exchange payments. GDP growth was down to 1.1 per cent, inflation up at 17 per cent, with 38 per cent of Indians below the poverty line.

Manmohan Singh went on to present a budget this year, within a month of assuming office, which shook India and positioned him at odds with both the BJP and the Left parties, vehement in their opposition to his policies.

> In December, in an interview to *India Today*, outlining his and his government's objectives, he said, 'I don't want to create the feeling that this country is out of danger yet. I look at the financial crisis in terms of our objectives – immediate, short- and medium-term. In June, we were on the verge of default. Our reserves were about ₹2,500 crore. My immediate objective was to reverse this trend. Our reserves exceed ₹8,000 crore today. More commercial banks are willing to look at India as a viable long-term proposition. It was essential to create a feeling of confidence in the international community. And we have done it. There has been a change in the mood from despondency and despair to hope and confidence.
>
> 'Secondly, I wanted to set in motion a process which would bring down the inflation rate in a short period. I would like to see single-digit inflation by the end of the fiscal year. I would have liked to see a sharper dip than has taken place. I think ours is a mixed record.'

This opening up of the economy was to have decisive and long-term effects on Indians, how they worked and how they saw the role of the state in meeting basic livelihood needs. The imperfect promise of a welfare state now, even in theory, appeared to have been jettisoned as the Indian state openly embraced an economic philosophy of the centrality of the private sector and of speedily integrating India into the global economy.

Some say it was Prime Minister Rao's desire to break completely away from the Nehruvian mould, others argue it was in the works with Rajiv having initiated the crucial process earlier. A third view is that it was what pragmatic politics would have dictated, as the Soviet Union was too consumed by its own existential crisis to be able to shore up and provide India the support it had traditionally given ever since the planning era was inaugurated in the country.

Liberalization changed the way people in India thought about not just goods and services but in how they viewed the state and its responsibility towards citizens. The initial loss of livelihoods led to much social turmoil. It fundamentally altered the amount or kind of things that Indians bought and sold.

Another development which would leave its mark on India was the refurbishing of the Model Code of Conduct in elections. This was an idea adopted by the Election Commission of India from Kerala in 1960. But it was only in this year that the Election Commission could consolidate norms and reissue them.

But another trend, which began in 1989, was also beginning to leave its impact on India. The BJP government in Lucknow saw its destiny in raising and raking the Ayodhya matter in a big way. It was this year that L.K. Advani rubbed home his larger idea of 'cultural nationalism' – Hindutva – when he said: 'I would like the words Hindu, Bharatiya and Indian to be synonymous.'

# 1992: *Aa Gaye Hum Kahaan*

*Yeh haseen vaadiyaan yeh khula aasmaan*
*Aa gaye hum kahaan aye mere saajna*
*In bahaaron mein dil ki kali khil gayee*
*Mujhko tum jo mile har khushi mil gayee*

Lyrics: P.K. Mishra
Music: A.R. Rahman
Singers: S.P. Balasubrahmanyam and K.S. Chithra
Film: *Roja*

'YEH *haseen vaadiyaan* ...' is perhaps not the most well-known song of the movie, let alone of the year. The title song of the movie *Roja* captured the imagination of the people, and for the first time ever, a Tamil movie – dubbed in Hindi – did so well across India. Mani Ratnam and A.R. Rahman became household names, and coming at a time of great and momentous change, they were to remain imprinted in public memory for a long, long time.

Kashmir had been a popular location in Indian movies throughout, reaching its high point in the 1960s. With the onset of militancy in the late 1980s, Kashmir no longer figured in the movies. With movies not being shot in the strife-torn land, there was little chance of it forming a part of a movie storyline. *Roja* reversed that – and in ways more significant than

Mani Ratnam had then imagined. Kashmiri militancy formed the plot of the script, which was planned to be shot in that state but eventually was shot largely in Himachal Pradesh. It was a low-budget movie but ended up getting dubbed in Hindi, Marathi, Telugu and Malayalam.

*Roja* brought Tamil cinema to the north Indian mainstream and in a period of great social, political and economic turmoil across India, it provided a narrative about Kashmir. '*Yeh haseen vaadiyaan …*' celebrated the beauty of Kashmir as it argued against the violence being perpetrated by the separatists. Pakistan wasn't spared either; its perfidious ways were a turning point in the script of the movie. And the movie made nationalism cool, when the hero, despite his hands and legs being tied, rolls over the tricolour which has been set afire by the terrorists.

Besides being a Tamil movie, *Roja* was different in other ways too from the prevalent crop of Hindi films. The year also had *Jo Jeeta Wohi Sikandar*, bringing back the hit combination of Aamir Khan and his cousin, director Mansoor Khan, after *QSQT*, in a movie straight out of Archie comics. Like *Roja*, *Jo Jeeta* was also shot well and had great music, which remains popular to this day. Both films also had different storylines from the movies that were being made in those times, and have acquired a cult status.

It is often forgotten now but 1992 was the year the then BJP president, Murli Manohar Joshi, took out the Tiranga Yatra, from Kanyakumari to Kashmir. The man accompanying Joshi as he hoisted the national flag under very heavy security at Srinagar's Lal Chowk was Narendra Modi. Nationalism, especially because the insurgency in Kashmir was led by Muslims, also became a proxy for majoritarianism in the BJP lexicon. It fused in with the Ram mandir movement, which was at its peak, eventually resulting in the demolition of Babri Masjid on 6 December 1992.

The BJP government of UP under Chief Minister Kalyan Singh, contrary to its undertaking given to the Supreme Court to protect the mosque, watched – and abetted – the destruction of the sixteenth-century Babri Masjid by a mob of kar sevaks. Kalyan Singh was dismissed as chief minister and was imprisoned for a day. Thousands lost their lives in the riots that followed. The Congress party led by Narasimha Rao was never able to live down this blot on its record in government. If the 1990s were the years India changed, 1992 was the year which acted as the marker of that change.

All this was happening in the aftermath of the end of the cold war, where the Soviet Union – India's ally for nearly two decades – had been wiped out. India's own economy was in a shambles and former prime minister Rajiv Gandhi had been blown up by LTTE in 1991. The Congress party had its first non-Nehru-Gandhi prime minister, and a minority government. Besides Kashmir, Punjab was also in the grip of terror and violence, although it saw successful assembly elections in 1992. The rumour that the government could attempt elections in Kashmir led to a renewed bout of violence that year.

India's struggle to find its moorings was reflected in sports. It came back empty-handed from the Barcelona Olympics and failed to qualify for the semi-finals in the cricket World Cup. India, however, defeated Pakistan in the league stage but Pakistan had the last laugh when it miraculously won the cup under the leadership of a back-from-retirement Imran Khan.

The lyrics of the songs in *Roja* stand out in complete contrast to the grimness of the movie. They also stand out in contrast to the grimness of the uncertain times in 1992. '*Yeh haseen vaadiyan, yeh khula aasmaan, ... aa gaye hum kahaan*'. *Aa gaye hum kahaan* (where have we come) was a question most Indians were asking that year.

# 1993: *Dil Hoom Hoom Kare, Ghabaraae*

*Dil hoom hoom kare, ghabaraae*
*Ghan dham dham kare, dar jaae*
*Ek boond kabhi paani ki*
*Mori ankhiyon se barasaae*

Lyricist: Gulzar
Music: Bhupen Hazarika
Singers: Lata Mangeshkar and Bhupen Hazarika
Film: *Rudaali*

RUDAALI or the professional mourner, used to be asked to weep at deaths of mostly upper-caste and powerful men, as their women could not possibly grieve in public. The story of one such woman, her friendship with another woman and her other loves and life, finds soulful expression in this song, written by Gulzar and set to music, with some strong Assamese folk influence, by Bhupen Hazarika.

*Dil hoom hoom kare, ghabraae* – the somewhat premonitory warnings and the echo of the impending gloom that make the heart flutter are powerfully depicted in this song, with the classic combination of Gulzar's lyrics and Bhupen Hazarika's haunting music. This is among Lata's finest renditions and Hazarika's version too is captivating. Gulzar has written powerfully, if somewhat pithily. Bhupen Hazarika set this song to Raga Bhopali. All the other songs in the film too have a classical base. In this song, complex feelings, bottled emotions, of being in love, yet being hesitant to express it further are recounted in a way that is hard to forget. The songs from *Rudaali* are counted by Lata Mangeshkar as among her favourites.

Mahasweta Devi's short story of the same name was brought to life in this Kalpana Lajmi film. Dimple Kapadia won the National Award for Best Actress for her role as the unfortunate Shanichari. The soundtrack went a long way in making this film memorable. *Rudaali*'s music ensures that it has a ring here and now, and is also deeply representative, with its pathos, of its time of release.

Plenty had already happened in India by August 1993 when this song was released. A lot of what was happening had the lament and echo of the melancholy that Hazarika–Gulzar and Lata got into this tune.

The year started with the blowback continuing from the destruction of the Babri Masjid the previous year. About a thousand people had already lost their lives across the country in December 1992, but 1993 was about what this event in UP did to the most cosmopolitan city in India, Bombay. The shadow it cast on the western metropolis was both long and dark.

Sometimes mobs of Hindus celebrating the fall of the mosque and at other times defiant Muslims, convinced that rioting was the answer, would spark off riots. But nothing lasts unless there is a sustained political push and pressure, and the Shiv Sena and the BJP in Maharashtra stepped on the gas. A deeply provocative editorial in *Saamna* by Bal Thackeray in 1992 had already made it acceptable to 'point out Muslim houses' and enable fine targeting. Two dock workers were killed on 5 January in a Muslim locality. Whatever may have been the reasons for that, in Dharavi, Muslim shops were gutted in retaliation and in Jogeshwari, a Hindu family was burnt to death. Another *Saamna* editorial calling for Muslims to be 'taught a lesson' ensured that fires raged on Bombay's streets for a week at least. About 900 people died in the riots and the Justice Srikrishna Commission report noted that of them, 575 were Muslim. The report went on to state:

> From 8th January 1993, at least there is no doubt that the Shiv Sena and Shiv Sainiks took the lead in organizing attacks on Muslims and

their properties under the guidance of several leaders of the Shiv Sena from the level of Shakha Pramukh to the Shiv Sena Pramukh Bal Thackeray who, like a veteran General, commanded his loyal Shiv Sainiks to retaliate by organized attacks against Muslims. The communal violence and rioting triggered off by the Shiv Sena was hijacked by local criminal elements who saw in it an opportunity to make quick gains. By the time the Shiv Sena realized that enough had been done by way of 'retaliation', the violence and rioting was beyond the control of its leaders who had to issue an appeal to put an end to it.

Effete political leadership, vacillation for political reasons and conflicting orders issued to the commissioner of police and percolated downwards created a general sense of confusion in the lower ranks of the police, resulting in the dilemma, 'to shoot, or not to shoot'. Four precious days were lost for the Chief Minister to consider and issue orders as to effective use of army for controlling the riots.

The uneasy limp back to normalcy did not last long in Bombay as on 12 March 1993, serial bomb blasts, starting from the Bombay Stock Exchange in Dalal Street, tore the city apart. RDX was used and the intention was clearly to inflict maximum damage. It was set off by two big underworld dons based in Dubai as an apparent counter for the attack on Muslims. About 250 people died and several hundred were injured in the gruesome blasts.

This entire sequence of attacks and counter-attacks post the demolition of the Babri Masjid did pause after March. But the cleavage in India, for the first time after 1947, became sharp and was there for those who wanted to deepen it and profit from it. The idea that politics would and could be solely about whipping up communal passions once again became a dominant theme. It was a disturbing political and social landmark in independent India.

But this is not to deny the other deep changes set in motion this year. While Jawaharlal Nehru had set up India's first panchayat in 1959 at Nagaur in Rajasthan, it was in this year that the Constitution (Seventy-

Third Amendment) Act that systematically devolved powers to the panchayats as part of a three-tier system of local self-government was passed. This ensured money flows, the necessity of elections, reservation for women and well-delineated functions. While appearing routine at one level, this revolutionized the idea of training leaders for democracy in remote villages, blocks and talukas; women too got a leg-up and its impact in terms of political literacy, expectation and empowerment continues to be salutary. A sea of trained younger people conversant with issues, rights and their responsibilities were thrown up who could dream of bigger things.

The process of trying to control insurgency in Kashmir had been on for some time. As the overt role of older groups in Kashmir giving either moral or physical succour to the insurgency faded, on 9 March 1993 the state saw the significant development of the formation of the twenty-six-group umbrella organization, the All Party Hurriyat Conference (the term Hurriyat means 'freedom'), designed to push itself as the representative of the Kashmiri people, and a fount of information and support for all those who opposed the Indian claim on Kashmir.

In July, a no-confidence motion against the incumbent but minority government was defeated with the help of some Jharkhand Mukti Morcha MPs, who, the Supreme Court decreed years later, were bribed to vote as they did. However, the court refused to 'intervene' and decided that parliamentary privilege covered their actions. This led to Fali Nariman saying that 1993 was the year when corruption was 'institutionalized'.

The year saw one of the worst earthquakes so far to hit Maharashtra. Latur and Osmanabad were shaken and about 10,000 people died. Thousands of homes were razed to the ground and 30,000 people were injured. As it occurred in the early hours of the day, at 3.56 a.m., in densely populated areas, the damage to human lives was intense. Fifty-two villages were demolished instantaneously.

*Rudaali*, its lead character Shanichari and the song '*Dil hoom hoom kare, ghabraae*', all three are unrelentingly melancholic. But there was no better fit to the mood and feel of 1993. This year, with the deaths and strife it rung in, is best remembered through the slow and haunting wail of Lata Mangeshkar. To seek a mourner seemed most apposite that year.

# 1994: *Didi Tera Devar Deewana*

*Didi tera devar deewana,*
*Hai Ram, kudiyon ko daale daana,*
*Dhandha hai yeh uska puraana,*
*Hai Ram, kudiyon ko daale daana.*

Lyrics: Dev Kohli
Music: Raam Laxman
Singers: Lata Mangeshkar and S.P. Balasubrahmanyam
Film: *Hum Aapke Hain Koun* (*HAHK*)

As 1994 rolled in, it brought with it Sooraj Barjatya's *Hum Aapke Hain Koun* (HAHK). The first film to be turned into a four-letter abbreviation, it merely followed up from *Maine Pyar Kiya*, the slightly older Salman Khan-starrer, with its flair for combining family, white goods, love and conservatism.

Today, *HAHK* with its extravagant and super-hit wedding songs is seen as an important expression of life in India three years after the 1991 liberalization. It marked the kick-starting of the big, all-season wedding with its opulence and high expense.

'*Didi tera dewar deewana*' is energetically performed by Madhuri Dixit in her signature purple sari with embroidery. She was the bigger of the two stars at the time and her name comes up on the roller before Salman Khan's does. The song is a ditty, to mark her sister's first child; it is coy, raunchy and oddly romantic, all at the same time. The grind that Madhuri performs, the constant targeting of her back through catapults by Salman and other singers in the extremely crowded frame keeps alive the idea of an attractive woman, not afraid of her sexuality. But the woman is, of course, portrayed by Barjatya in the most acceptable and conservative family clothes, a *seedha palla* (UP/Gujarati-style) sari in this case.

The lyrics could not have been simpler and the simplicity may have enabled this song to become a blockbuster hit. Lyrics by the Lahore-born Dev Kohli kept it basic. The music, supplied by composer Raam Laxman, is catchy and pacey. Raam Laxman did best in the Barjatya stable, though he had his beginnings in Marathi cinema. He was also the *Maine Pyar Kiya* composer and brought the same sensibility, lilt and often the musical refrain too to *HAHK*.

In 1994, as lyricist Indeevar justified the direct allusion to sex-infused lyrics to *India Today*, saying, 'I would rather write about sex than violence,' others did not need to justify them and merely said, like Bappi Lahiri, that 'people like them'. What films like *HAHK* and their music did was to provide an ideal super-conservative framework as relief while India struggled to deal with cataclysmic change in the way people lived, worked and consumed. This also coincided with cable and satellite TV now slowly creeping over the leisure time of households and their imagination.

Plague made a serious comeback in Gujarat's industrial hub Surat and in Beed in Maharashtra, nearly three decades after it had last broken out in India. It was a big challenge to India's public healthcare system and there was chaos in Surat as there were forty-six deaths in the first three days. Panic resulted in nearly four lakh people fleeing the town. Beed and Surat and surrounding areas saw masked people amidst DDT and other pesticides sprayed in a desperate bid to snuff out the infection.

This was the year of what is still a benchmark in Centre–state relations – the so-called Bommai judgment. The Supreme Court delivered a ruling in March on the scope of Article 356 of the Constitution and specified the conditions under which states could be brought under president's rule. Declaring that state governments could be dismissed if they worked against secularism, a basic feature of the Constitution, the court upheld the dismissals of the BJP governments in Madhya Pradesh, Rajasthan and Himachal Pradesh in the wake of the demolition of the Babri Masjid. The imposition of president's rule in Nagaland in 1988, in Karnataka in 1989 and in Meghalaya in 1991 was held to be invalid, but no remedial action was spoken of, as elections had been held after the dismissals.

In October, the Supreme Court also refused to answer a presidential reference on whether a temple existed on the spot in Ayodhya where the Babri Masjid had stood till 1992. The court termed the question superfluous and unnecessary. It held as valid the Centre's acquisition of land at and around the site just after the demolition.

In December, three members of the Central cabinet who had been accused of corruption resigned, two for their role in securities irregularities and the third named in a sugar scandal. At the same time, Narasimha Rao's then principal rival, Arjun Singh, also left the cabinet, charging the government with corruption. This was also the time when N.D. Tiwari left the Congress and formed the Congress (T).

The first indigenously produced surface-to-surface missiles called Prithvi was inducted into the armed forces from this year. Three variants, one each for the army, navy and the air force, were developed. A.P.J. Abdul Kalam, then sixty-two years old, was credited with having fired the programme and mission of indigenous research and, eventually, Prithvi. It was developed under the Integrated Guided Missile Development Programme. A scandal, known as the ISRO spy scandal, also made news this year. It led to both comment and unease in India's defence and space circles.

In 1994, India won the Miss Universe title for the first time, with Sushmita Sen being taken around central Delhi in a horse carriage like a gold medallist from the Olympics. Aishwarya Rai won the Miss World title this year.

This year, as far as film songs go, Raveena Tandon gyrating to '*Tu cheez badi hai mast mast*', composed to the tune of a famous qawwali made internationally popular by Nusrat Fateh Ali Khan, also struck a chord and held sway with audiences.

# 1995: *Tujhe Dekha Toh Yeh Jaana Sanam*

*Tujhe dekha toh yeh jaana sanam*
*Pyaar hota hai deewana sanam*
*Ab yahaan se kahaan jaaye hum*
*Teri baahon mein mar jaaye hum.*

Lyrics: Anand Bakshi
Music: Jatin–Lalit
Singers: Kumar Sanu and Lata Mangeshkar
Film: *Dilwale Dulhaniya Le Jaayenge* (*DDLJ*)

THE signature song of a blockbuster hit, *Dilwale Dulhaniya Le Jayenge* (*DDLJ*), '*Tujhe Dekha Toh Yeh Jaana Sanam*' was much more than just that. Sung in mostly verdant green-and-yellow mustard fields of Punjab, it was very much a Yash Chopra idea of love and its expression. But this film importantly launched his son, writer-director Aditya Chopra, who apparently wrote the script in 3–4 weeks.

The song captured both hearts and charts and remains an anthem for lovers. But there are two things that made it more special even though not immediately evident at the time. First, it was a project that addressed the modern NRI in Europe and the US, as lead characters in the film, as well as from the sales point of view. The NRI market as an idea to change Hindi cinema was to stay on from here. The other and more significant reason why this film was a showcase for the times was that it was again, like *HAHK* just one year before it, a validation of some of the old India that stuck on, especially as winds of change engulfed the country.

So, far from the defiance of Madhubala as she sings '*Pyaar kiya toh darna kya*' in Emperor Akbar's court or even *Qayamat Se Qayamat Tak* where the two young lovers pick death over conformity, this celebrates the idea of an arranged marriage and 'Bauji' must 'hand over' the girl Simran, played by Kajol, to Raj, played by Shah Rukh Khan (SRK). In earlier interviews during the shooting of the film, SRK is said to have remarked on how he thought Raj was 'a pansy'.

Despite Simran and her mother urging Raj to run away and just escape the arranged marriage with Kuldeep, Raj insists on parental approval and staying within the boundaries circumscribed by arranged marriages between NRIs and Indians back home.

It is this, change but such little change, that was to mark the tussle of modern India after the 1990s, that had so much on its plate. Economic liberalization changed lives and livelihoods, and the social upheaval created in the largely static north Indian states with the Mandal Commission's report being implemented and the Babri mosque's demolition wreaked havoc with the idea of India.

While P.V. Narasimha Rao's minority government (a first for the Congress party) continued to hold office, plenty happened that was to be significant and leave an impact on the years to come.

The first startling developments came from the largest Indian state of UP. The path-breaking coalition between the Bahujan Samaj Party (BSP), the Ambedkarite party under Kanshi Ram that was quickly unsettling older political formations, and the Samajwadi Party (SP), another new party but with an old, tested socialist imprint, was itself startling. But this year, it was to implode in a way that was to ensure that they wouldn't come together again for a long time.

The alliance struck in the wake of the challenge of the BJP's formidable rise after the Babri mosque was demolished had managed to sweep up Dalits, OBCs and Muslims and formed a surprise coalition government in the state in 1993. But after Mayawati said she would want to withdraw support, some Samajwadi Party members attacked her in a now notorious 'Guest House incident' with a view to humiliating and intimidating her and the party, and the result was a complete rupture in trust and ties. Importantly, the BJP moved in smartly to strike an association with the BSP, on the basis of CMs-by-rotation, making Mayawati UP's first ever Dalit chief minister.

Another event that shook up politics in another large state of western India, Maharashtra, was the first ever victory of the Shiv Sena, in association with the BJP. Despite getting 31 per cent of the vote share, the Congress sat in the opposition and the Shiv Sena–BJP combine reaped the full benefit of the turmoil, anger and disenchantment with the Congress's handling of the past year's cataclysmic events – the riots and the serial bomb blasts. Immediately after assuming office, the Shiv Sena–BJP Juti (alliance) changed the name of Bombay to Mumbai. They declared it was being done as 'Mumba Devi' was the patron saint of the city. The name change was also seen as part of the Marathi makeover of the city and its innate cosmopolitanism. The excuse bandied was also to make it less Portuguese/English and more local. But the name change, defended almost violently by Shiv Sena cadres, who often went on a rampage if 'Bombay' was used, proved Shakespeare's adage wrong of there not being anything in a name. There was much more to one, it was clear. The battle for the soul of Bombay or Mumbai was waged via the change of name and it was a significant flag for the Hindutva parties to plant in an important state of India, that too in its financial capital.

The killing of Beant Singh, the chief minister of Punjab, on 31 August this year in a bomb blast, also signified how deeply the consequences of a fundamental rupture in societal ties can go. The Khalistan movement was dealt with by the Indian state in a way then deemed most effective, but it left a trail of blood in its wake, which included that of not just a prime minister or army chief but also a sitting chief minister. The reason cited was Beant Singh's role in suppressing the remnants of separatism under his watch. It was a violent blast suddenly reminding India of the horror in Punjab they thought they had put to sleep. A total of eighteen people died in the explosion outside the secretariat.

This year was also known for a set of unique incidents where Lord Ganesha was believed to be sipping milk. Some rationalist associations said it was capillary action that could have created an illusion of idols in several places drinking milk, but what was truly intriguing about this was the efficiency with which the rumours spread. It was still one year before the mobile phone was to hit India, but even without all those devices and connectivity, large sections of the country seemed hostage to the idea that idols of Lord Ganesha could drink milk. It was a spectacle of faith versus reason, where mass belief was successfully stirred for significant sections, faith winning this round.

Analysts in later years have equated this to belief in Mother Mary's statue crying tears of blood and other events surrounding the Prophet's hair. But what stood out in this was that this was not centred on any one idol or temple, but faith had it that Lord Ganesha's idols generally were drinking milk, making this a truly intriguing moment.

In the state of West Bengal, where the Left Front government under Jyoti Basu was in its eighteenth year, a consignment of 2,500 AK-47 rifles was mysteriously air-dropped over Purulia by a Russian plane with a Latvian crew. A British arms dealer, Peter Bleach, and a Danish smuggler Kim Davy too were on board. While the rest of the passengers were arrested in Delhi on landing and spent years in a Calcutta jail, the Danish smuggler escaped to Denmark, with bids to extradite him having come a cropper. While the real reason remains a mystery, the most commonly believed account is that it was a plot to destabilize the Marxist government in Calcutta. By whom? A whistle-blower claims it was by the government in Delhi.

The talented A.R. Rahman – one of the brightest stars on the Tamil music firmament – was discovered in all his splendour by the Hindi music world this year with the release of Ram Gopal Varma's *Rangeela* – Rahman's first Hindi soundtrack. Watching Urmila Matondkar, Jackie Shroff and Aamir Khan move uninhibitedly to his tunes was reason enough to feel happy to be alive in India in 1995.

# 1996: *Chhod Aaye Hum Wo Galiyaan*

*Jahaan tere pairon ke kanwal gira karte the*
*Hanse toh do gaalon men bhanwar pada karte the*
*Chhod aaye hum wo galiyaan*

Lyrics: Gulzar
Music: Vishal Bhardwaj
Singers: Hariharan, Suresh Wadkar, KK, Vinod Sehgal
Film: *Maachis*

WHEN Gulzar wrote '*Chhod aaye hum wo galiyaan*', he might have been writing about Punjab, which had almost grown tired of its militant ways with the insurgency winding down. But he wasn't. He was writing a song about nostalgia and the loss of the innocence of youth. When he returned to directing a film after *Lekin* (1990), he chose to talk about the youth in Punjab, which according to him had become a victim of that much-abused term, 'system'.

In typically Gulzar fashion, he managed to make the country sing his deeply philosophical and incisive poetry in his own film, *Maachis*. Listeners all over the country sang '*Chappa chappa charkha chale*' and '*Chhod aaye hum wo galiyaan*'. The latter starts on a happier note with the protagonists remembering the good times gone by and then transitions into a more melancholic interlude before it moves to a despondent hue. Sung by four singers, Hariharan, Suresh Wadkar, Vinod Sehgal and KK, the song was a runaway hit.

With its fresh, melodious music, *Maachis* introduced to Hindi cinema Vishal Bhardwaj, who went on to win the R.D. Burman Filmfare Award for New Musical Talent after *Maachis*. After Burman's demise in 1994, Vishal Bhardwaj began his musical partnership with Gulzar with *Maachis*; a partnership which India would hear more and more of in the years to come. Vishal brought a fresh, earthy and uncomplicated sound to Hindi film music. His focus on good lyrics and high-quality rendition by singers was evident in *Maachis* and became his calling card before he evolved into a film director.

Despite its melodious and high-quality soundtrack, *Maachis* wasn't the only soundtrack to make a mark in 1996. Hindi film music was in the middle of a revival with new composers giving it a new lease of life. Jatin–Lalit showed their class with songs like '*Baahon ke darmiyaan*' and '*Yeh dil sun raha hai*' in Sanjay Leela Bhansali's directorial debut, *Khamoshi – The Musical*.

Jatin Pandit and Lalit Pandit are brothers who formed a pair and had a remarkable run in Hindi film music that lasted sixteen years. Their first major success was '*Pehla nasha*' for the film *Jo Jeeta Wohi Sikandar* in the year 1992.

While Gulzar penned the songs for *Maachis*, it was Majrooh Sultanpuri who did the same for *Khamoshi*. There was also Javed Akhtar giving expression to young love with songs like '*Ghar se nikalte hi*' in *Papa Kehte Hain* which had music by Rajesh Roshan. He went on to win the Filmfare Award for Best Lyrics for this song for the year 1996.

While these were really popular soundtracks in the year, they weren't able to match the popularity of another film. This was Dharmesh Darshan's Aamir Khan-starrer *Raja Hindustani*, the biggest box-office success of the year. *Raja Hindustani* had music by Nadeem–Shravan and recreated traditional Hindi film music sound and arrangement. It ended up getting the earworm of the year with '*Pardesi pardesi*' sung by Udit Narayan and Alka Yagnik.

As a new musical philosophy was taking root in Hindi cinema, India too was transitioning during this decade, and 1996 was an important year in this transition. India, which had faced economic headwinds at the start of the decade, responded by liberalizing the economy and opening up to the rest of the world. The nation was now open for business. While its industry and business responded positively to a less restrictive economic environment, Indian society was also affected by this huge economic change.

India went to polls in 1996 for the first time after economic liberalization and the ruling Congress party had its back to the wall. Having been hit by the biggest corruption scandal in its tenure, the Hawala scandal, the ruling party led by Prime Minister P.V. Narasimha Rao was in disarray. Seven ministers of the Narasimha Rao government were charge-sheeted by the CBI. '*Hawala kaand*' became a byword for corruption in the country in that period. It didn't help Rao's electoral prospects that the CBI raided the official bungalow of the telecom minister in his government, Sukh Ram, in 1996 and recovered ₹2.54 crore in hard cash. The Hawala scandal did not just concern Congress politicians though. Also mentioned in the scam were opposition leaders like L.K. Advani and Sharad Yadav.

The Hawala scandal and the Sukh Ram raids weren't the only reasons why corruption became the biggest issue in the general elections in 1996. The fodder scam in Bihar was also making news with accusations of embezzlement worth ₹900 crore shocking the public. The Patna High Court ordered the CBI to start investigations in the case in 1996.

When the results for the general elections were declared in May 1996, Rao found that people had lost confidence in him. The Congress party was reduced to 140 MPs while the BJP emerged as the single largest party with 161 MPs. L.K. Advani's steering of the Hindutva rath that began after his party's humiliating loss in 1984 (reduced to two Lok Sabha seats) finally brought BJP to the national centre stage. Indian politics seemed to echo '*Chhod aaye hum wo galiyaan*' as Atal Bihari Vajpayee was sworn in as prime minister. But Vajpayee's government failed to prove its majority in the Lok Sabha as other parties did not want to be associated with the BJP, which had been accused of fanning communal fires through the Ram Janmabhoomi movement. Having failed to gather the support of other parties in parliament, it had to quit after thirteen days in power. A post-poll alliance of parties was then cobbled together with the name United Front. The Congress party announced outside support to the UF government and Chief Minister H.D. Deve Gowda of Karnataka was sworn in as the eleventh prime minister of the country.

The Kashmir Valley had been thrown into spiralling violence after the alleged mass rigging of the 1987 assembly elections. As the Indian Army brought things under control by 1996, the Central government decided to give the democratic process another chance. Elections to the Jammu and Kashmir assembly were held in September–October 1996 under the constant threat of attacks by separatists. The National Conference led by Farooq Abdullah won fifty-seven seats in the polls in a House of eighty-seven and he was sworn in as the chief minister of the state.

In the world of sports, 1996 saw two big events. These were the 1996 Cricket World Cup hosted jointly by India, Pakistan and Sri Lanka and the summer Olympics held in Atlanta, USA. The Cricket World Cup was the scene of heartbreak for Indian fans who saw their team lose to Sri Lanka, the eventual winner, in the semi-final match held at Eden Gardens in Calcutta on a pitch that was turning square. India failed to chase and the match had to be abandoned midway in favour of Sri Lanka as the crowd started rioting. The Indian team had earlier beaten arch-rival Pakistan in a memorable quarter-final match held in Bangalore.

If the Cricket World Cup was a scene of heartbreak, the summer Olympiad was the scene of some unexpected success for the Indian sports lovers. Leander Paes surprised by winning the bronze medal in the men's singles tennis event; the first individual medal won by an Indian athlete since 1952. The Indian contingent had returned without medals in the previous three editions of the summer Olympics. Paes was awarded India's highest sporting honour, the Rajiv Gandhi Khel Ratna, for his performance in Atlanta.

India was changing in 1996. It was leaving something behind and finding a new way. Like Leander Paes, its youth was full of hopes and aspirations. It wanted to croon, '*Chhod aaye hum wo galiyaan*', this time with hope.

# 1997: *Arre Re Arre Yeh Kya Hua*

*Tum chale jaao zara hum sambhal jaayein*
*Dhadkanein dil ki sahi naam chal jaayein*
*Waqt ke aage kahin na hum nikal jaayein*
*Arre re arre yeh kya hua koi na pehchaana*

Lyrics: Anand Bakshi
Music: Uttam Singh
Singers: Lata Mangeshkar and Udit Narayan
Film: *Dil Toh Pagal Hai*

THE sheer energy of the musical *Dil Toh Pagal Hai* made it a standout film of 1997. '*Arre re arre yeh kya hua*' comes at a time in the story when the two lovebirds, played by Shah Rukh Khan and Madhuri Dixit, are in full flow and in sync, with their love almost fully expressed to the other. Anand Bakshi, the most prolific lyricist in Bombay so far, composed rhymes and a tune that was both energetic and intimate. The magic of love being discovered by two members goes through many moods in this one song. Anand Bakshi brought to this song an almost deceptive simplicity of easy words often camouflaging complex emotions – '*Tum chale jaao, zara hum sambhal jaayein*' (Leave, so I may find my feet).

The catchy melody in this song was composed by Uttam Singh, who started out as a violinist and a music arranger, and worked with R.D.

Burman as his main violinist for many years, till he got his break. He has also worked with Ilaiyaraaja for numerous Tamil films, a stint he values a lot. His music, ex-soldier Bakshi's words, the classic Yash Chopra 'situations' and the stars then at their peak ensured that this film's songs, especially this one, found their way on most lips.

This was at a time when Hindi films were continuing their romance with athletic prowess and sensual moves rolled into one. Troupes trained by Shiamak Davar made for workout-style regimes and entire groups bearing witness to a tender moment between the leading protagonists.

Two important events, politically speaking, which would impact on the future course, took place in 1997. Sonia Gandhi, the widow of Rajiv Gandhi, reluctantly enrolled herself as a primary member of the Congress party. Also, investigations were started (sanctioned by the Bihar governor) into the corruption charges against Lalu Prasad Yadav. Both events would shape the future in ways unimaginable at the time.

Sitaram Kesri, treasurer of the All India Congress Committee (AICC) since 1980, was elected as the president of the Congress party, in an election for this post that had not taken place in four-and-a-half decades. This was after P.V. Narasimha Rao stepped down as president. Minus the Nehru-Gandhi family at the helm, since the assassination of Rajiv Gandhi, the Congress's fortunes began to decline, with Kesri being adamant about doing things his way.

The Janata Dal-led United Front government, the first to be led by an OBC, H.D. Deve Gowda – a unique experiment of the Congress lending support from outside to a group of regional parties, also supported from the outside by the communists – suffered a jolt when the Sitaram Kesri-led Congress decided to withdraw support early on. Political and personal reasons as well as a fundamental misunderstanding between Kesri and Gowda led the arrangement to the brink and to the surprise of many even in the Congress, Kesri did not hesitate to pull the rug from under Gowda's feet.

In the vote of confidence on 11 April, the Ayes in the Lok Sabha, favouring the government, were just 190 and the Noes that voted against it were 338. Analysts say it was a vote to remember as there were no defections, or party hoppers. Kesri could not succeed in breaking the United Front and neither could Gowda woo sections of the Congress to defy Kesri. However much the Congress did this to appear 'tough' and as an 'opposition', they agreed to a change of guard to avert a mid-term poll and I.K. Gujral took charge as prime minister, after the eleven-month-old Deve Gowda government fell.

Other parts of the political map too were marked by trouble and excitement. In Uttar Pradesh, the unexpected coalition between the BSP and the BJP collapsed with BSP withdrawing support. BJP's Kalyan Singh continued in power with the help of defectors all of whom he inducted into his council of ministers – the largest ministry of all times with ninety-three ministers.

The CBI decided to go ahead and prosecute fifty-six persons in connection with the fodder scam, including Lalu Prasad Yadav. Rabri Devi took charge as chief minister, the first and only woman chief minister of Bihar, on 25 July.

The indigenous polar satellite launch vehicle PSLV-CL was launched this year, which meant that India joined the select group of nations which had the capability to launch heavier satellites. But India lost its Insat-2D communication satellite which was in orbit for just four months. This was also the year when an Indian-origin woman astronaut, Kalpana Chawla, went into space for the first time.

The All India Radio went online in 1997. These were early days of television but state radio was already struggling to innovate to be relevant as widely as it was before.

This year will also be remembered for the first lung and liver transplants in the country. The All India Institute of Medical Sciences in New Delhi carried out India's first liver transplant while surgeons in Madras did the country's first lung transplant. Scientists in Lucknow came up with 'Sujata', an opium-free poppy, which could be harvested for seed and seeds' oil. Scientists also developed, for the first time anywhere outside the US, liposome-based drugs to treat Kala-azar and fungal infections. A.P.J. Abdul Kalam, known as the mover behind India's missile programme, was awarded the Bharat Ratna at the end of the year.

Politically speaking, the excitement did not really end till the year did. On the issue of the Jain Commission report on the assassination of the former prime minister Rajiv Gandhi and remarks made in it regarding the DMK, the Sitaram Kesri-led Congress again pulled support from the Inder Kumar Gujral government. The United Front government fell and polls could not be averted this time around as the eleventh Lok Sabha was dissolved on 4 December 1997.

So, the '*Arre re arre yeh kya hua*' song, where leotards worn by the lead actress Dixit find a place along with her alternating in the red chiffon sari, smouldering with passion, was a fitting parable for 1997 – a mish-mash year which was a bit of this and a bit of that – and something which was to set the stage for much of the future momentum, political and social.

# 1998: *Kuchh Kuchh Hota Hai*

*Tum paas aaye yoon muskaraye*
*Tumne na jaane kya sapne dikhaye*
*Ab toh mera dil jaage na sota hai*
*Kya karoon haye kuchh kuchh hota hai*

Lyrics: Sameer
Music: Jatin–Lalit
Singers: Udit Narayan and Alka Yagnik
Film: *Kuch Kuch Hota Hai*

'A*B toh mera dil jaage na sota hai/ Kya karoon haye kuchh kuchh hota hai*' would have ended up as another melodious musical hit from the 1990s but it became special by being part of Karan Johar's debut film, *Kuch Kuch Hota Hai*. In a year that saw musical blockbusters such as *Dil Se* and 1947: *Earth*, the title song of this Shah Rukh-Kajol-Rani-starrer won Alka Yagnik the National Award for the Best Female Playback Singer. Sameer's lyrics were clean and simple, in an era where double-meaning lyrics in Govinda songs had been ruling the roost. The composer duo of Jatin and Lalit was at the peak of their career, having composed music for blockbusters like *Dilwale Dulhania Le Jayenge* and *Jo Jeeta Wohi Sikandar*.

The catchy melody of the song, which was easily hummable unlike the title song of *Dil Se*, gained from the glossy picturization of the song – and the film – by Karan Johar. Johar revelled in the youthful world of glamorous mass consumption which had caught on with *Hum Aapke Hain Koun* and *Dil Toh Pagal Hai*, but took it to another level with logos of top brands on clothes. The college was transported straight out of Archie comics, with a dash of *Beverly Hills, 90210* thrown in. It was essentially a feel-good film that reunited the romantic lead pair of Shah Rukh Khan and Kajol, but extended the trend by introducing a few more serious elements, such as a widower, a motherless child and a broken heart. The result was an unexpectedly subtle mix of light, sometimes silly entertainment built upon emotions that felt quite genuine. Even as the characters grew up, the glamour quotient never went down and the title song itself was filmed over a ten-day period in several picturesque locations in Scotland.

If *Kuch Kuch Hota Hai* was a blockbuster, Mani Ratnam's *Dil Se* was a box-office disaster. The concluding part of a trilogy featuring *Roja* and *Bombay*, the Shah Rukh-starrer boasted of outstanding and extremely popular music by A.R. Rahman. It also marked Gulzar's rebirth as a lyricist in modern Hindi cinema. '*Chaiyya chaiyya*', filmed on top of a train, achieved a cult status rarely witnessed in Hindi cinema of the 1990s. Filmed exquisitely, *Dil Se*'s songs qualified as the top video album of the year. The year also saw A.R. Rahman compose for Deepa Mehta's *1947: Earth*, a film based on Bapsi Sidhwa's novel, *Ice Candy Man*. Indian entry to the Oscars for the best foreign film, *1947: Earth*, was described by the *New York Times* as 'a powerful and disturbing reminder of how a civilization can suddenly crack under certain pressures'.

To many in India, 1998 seemed like that year. On New Year's Day, the Election Commission announced that general elections would be held from 16 to 28 February. Sonia Gandhi launched Congress party's election campaign from Sriperumbudur in Tamil Nadu, where her husband Rajiv Gandhi had been killed by a suicide bomber in 1991. On being denied a ticket to contest, former prime minister Narasimha Rao lamented: 'My plight is like Draupadi's. Everyone watched her being disrobed but no one helped.' The first phase of polling began amidst the backdrop of bomb blasts in Coimbatore during 14–15 February. A series of car bombs killed at least sixty people on the day BJP president Lal Krishna Advani was scheduled to campaign in the southern city. Poll-related violence saw the death of more than 150 people and when the results were announced on 2 March, no group had a majority to form the government. The BJP-led National Democratic Alliance (NDA) had won 251 seats, the Congress-led alliance 166 and the incumbent United Front, ninety-six.

Attempts by the Congress to form the government with United Front's support did not gain sufficient traction, as Jayalalithaa's All India Anna Dravida Munnetra Kazhagam (AIADMK) continued to dither. As BJP was the single largest party, Atal Bihari Vajpayee was called by the president to form the government and was given ten days to prove his majority. On 19 March, Vajpayee was sworn in as the prime minister of a thirteen-party coalition which had the support of the AIADMK. The NDA government won the vote of confidence in the Lok Sabha on 28 March by thirteen votes as Telugu Desam Party decided to back it at the last moment. Meanwhile, there was a change at the helm of the Congress party as Sitaram Kesri resigned from the presidentship on 9 March and Sonia Gandhi was elected the party president on 14 March, bringing the leadership of the party back to the Gandhi family after seven years.

When Vajpayee government came to power, it had announced that it would 're-evaluate India's nuclear policy and exercise the option to induct nuclear weapons'. On 11 and 13 May 1998, India conducted five underground nuclear tests code-named 'Shakti', at Pokhran, Rajasthan, catching everyone by surprise. This needed extensive camouflage and concealment to keep the preparations for the test secret from the prying eyes of the CIA. In December 1995, US satellites had detected activity at Pokhran suggesting that a test was being readied, but under American pressure, the Narasimha Rao government cancelled the test. In October 1996, preparations for a nuclear test at Pokhran were once again revealed by reconnaissance photos, but India decided again not to test and the site was cleared by mid-December.

On 28 and 30 May 1998, Pakistan followed suit, with alleged six tests of its own. While this made India and Pakistan declared nuclear weapon states, it brought in extensive economic sanctions from the Western countries, notably the US and Germany, as also Japan, Canada and Australia.

Due to economic sanctions and the Asian economic crisis, food inflation shot through the roof. The very high prices of onion became emblematic of the crisis, and the BJP lost assembly elections for Madhya Pradesh, Delhi and Rajasthan to the Congress in November. It lost power in Delhi and Rajasthan while the Congress retained the state of Madhya Pradesh. Prior to that, in September, the Vajpayee government recommended the dissolution of the Rabri Devi government in Bihar and imposition of president's rule. President K.R. Narayanan returned the recommendation after three days, asking the Union cabinet to reconsider its decision, which did not press the case any further.

The year ended on a tough note for the government, as it sacked the navy chief, Admiral Vishnu Bhagwat, the first instance of a service chief's sacking in independent India's history. This happened two days after he had taken over as chairman of the Joint Chiefs of Staff Committee, on the grounds that a series of actions by Admiral Bhagwat 'were in deliberate defiance of the government'.

In October, India got a pleasant surprise when Amartya Sen became the sixth Indian to be awarded the Nobel Prize, after the Swedish Royal Academy of Sciences selected the noted economist for the 1998 Bank of Sweden Prize in Economic Sciences. Sen was honoured for a lifetime's work in economics on social choice, poverty index and studies of famine.

Sen also had a connection with another Indian Nobel laureate, Rabindranath Tagore. In 1933, when Tagore, the first Asian Nobel laureate, was asked to name the baby born to the daughter of his secretary, he chose 'Amartya', meaning 'immortal' 'It's an outstanding name. I can see the boy will grow into an outstanding person,' the poet told the parents. In a year in which so much happened, the last thing one would have wanted to say was '*kuch kuch hota hai*'.

# 1999: *Hum Dil De Chuke Sanam*

*Umeedein tumhin se hain mere sanam*
*Thaama hai tumhara hi yeh daaman*
*Oh bhoolenge kabhi na ab tumhein hum*
*Oh hum dil de chuke sanam*
*Tere ho gaye hain hum*
*Teri kasam*
*Teri kasam*

Lyrics: Mehboob
Music: Ismail Darbar
Singer: Kavita Krishnamurthy
Film: *Hum Dil De Chuke Sanam*

'HUM *dil de chuke sanam, tere ho gaye hain hum*' is the title song of the Sanjay Leela Bhansali film, which comes at the climax of the movie. With this film, Bhansali introduced a new music director, Ismail Darbar, who had been playing the violin for many music directors before he got this break. The music of the film, which consisted of eleven songs and had taken two years to produce, was one of its highlights. It was also praised for its lavish set designs and exquisite cinematography.

All the songs, which encompassed a range of emotions while driving the story of the love triangle forward, were chartbusters. But it was after a long gap that a somewhat low-key song – playing in the background – formed the climax of the film. Simple lyrics by Mehboob, a melodious tune which conveyed a soft longing, good acting by Aishwarya Rai displaying her conflicted emotions, and the stunning locales of Budapest in Hungary – shown as Italy in the film – made the title song the most hummable of the numbers in the film.

Darbar won the National Award for the Best Music Director for the blockbuster, which also won the National Awards for Best Cinematography, Best Production Design and Best Choreography. The film, however, boasted of a regressive theme where the wife chooses to stay with the husband, forsaking her lover. The symbolism of a red sari and a mangalsutra were fully exploited by Bhansali in the song which established Rai, the erstwhile beauty queen, as an actor. Rai also had another musical success in Subhash Ghai's *Taal*, which had A.R. Rahman as music director. Sooraj Barjatya released his multi-starrer, *Hum Saath Saath Hain*, which could neither replicate the musical nor the box-office success of his previous film, *Hum Aapke Hain Koun*. Unlike these romantic musical hits, the Aamir Khan-starrer *Sarfarosh* was a thriller which dealt with the issue of cross-border terrorism from Pakistan. It was released in April, just weeks before Indians were to learn of Pakistan's cross-border perfidy in Kargil.

During late 1998 and early 1999, the Pakistan Army launched Operation Badr, under which it sent troops and paramilitary personnel into Indian territory in the Batalik-Kargil-Dras region. The operation, which was approved by Gen. Pervez Musharraf, the then army chief, aimed to sever the link between Kashmir and Ladakh and cause Indian forces to withdraw from the Siachen Glacier, thus forcing India to negotiate a settlement of the broader Kashmir dispute. Rawalpindi also believed that any tension in the region – between two nuclear powers – would internationalize the Kashmir issue, helping it to secure a speedy resolution.

This infiltration was going on while Indian Prime Minister Atal Bihari Vajpayee had gone on a bus to Pakistan on 20 February. Vajpayee, who was accompanied by twenty-two accomplished Indians, was travelling in the inaugural bus service from Delhi to Lahore. He was received by his Pakistani counterpart, Nawaz Sharif, at Wagah, where he was given a ceremonial welcome. By visiting Minar-e-Pakistan, a 60-metre high tower erected at the place where the All-India Muslim League had adopted the resolution for the creation of Pakistan in 1940, Vajpayee stamped the seal of approval on Pakistan, as his party had opposed Partition and believed in the concept of Akhand Bharat (United India). The visit was marked by great bonhomie from both sides. At the official banquet, Vajpayee quoted a verse of the eleventh-century poet Mas'ud bin S'ad bin Salman: '*Shud dar gham Lohur rawanam Yarab! Yarab! Ki dar arzu-e anam Yarab!*' ('My soul goes out in longing for Lohur, O God! How I long'), Nawaz Sharif quoted from Vajpayee's poem '*Ab jang na hone denge*' ('We will not allow war'). The visit ended with the Lahore Declaration between the two sides.

But the ink on Lahore Declaration had not even dried when the Pakistani intrusions were detected by local shepherds. On 5 May, a five-member patrol led by Captain Saurabh Kalia was captured by the intruders who tortured and killed them. The initial estimates of intrusions were not taken seriously by the army, who assumed that these were some militants who would soon be thrown out. But as the extent of intrusions became clear, the air force was deployed and the army deployed more troops as part of Operation Vijay. By end-May, the IAF had lost two MiGs and a helicopter and the army's attempts to recapture the posts led to heavy casualties. The government released proof of Pakistani involvement, including a telephone conversation between Musharraf in Beijing and his chief of general staff Lt Gen. Aziz Khan in Rawalpindi. Deft diplomatic moves brought global pressure upon Pakistan for violating the sanctity of the Line of Control (LoC), while the army sent in even more troops and extensively used Bofors guns to pummel the Pakistani positions.

These moves started yielding results as the Indian Army captured Tololing in Dras by mid-June, while US president Bill Clinton telephoned Sharif to express his displeasure. Sharif eventually flew to Washington DC on 4 July, where Clinton admonished him and Pakistan announced unilateral withdrawal from the occupied areas. Fighting, however, continued as Pakistan Army conducted its withdrawal. On 14 July,

Vajpayee declared Operation Vijay a success, which concluded on 26 July, a day that was declared as the Kargil Vijay Diwas. The highlight of the Kargil war was its detailed media coverage in India, particularly on television, which ended up giving rise to jingoistic feelings.

The media coverage of the Kargil war came to Vajpayee's rescue when he was in the middle of an election campaign, following the dramatic defeat of the government in a vote of confidence in the Lok Sabha by a single vote on 17 April. The voted was necessitated after the AIADMK withdrew its support. Although Sonia Gandhi publicly claimed to have the numbers to form a government, Mulayam Singh Yadav backed out from supporting her, resulting in the general elections. The results of elections held in September–October gave Vajpayee's NDA 298 seats, as the Congress-led Alliance won 134 and others 105.

But the election results brought no solace to what continued to be a tragic year. Christian missionary Graham Staines and his two young children were burnt alive by Hindu fundamentalists in Orissa in January, while a super cyclone hit the eastern state in October killing nearly 10,000 people. In August, the Pakistan Navy's reconnaissance plane, *Atlantique*, was shot down in the Rann of Kutch killing all on board, furthering tensions between the two countries. On Christmas eve, Pakistani terrorists hijacked an Indian Airlines Airbus flight IC-814 carrying 189 people from Kathmandu to New Delhi. After landing at Amritsar and a detour to the United Arab Emirates, it landed at Kandahar, Afghanistan, on 25 December. On 28 December, the hijackers made three demands, including the release of 35 terrorists and a sum of $200 million. The Vajpayee government negotiated with the hijackers, eventually agreeing to release three Pakistani terrorists, who were accompanied to Kandahar by Minister for External Affairs Jaswant Singh. On 31 December, the hijackers, who had stabbed a man on the plane to death, freed their hostages. It was quite a slap in the face of a government which boasted of a very hard line on terrorism. Perhaps the government assumed that it had nothing to worry after the voters had sung to Vajpayee during the elections, '*Hum dil de chuke sanam*'.

# 2000s
# India Shining
## Phir Bhi Dil Hai Hindustani

Three new states are carved out. Gujarat riots shake the conscience of the nation. Rights-based laws from 2004: right to information and right to work. India's economy booms. The telecom revolution is upon us.

1.

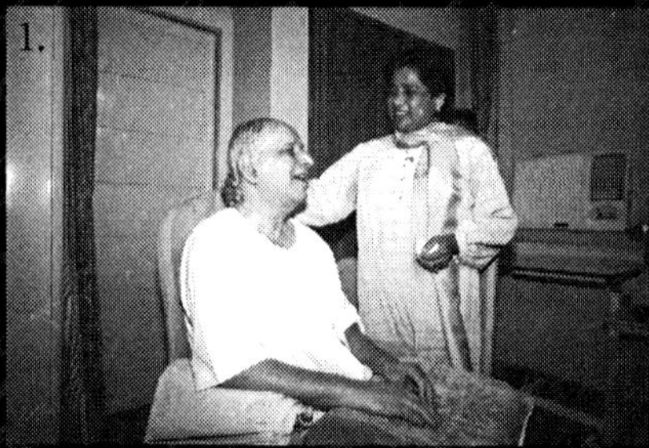

2.

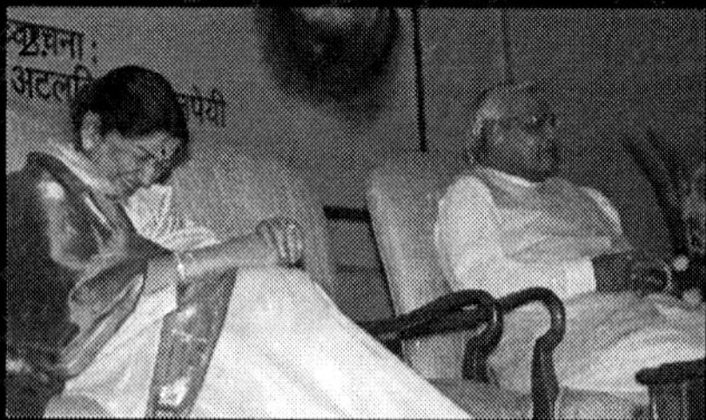

3.

4.

1. The icons of Dalit politics: Kanshiram and Mayawati. (Photo: Pravin Jain)

2. Prime Minister A.B. Vajpayee with the legendary singer, Lata Mangeshkar, at a function. (Photo: Pravin Jain)

3. Prime Minister Vajpayee and the Pakistani dictator Pervez Musharraf during the failed Agra summit. (Photo: Pravin Jain)

4. Mumbai burns as Pakistan-based terrorists strike iconic landmarks in November 2008.

5. The UPA returns: Sonia Gandhi felicitates Manmohan Singh after the 2009 election results. (Photo: Pravin Jain)

5.

# 2000: *Phir Bhi Dil Hai Hindustani*

*Ulti seedhi jaisi bhi hai apni yahi kahaani*
*Thodi hum mein hoshiyaari hain, thodi hai naadaani*
*Thodi hum mein sachchaai hai, thodi beimaani*
*Phir bhi dil hai Hindustani*

Lyrics: Javed Akhtar
Music: Jatin–Lalit
Singer: Udit Narayan
Film: *Phir Bhi Dil Hai Hindustani*

'PHIR *bhi dil hai hindustani, phir bhi dil hai Hindustani*', the title song of Aziz Mirza's film, has moved into the pantheon of patriotic songs that are religiously trotted out on every Republic Day and Independence Day. But Javed Akhtar's lyrics were more tongue-in-cheek and humorous than in-your-face patriotic, and conveyed a spirit of fun not linked to the idea of flag-waving nationalism popular in Hindi cinema. The video of the song, shot in an irreverent manner with bright colours, made the lilting tune by Jatin–Lalit catchier. Conceived as a promotional number before the film's release, it became so popular that it had to be featured in the opening credits of the film to meet popular expectations. The song also played in the background during the climax of the film, as a tune that exhorts the average Indian to come together for a public cause.

Wrapped around a rivalry between two TV journalists, played by Shah Rukh Khan and Juhi Chawla, the film skewers the mass media, political parties, the justice system and corporate sponsorship. Rarely subtle – an executioner stopping to promote a product on his way to perform his work on the gallows – it nevertheless hits its targets with mud-splattered relish. Perhaps ahead of its time, the film, which was the first production by Shah Rukh, Juhi and Aziz under their new production company Dreamz Unlimited, didn't exactly set the box office on fire.

The biggest hit of the year was Hrithik Roshan's debut film, *Kaho Na ... Pyaar Hai*, while Mansoor Khan made his first film which didn't star his cousin, Aamir Khan – *Josh*. The film had Shah Rukh and Aishwarya Rai, not as a romantic pair but as siblings. Aditya Chopra returned after *Dilwale Dulhaniya Le Jayenge* with a multi-starrer *Mohabattein*, which was panned by the critics. Abhishek Bachhan and Kareena Kapoor made their debut in J.P. Dutta's *Refugee*, another film which failed at the box office. The year rounded up with Vidhu Vinod Chopra's *Mission Kashmir*, which boasted of its screenplay being written by Pulitzer Prize finalist Suketu Mehta. The film dealt with the complex issue of terrorism, particularly in the context of Kashmir and longed for the fast-vanishing idea of Kashmiriyat.

Kashmir continued to be at the forefront of the trouble with spiralling violence, as the effect of the Kargil war and Kandahar hijacking vitiated the environment between India and Pakistan. Early in the year, Prime Minister Vajpayee asked for Pakistan to be declared a terrorist state, as he accused it of being behind the Kandahar hijacking. When US president Bill Clinton visited India in March to improve ties, a massacre of thirty-six Sikhs took place in Chittisinghpura village in Kashmir. Lashkar-e-Taiba terrorists were believed to be behind the massacre but the muted US reaction to the Indian charge led to a lot of heartburn in India. In her 2006 book *The Mighty and the Almighty: Reflections on America, God, and World Affairs*, Clinton's Secretary of State Madeleine Albright accused 'Hindu militants' of perpetrating the act. The reference to 'Hindu militants' was deleted in subsequent printings.

But Clinton's visit was significant not because of what he did in Delhi but also because of what he did in Islamabad. Pakistan used to be treated at par with India as far as the United States was concerned, but Clinton landed secretly off-schedule in an unmarked plane, taking with him the smallest functional entourage at the end of his five-day trip to India. On live television, he told the people of Pakistan that 'Democracy cannot develop if it is constantly uprooted ...', while he negotiated privately with the military dictator, Gen. Pervez Musharraf, over other issues. He flew away, after spending less than six hours on Pakistani soil, and set the template for his successors who did not even keep up the pretence of visiting Pakistan while visiting India.

Alongside New Delhi's diplomatic joust with Islamabad, Vajpayee tried to open various channels of communication with Kashmiri groups. In a bold move in July, the government initiated a ceasefire with the Hizbul Mujahideen. But it fell apart after only fifteen days, after accusations from the group that the government had fired on some of the group's members. The J&K state assembly passed a resolution to restore the pre-1953 status of the state but the Centre dismissed it outright, and refused to discuss it in parliament. On 19 November, Vajpayee made a unilateral declaration of cessation of combat operations against terrorists in Jammu and Kashmir for a period of one month, co-terminus with the Islamic holy month of Ramzan. Pakistan reciprocated by exercising restraint and relocating some of its troops on the Line of Control. This 'ceasefire' was then extended three times, till it was withdrawn in May 2001. The withdrawal announcement was accompanied by an invitation to Musharraf to visit India for talks.

In June, a massacre of thirty-four Yadavs in Aurangabad district of Bihar by the upper-caste Ranvir Sena again highlighted the fragile state of law and order in the eastern state. By then, the state government had already agreed to the creation of a new state of Jharkhand from its southern parts, bringing to fruition a long-standing demand of the tribals of the region. Patna again made the headlines in July when more than fifty people were killed as a Boeing 737 passenger plane crashed in a residential area of Bihar's capital city. Bihar was to also witness an unprecedented strike by the state police, demanding better compensation for the families of fallen comrades, and less 'political interference' in their work.

Ageing Kannada film star Rajkumar was part of a group taken hostage by notorious bandit Veerappan. A popular outcry put the state government under strong pressure to negotiate Rajkumar's release, but Supreme Court ruled out a deal involving the release of imprisoned members of Veerappan's elephant- poaching and timber-smuggling group. In November, after three months of grave embarrassment for the state governments of Tamil Nadu and Karnataka, Veerappan suddenly released the veteran actor. The exact cause for his release was never known, although the Karnataka state government conceded some of the brigand's demands.

India's improved relations with Bangladesh were reflected in the restoration of the passenger railway link from Benapole in Bangladesh to Petrapole in West Bengal, which had been closed due to lack of commercial interest in 1974. India also signed agreements with Russia and South Africa, and opened trade negotiations with the European Union.

International cricket entered into one of its darkest phases when Delhi police charged South African captain Hansie Cronje with match fixing. After some initial denials, Cronje accepted the charge which was proved by an inquiry commission in South Africa. Cronje was handed down a life ban, while some other South African cricketers were also banned. Names of two former Indian players, Mohammad Azharuddin and Ajay Jadeja, also figured in the allegations.

As three new states of Uttaranchal, Jharkhand and Chhattisgarh came into being in November, the world's longest elected communist leader, Jyoti Basu, the chief minister of West Bengal, decided to hang up his boots. He was succeeded by Buddhadeb Bhattacharjee. Meanwhile, Sonia Gandhi was challenged for the post of Congress party president by Jitendra Prasada. She won with a margin of 7,448 to 94.

Indians dominated the beauty pageants this year with the selection of Lara Dutta as Miss Universe, Priyanka Chopra as Miss World, Diya Mirza as Miss Asia-Pacific and Aditi Gowitrikar as Mrs World. But a world away from the glamour, a drought affected ten crore people inside the country. This fit in perfectly with the glamour-laden song masking the harsh realities, '*Phir bhi dil hai Hindustani*'.

# 2001: *Radha Kaise Na Jale*

*Madhuban mein jo Kanhaiya kisi gopi se mile*
*Kabhi muskaaye, kabhi chhede, kabhi baat kare*
*Radha kaise na jale, Radha kaise na jale*
*Aag tan mann mein lage*
*Radha kaise na jale, Radha kaise na jale*

*Madhuban mein bhale Kanha kisi gopi se mile*
*Mann mein toh Radha ke hi prem ke hain phool khile*
*Kis liye Radha jale, kis liye Radha jale*

Lyrics: Javed Akhtar
Music: A.R. Rahman
Singers: Udit Narayan, Asha Bhosle, Vaisali and chorus
Film: *Lagaan*

'RADHA *kaise na jale*' was part of the film *Lagaan* which was set in the nineteenth century. Although based on the Raas Leela played on the full-moon night of the month of Kartik, in the movie the song takes place on the occasion of Janmashtami, the day celebrated as Lord Krishna's birthday. A.R. Rahman's music is traditional, while Javed Akhtar tried to approximate the language of that era with a colloquial flavour. Javed got a National Award for the lyrics while Rahman won it for the music of the film, which was shortlisted for the Oscars in the best foreign film category.

The choreography of '*Radha kaise na jale*' by Saroj Khan is a mix of traditional dandiya and classical dances. The song is presented as a light-hearted duet, where Radha is jealous to see Krishna (or Kanha, his pet name) always flirting with the gopis, while Krishna tries to pacify her by reassuring her of his love. In the song, the heroine of the film is displaying her insecurities about the hero – played by Aamir Khan – falling for the English girl more than for his flirting with the other gopis. This was part of the romantic track of the film which weaved it with the cricket-based climax in the context of British colonial rule in India. A bold departure from the films being made during those times, it was risky of Aamir to produce this movie. The success of the 222-minute-long film established him as an actor-producer-director with a difference, who could pull off unusual themes in the format of commercial cinema.

If *Lagaan* was rustic and set in the past, Aamir's other movie this year, *Dil Chahta Hai*, was urban and more contemporary. Directed by Javed's son, Farhan Akhtar, the film was about three upper-class boys and an emotional exploration of their existential angst. The language, the grammar, the narrative and the theme were radically modern and ushered in a fresh style of urban movie-making which appealed to the youth.

As in the world of Hindi films that touched extremes, the country saw some real highs and some deep lows during the year. The 9/11 terror strikes in the United States finally drove home the truth of India's suffering from terror to the Western world. Within a couple of months of the horrific attack on the twin towers in New York, the Indian parliament was attacked by six terrorists from Pakistan-based terror groups, Lashkar-e-Taiba and Jaish-e-Mohammad. The dramatic suicide attack on 13 December saw six security officials die, even as the top political leadership was fortunate to remain unhurt. This followed another ghastly attack on the Jammu and Kashmir state legislature on 1 October, wherein thirty-eight people were killed by a Pakistani suicide bomber from the Jaish-e-Mohammad. He detonated a government jeep packed with explosives at the entrance of the building, while other terrorists disguised as policemen entered the complex and began firing. The two incidents, particularly the terror attack on parliament, angered the Vajpayee government, which asked Pakistan to take exemplary action against the terrorist groups involved in the attacks. As the year ended, the possibility of the war was in the air.

The year had started on a tragic note with a massive earthquake striking the state of Gujarat on Republic Day. More than one million were rendered homeless and the death toll in the Kutch region was 12,300 as the earth cracked open in the western state. Bhuj, which was situated only 20 km away from the epicentre, was completely devastated while many buildings were damaged in Ahmedabad. The Indian armed forces moved in to undertake relief and rehabilitation work, in which they were supported by many international NGOs including the Red Cross. Relief material and aid also came in from foreign countries, which included thirteen tonnes of relief material from Pakistan. An exhaustive reconstruction and rehabilitation policy was announced by the state government in May to build the destroyed areas.

While the country was recovering from the grave human tragedy in Gujarat, a political earthquake was caused by a news website. On 13 March, *Tehelka* released video CDs of the sting operation which showed politicians and military officers accepting gifts from journalists posing as arms dealers and middlemen. The BJP's national president Bangaru Laxman, who was seen on camera accepting cash, had to resign from his post. Defence Minister George Fernandes and his Samata Party's national president Jaya Jaitly also resigned. Retribution was swift from the BJP government, which booked *Tehelka* under many sections of the penal code. It unleashed the Income Tax Department, Enforcement Directorate and Intelligence Bureau on them but could not find any proof of wrongdoing. *Tehelka*'s financier Shankar Sharma was imprisoned without any charge and the journalists who carried out the sting operation were also put behind bars. George Fernandes returned to his post in November.

Jaswant Singh became the first foreign minister to visit Myanmar after the military junta grabbed power, but India's relations with Bangladesh took a nosedive when in April 2000, sixteen BSF troopers were killed in a firefight with Bangladesh Border Guards. The cause of the clash was simmering tensions between the two forces guarding the border but the immediate provocation came from disputes over a poorly demarcated international border between the two countries. The Indian government came under pressure from a national outrage when news came of medical reports which suggested that many of the sixteen troopers killed by Bangladeshi forces were mutilated and tortured before being murdered. Although tensions remained, the situation was restored to status quo ante after intervention by the top political leadership of both countries.

The BJP government continued to suffer electoral reverses as it lost assembly elections in Assam, Kerala and Pondicherry to the Congress; in Tamil Nadu to the AIADMK, which was allied with the Congress; and in West Bengal, where the Left Front returned to power, continuing its record as the world's longest-serving elected communist government.

In July, Pakistan president Pervez Musharraf came to India for summit-level talks at Vajpayee's invitation but the talks collapsed without making any breakthrough at Agra. In anticipation of the talks, certain entry points on the Line of Control in Jammu and Kashmir were opened. The talks ended rather acrimoniously when Musharraf unleashed a PR coup as he spoke at length to Indian editors on live television, taking the Indian government by surprise. Three years after the nuclear tests, and needing international support after 9/11, the US government lifted the sanctions imposed on India and Pakistan.

Meanwhile, provisional results of the 2001 census confirmed that the country's population had crossed one billion. And cricket rivalry between India and Australia was established with a three-Test series which the hosts won in a dramatic fashion after losing the first Test and following on in the second one at Kolkata. V.V.S. Laxman and Rahul Dravid played epic innings in what is rated by many as the best Test match ever to turn the match around, as Harbhajan Singh's hat-trick sealed for India an improbable victory. It was a fitting tribute to a year in which *Lagaan* did the improbable too, when the nation hummed the line, '*Radha kaise na jale* ...'

# 2002: *Saathiya Saathiya*

*Peeli dhoop pehenke tum*
*Dekho baag mein mat jaana*
*Bhanwre tumko sab chhedenge*
*Phoolon mein mat jaana*

Lyrics: Gulzar
Music: A.R. Rahman
Singer: Sonu Nigam
Film: *Saathiya*

STARTING in 1993, Allah Rakha Rahman won the Filmfare Award South for Best Music Director every year till 2001. Having won nine consecutive awards for blockbuster Tamil soundtracks, he failed to win the tenth in the year 2002. He compensated by winning his fifth Filmfare Award for Hindi Film Music for that year though. That was for *Saathiya*. The title song of the film, sung by Sonu Nigam, became quite a rage. The lyrics were written by Gulzar.

*Saathiya* was neither an original film nor had an original soundtrack. It was a remake of Mani Ratnam's Tamil film *Alaipayuthey*, which was released in 2000. The film was a romantic drama, dealing with the evolution of a romantic relationship into a marriage with its tensions weighing on the couple. Out of nine tracks in *Alaipayuthey*, seven were retained in the

Hindi remake. The song '*Pachai nirame*' sung by Hariharan became '*Saathiya Saathiya*' in the film without losing its charm as a soft, syrupy song. *Saathiya* was Rahman's second collaboration with Gulzar after *Dil Se* in 1998 and it lived up to expectations.

The year 2002 also saw another film, which was remade for the third time in Hindi. This was *Devdas*, directed by Sanjay Leela Bhansali. Set in the early twentieth century and based on a novel written by Bengali writer Sarat Chandra Chattopadhyay in 1917, this romantic period drama had music by Ismail Darbar. If *Saathiya* had music which was modern, *Devdas* was more rooted in Indian classical music. Featuring imaginative poetry by Nusrat Badr, Darbar was able to weave magic with his tunes and arrangement. The singing matched the quality of compositions with Shreya Ghoshal making her debut with the mesmerizing '*Bairi piya*'. Ghoshal won the National Award for her rendition. *Devdas* was an ambitious project for both Bhansali and Darbar but they managed to pull it off by creating an album that had both range and freshness. While Udit Narayan and Vinod Rathod sang '*Chalak chalak*', a song swinging from joyful inebriation to mournful longing, dance maestro Birju Maharaj sang the prelude to '*Kaahe chhed chhed mohe*' before Kavita Krishnamurthy took over and took this thumri to great heights.

Ram Gopal Varma's crime thriller *Company* was also released in 2002. Loosely based on the story of gangster Dawood Ibrahim, the film narrated the story of how a criminal mastermind converted the underworld to a well-oiled machinery resembling a corporate set-up. If Varma's *Satya* was about a character's initiation into the underworld, *Company* was about consolidation.

The year hadn't arrived quietly for India though. The nation was still feeling the after-effects of the terrorist attack on the Indian parliament on 13 December 2001. The Indian government had ordered mobilization of Indian armed forces in December and by January, 500,000 troops had been mobilized with three armoured divisions concentrated on the Line of Control in Kashmir. Pakistan had responded by mobilizing 300,000 of its troops. This deployment, known as Operation Parakram that lasted nearly eleven months, claimed the lives of 1,874 Indian military personnel.

Even as the spectre of war hung over the world thanks to this military deployment between two nuclear powers, it wasn't the most terrifying thing that took place in the year 2002 in India. That mantle was claimed by events which unfolded in Gujarat. The events were sparked off by a ghastly incident that took place on the morning of 27 February 2002 at the Godhra railway station in Gujarat. As per the commission set up by the Gujarat government, a mob descended on the Sabarmati Express as it was heading out of the Godhra station and set four coaches on fire. The train had a large contingent of devotees returning from a religious function at the disputed Ram Janmabhoomi site in Ayodhya. Fifty-nine people were killed. This incident set off a chain of events whose echoes continue to be heard.

The news of the Godhra train carnage led to widespread anger among sections of Hindus in the state against the Muslim minority, whose members were accused of having attacked the train. What followed over the next three days was a pogrom in which Muslims were targeted and their homes burnt. The state government was accused of being complicit in this pogrom with the police asked to look the other way. When asked about the violence in the state under his watch, Chief Minister Narendra Modi leaned on Newton to explain what had happened. He said, 'Every action has an equal and opposite reaction'. As per official figures, nearly 1,050 people died in these riots while unofficial figures claimed that nearly 2,000 people had died.

Scholars and commentators who studied the violence in Gujarat accused the state machinery of abetting the targeting of the Muslim population in order to secure electoral success for the BJP in the assembly elections to be held later in the year. The government was also accused of not providing relief to the displaced Muslims in the state. Prime Minister Atal Bihari Vajpayee visited Gujarat and when the media asked him if he had any advice for the chief minister, he said, 'The only advice I have for the CM is that he practise "Raj Dharma". The ruler cannot differentiate between the people on the basis of caste or religion.' It was a stinging indictment of the conduct of the state government by a PM who was from the same party that ruled over Gujarat, the BJP. Sporadic violence targeting the Muslim minority continued for months after that.

Facing flak from all over the country for this large-scale violence which was covered widely by television news media, Narendra Modi resigned in July 2002, eight months before the assembly's tenure was supposed to end. The elections were advanced. Modi accused his opponents of tarnishing the reputation of Gujarat and Gujaratis and launched a Gujarat Gaurav Yatra in September just before the state went to polls in October. The BJP returned to power in the state winning 127 seats out of 182. Modi was appointed the Gujarat chief minister.

Even as India stood shocked looking at the scale of violence in Gujarat, there were some moments of cheer as well. Travelling to England, the Indian cricket team beat England in the finals of the triangular NatWest Series. Chasing a difficult target of 326 in the final held at Lord's on 13 July, India took a solid start before losing its way after the fielding restriction were removed after fifteen overs. It lost half the side for 146 with all the experienced batsmen back in the dressing room. The young partnership of Yuvraj Singh and Mohammad Kaif then rebuilt the Indian innings run by run, playing a very mature game. Kaif stood not-out till the end as India stole victory from the English team.

July 2002 also saw an Indian son depart. Dhirubhai Hirachand Ambani had quit his job as a clerk in Aden and returned to India where he set up an import-export business in Bombay. He was twenty-six years old then and over the next forty years, Ambani established Reliance Industries Limited. Through his life, Dhirubhai was often accused of not playing by the rules or rather bending them to suit his plans, but what cannot be ignored is the influence Reliance had on the Indian industrial scene and the stock markets where Ambani came to be known as the messiah of small investors. When he died at the age of sixty-nine in 2002, Reliance Industry Ltd was a ₹55,000-crore behemoth.

In Delhi, the city was taking its first steps towards an infrastructure renaissance as the first segment of the Delhi Metro between Tis Hazari and Shahdara was inaugurated on 25 December. Built with Japanese assistance, the Delhi Metro Rail Corporation had been incorporated in 1995 even though construction began only in the year 1998.

For India, the year 2002 had begun on an ominous note and it did not go away without taking a toll. It had a been tough year for the country, its politics, its faith in a state that was fair to all its citizens. It could have ended the year with the hope that sang:

*Mausam mausam hanste rehna*
*Maddham maddham hanste rehna*

# 2003: *Har Pal Yahaan, Jee Bhar Jiyo*

*Har pal yahaan, jee bhar jiyo*
*Jo hai sama, kal ho naa ho*
*Har ghadi badal rahi hai roop zindagi*
*Chaanv hai kabhi kabhi hai dhoop zindagi*

Lyrics: Javed Akhtar
Music: Shankar–Ehsaan–Loy
Singer: Sonu Nigam
Film: *Kal Ho Naa Ho*

TWO years after crooning '*Suraj hua maddham*' in *Kabhi Khushi Kabhie Gham* for Shah Rukh Khan, Sonu Nigam reprised that role for the title song of the film, *Kal Ho Naa Ho*. This song, composed by the trio Shankar, Ehsaan and Loy to the words of Javed Akhtar, underlines the ephemeral nature of life and asks the listeners to make the most of each moment. This gentle melody was one of the biggest hits of the year 2003 and earned both the singer and the lyricists many awards, including the Filmfare Awards. The film starring Shah Rukh Khan, Preity Zinta, Saif Ali Khan and Jaya Bachchan was another of Karan Johar's productions that revolved around NRIs, this time in New York. It was directed by Johar's former assistant, Nikhil Advani.

Even though *Kal Ho Naa Ho* was a huge success, it wasn't the only good soundtrack released in the year. *Chalte Chalte*, another film starring Shah Rukh Khan – this time paired with Rani Mukherji – was another roaring success at the music charts. The music was composed by Jatin–Lalit and Aadesh Shrivastava and was full of the soft, romantic songs that were their hallmark. The year also saw Vishal–Shekhar making their debut with the soundtrack for the musical comedy *Jhankaar Beats*. The music and the film paid tribute to the genius of R.D. Burman. Even though the tunes they composed were new, they took inspiration from RD's rhythms and sound patterns in this album. The movie and its music were surprise hits in the year.

The year 2003 was also remarkable because of a film starring actors Sanjay Dutt and Arshad Warsi. The duo played the roles of sweet rogues in director Rajkumar Hirani's debut film, *Munna Bhai M.B.B.S*. This comedy film was a major hit and established Hirani as a director to contend with.

In the non-film world, 2003 was a year when India decidedly moved away from the acrimonies of 2002. While 2002 had been punctuated by a stand-off between India and Pakistan, 2003 saw the two sides turn around and focus on confidence-building measures. Diplomatic relations between the two countries were restored in May. In July, the Lahore–Delhi bus service was resumed and in this bus travelled a two-and-half-year-old child, Noor Fatima. Noor Fatima was travelling from Pakistan to India for an open-heart surgery. Her parents chose a hospital in Bangalore for this surgery. Little Noor Fatima became the symbol of a turnaround in India–Pakistan relations. Confidence-building measures between the two countries culminated in a ceasefire on the Line of Control in Kashmir.

As India was warming up to its western neighbour, relations with China were also being reinvigorated in the year 2003 with Prime Minister Vajpayee visiting the communist nation in June. The visit led to India conceding that Tibet was a part of China while China recognized Sikkim as a part of India. The visit gave a strong push to trade between the two countries which was stuck at just over $6 billion in 2003.

Even as India's push for external security was getting stronger, there were other challenges that remained. On 25 August 2003, the financial capital of India, Mumbai, was struck by two bomb blasts that killed fifty-four people and injured 244. One blast took place at Gateway of India while the other struck Zaveri Bazar near the Mumba Devi temple. Later, three of the accused were sentenced to death for these blasts and the verdict was upheld by the Bombay High Court in 2012.

While India was mending its relations with both Pakistan and China, it was faced with external pressure of a different kind this year. In March 2003, American president George W. Bush announced that a coalition of forces would invade Iraq to unseat Saddam Hussein. The invasion was justified by claims that Iraq possessed weapons of mass destruction (WMD). Washington requested India to contribute to the invasion of Iraq by sending troops to the Middle Eastern country. As the Indian government internally debated whether India could commit troops to the Iraqi invasion, Americans mounted considerable pressure on it. Members of the Vajpayee government led by Home Minister L.K. Advani wanted India to contribute to the effort of the American alliance in Iraq. Some Indian strategic affairs commentators also wanted India to 'not miss this opportunity' but the Lok Sabha passed a resolution to the effect that India should not send troops.

The year 2003 also gave some bittersweet memories to Indian cricket fans. Before leaving for the ODI World Cup in South Africa in February, the Indian cricket team had visited New Zealand for a bilateral cricket tour. The series had been planned long in advance in order to help India get used to fast, bouncy pitches that would help it cope with such pitches in the World Cup. The New Zealand tour turned out to be an unmitigated disaster for the Indian team which lost the seven-match One-Day series to the New Zealand team 5–2. Only Virender Sehwag could manage to score two centuries as all the other batsmen suffered a loss of self-confidence.

As India began their World Cup campaign, their batsmen struggled in the first two matches with India losing the match against Australia. This led to a backlash at home with violent attacks on the homes of some of the Indian cricketers while others saw their effigies being burnt. India came back in the tournament registering memorable victories over England and arch-rival Pakistan. The turnaround propelled India to the finals. The final was an anticlimax as the Australian team demonstrated why they were the best team in the game at that time. Australia had remained unbeaten throughout the tournament and its victory in the final was a crushing defeat for the Indian team.

India was to take revenge for this loss later in the year when they visited Australia for a bilateral series of four Test matches. Against the overwhelming favourite home team, India began strongly in the Test series, drawing the first match which saw captain Sourav Ganguly score a century. This was followed by a memorable Test match win at Adelaide thanks to Rahul Dravid's heroic efforts.

For India, 2003 did not bring any dramatic successes but neither did it bring with it any tragic upheavals. It was quite a change from the tension of 2002, even if it didn't quite break the shackles of the recent past. The year seemed to agree with Javed Akhtar's words however:

*Har ghadi badal rahi hai roop zindagi*
*Chaanv hai kabhi, kabhi hai dhoop zindagi*
*Har pal yahaan, jee bhar jiyo*
*Jo hai sama, kal ho naa ho*

# 2004: *Yeh Jo Des Hai Tera, Swades Hai Tera*

*Nayi nayi raahon mein, dabi dabi aahon mein*
*Khoye khoye dil se tere, koi yeh kahega*
*Yeh jo des hai tera, swades hai tera*

Lyrics: Javed Akhtar
Music: A.R. Rahman
Singer: A.R. Rahman
Film: *Swades*

A.R. Rahman and Ashutosh Gowariker had a successful partnership with *Lagaan* in 2001. When they teamed up again for Gowariker's second work, *Swades*, the expectations were high. *Swades* was not a period film, unlike *Lagaan*, but the soundtrack did not disappoint. Rahman sang the title track '*Yeh jo des hai tera*' himself. Javed Akhtar's lyrics talk about the unbreakable bond with one's country. A gentle rhythm punctuated by shehnai played by Madhukar Dhumal made this a unique song. The song had all the qualities that Rahman is famous for. It created a beautiful fusion of an Indian base with Western musical influences and a marriage of the music and lyrics where both glide in and out of each other. The chorus adds body to the song as it tapers off with a soul-stirring shehnai solo. The song earned Javed Akhtar another Filmfare Award even as Rahman lost out to Anu Malik for the Best Composer Award.

The year 2004 also saw a unique partnership between two old giants of Hindi films; one living while the other had passed away in 1975 – Yash Chopra and Madan Mohan. Yash Chopra returned to film direction with *Veer Zaara* starring Shah Rukh Khan, Preity Zinta and Rani Mukherji. Madan Mohan had passed away at the age of fifty-one in 1975. Having assisted S.D. Burman, Madan Mohan had struggled to break into the big league in Hindi film music. He was known as a talented composer who did not get his due. His talent lay in composing ghazals, with Lata Mangeshkar even calling him *Ghazal ka shehzada*, the prince of ghazals, while Kaifi Azmi praised his grip over the Urdu language. When Yash Chopra wanted special music for his directorial venture, Mohan's son, music industry executive Sanjeev Kohli, passed on the family secrets to him. These were home recordings of some compositions that had been hummed by Mohan but never used. Eleven tracks from these recordings were used to compose the music for the film. The music was arranged by R.S. Mani and produced by Sanjeev Kohli himself. Lata Mangeshkar, the favourite singer of Yash Chopra and Madan Mohan, lent her voice to the songs that became huge hits.

The *des* (nation) Rahman was singing about in *Swades* was shining in 2004. That was the assertion of the ruling party, the BJP, as India went into election mode in the first half of 2004. India Shining (Bharat Uday in Hindi) was the campaign created by the BJP to portray that India was finally emerging and there was a pervasive sense of optimism all around. Prime Minister Atal Bihari Vajpayee was the leader in whose name the BJP was seeking a return to power in the country. An old master of the political game, a gifted orator and a popular leader, Vajpayee had no apparent political challengers. Vajpayee asked the parliament to be dissolved ahead of schedule and called for elections.

The BJP built a campaign that was omnipresent and ensured that this message of optimism went around the country. The political brain behind this campaign, BJP general secretary Pramod Mahajan, even set up a call centre from which Vajpayee's taped voice called people all over the country, exhorting them to support the BJP in the polls. Facing this well-oiled machinery of the BJP and its alliance, the NDA, was an opposition in disarray, with Sonia Gandhi leading the Indian National Congress.

While Vajpayee was popular, Sonia Gandhi was targeted by the BJP for being a foreigner in India and therefore unfit to lead the country. She was born in Italy but had taken Indian citizenship after she got married to Rajiv Gandhi, who later became India's prime minister. The BJP kept up the attack on Sonia's foreign origins, her weak oratory and scoffed at her mass contact programme, which incidentally received a good response from the public.

Even as surveys indicated the elections to be a cakewalk for the BJP, the results on 13 May 2004 were a surprise. The NDA, was voted out with 181 seats while the Congress alliance won 218 seats. The Left Front won fifty-nine seats and announced its support to the UPA, led by Sonia Gandhi. Despite the RSS and the BJP's acrimonious campaign, Sonia Gandhi was set to be India's prime minister. BJP leader Sushma Swaraj, who had contested and lost against Sonia Gandhi in 1999 from Bellary in Karnataka, then went public with her opposition to a foreign-born person becoming India's prime minister. She said that if Sonia was made the PM, she would shave her head in protest, wear white clothes and start a mass movement against Sonia.

Having scaled all opposition to her anointment as prime minister, Sonia Gandhi did the unthinkable and relinquished the prime ministership. Her party, its allies and the party supporters protested loudly but she refused to change her mind, and former finance minister Manmohan Singh became the prime minister.

Even as Indian politics was witnessing high drama, there was no lack of drama elsewhere either. India's industrial sector witnessed two bitter battles in 2004. In an interview in November 2004, Mukesh Ambani, son of Dhirubhai Ambani, admitted that there were differences between him and younger brother Anil over ownership. This was the start of the Reliance ownership battle that was to embroil others in times to come. The other turbulence to hit Indian industry also had to do with succession. The chairman of the Birla Corporation, Priyamvada Birla, passed away in 2004. She had inherited ownership and estates of her husband Madhav Prasad Birla who had set up the corporation that had interests primarily in jute and cement. They had no children and contrary to expectations of the larger Birla family, she willed her shares and estate to a chartered accountant, Rajendra Singh Lodha, who was also the co-chairman of the Birla Corporation. While the corporation had modest profits of ₹41 crore, the estate Priyamvada Birla left was worth ₹5,000 crore in 2004. The Birla clan refused to accept the will and challenged it in the court.

While serious battles were being fought in India in the political and corporate worlds, the sports arena was also witnessing some marquee battles. In March 2004, after much debate about their security, the Indian cricket team embarked on a full tour of Pakistan, after a gap of fifteen years. India won the five-match One-Day series 3–2 and the three-match Test series 2–1. This was India's first Test series victory on Pakistan soil. The highlight of this series was a triple hundred scored by Virender Sehwag in Multan in the first Test match. Sehwag was in excellent form and demolished the Pakistani bowling effort. Just a shot away from becoming the first Indian batsman to score a triple century, Sehwag sashayed down the pitch to a Saqlain Mushtaq ball and hoisted him over mid-wicket for a six and crossed 300. Even as India won the match, it was not free from controversy. India under captain Rahul Dravid (filling in for an injured Sourav Ganguly) declared the first innings on 675. Dravid wanted Pakistan to face Indian bowlers for one full hour at the end of the second day. The reason this became controversial was that Sachin Tendulkar was left stranded on 194 at the other end. The Indian team had communicated twice to Sachin to hasten his scoring rate but when they saw time slipping away, Dravid stepped in and declared. While some hailed this as a great move underlining India's commitment to team victory rather than individual glory, it upset others no end as they considered it an affront to India's biggest batting star.

This debate about whether India should have allowed Tendulkar to score his double hundred underlined India's confused sense of propriety. It was part unique and part misplaced but it was thoroughly Indian, aptly summed by Javed Akhtar's line: '*Yeh jo des hai tera, swades hai tera*'.

# 2005: *Kaisi Paheli Zindagaani*

*Nayi nahin yeh baatein*
*Yeh baatein hai purani*
*Kaisi paheli hai yeh*
*Kaisi paheli zindagaani*

Lyrics: Swanand Kirkire
Music: Shantanu Moitra
Singer: Sunidhi Chauhan
Film: *Parineeta*

JAZZ legend Louis Armstrong performed the song '*A kiss to build a dream on*' in 1951 when it featured in the film *The Strip*. It wasn't Armstrong's own composition. It had been composed in 1935 by Bert Kalmar, Harry Ruby and Oscar Hammerstein II. But it was Armstrong's rendition that became the inspiration for *Parineeta*'s song '*Kaisi paheli zindagaani*' in 2005. Sarat Chandra Chattopadhyay's Bengali novel *Parineeta* is set in early twentieth-century Calcutta but the film *Parineeta* directed by debutant Pradeep Sarkar was based in the 1960s. This was not the first adaptation of the novel on the silver screen, not even the first Hindi adaptation. Bimal Roy had already made a Hindi film in the year 1953, starring Ashok Kumar and Meena Kumari. There had been Bengali versions too. For the 1960s, Armstrong's version of the song was a perfect fit. Sung by Sunidhi Chauhan and performed by Rekha on-screen, composer Shantanu Moitra tweaked the music to make it a jazzy cabaret song. *Parineeta* introduced actress Vidya Balan to film audiences and gave Shantanu Moitra and lyricist Swanand Kirkire a big break.

Before *Parineeta* happened, Pradeep Sarkar had made his name as an ad-film and music video director. His collaborations with the band Euphoria for their music videos had become very popular and they ended up drawing Vidhu Vinod Chopra's attention. For Shantanu Moitra and Swanand Kirkire, *Parineeta* was not their first collaboration. They had already partnered for *Hazaaron Khwaishein Aisi* for the song '*Bawra mann dekhne chala ek sapna*' which was also released in 2005. Kirkire also sang the song. Moitra's music received critical acclaim and became immensely popular as well.

The year also saw India dance along with Aishwarya Rai, Abhishek Bachchan and Amitabh Bachchan to the song '*Kajra re*' for their film *Bunty Aur Babli*. Gulzar penned the fun song. The song was a rage all over India and the film soundtrack also won the Filmfare Award for Music for the year 2005. '*Kajra re*' was included in the film as an 'item song', a song which may not have anything to do with the film plot. Composed by Shankar, Ehsaan and Loy and sung by Alisha Chinai, '*Kajrare*' became a rage. Gulzar wrote the song keeping the setting in mind and did not attempt to embellish it with high poetry. The song was not devoid of Gulzar's unique style of poetry though. Later in an interview, Gulzar spoke about the song and said, 'I don't think the words "*Teri baaton mein kimaam ki khushboo hai, tera aana bhi toh garmiyon ki loo hai*" are frivolous. Poetry with a serious thought doesn't mean it has to be serious in mood.'

The year 2005 also saw the rise of another musical phenomenon in the form of music director Himesh Reshammiya. He had been around for some time but found big success in this year for the music of the film *Aashiq Banaya Aapne* starring Emraan Hashmi. The album was a fusion of Sufi and Western music styles, and became a runaway success, establishing Reshammiya as a star composer.

While India was singing '*Kaisi paheli zindagaani*', the India–Pakistan relationship also seemed to be asking the same question as it continued to surprise the world. The relationship between the two nuclear powers went from strength to strength as a bus service was established between Srinagar, the capital of Jammu and Kashmir, and Muzaffarabad, the capital of Pakistan-Occupied Kashmir. It was the culmination of efforts made by President Pervez Musharraf's administration in Pakistan and the Indian government under prime ministers Atal Bihari Vajpayee and Manmohan Singh. Started on 7 April 2005, the bus travelled a distance of 170 km and allowed Kashmiri families that were divided by the Line of Control to come together.

Even as things seemed to be fine on the external front for India, internally there were other challenges. The metropolis of Bombay is no stranger to heavy rains as the city gets torrential rains during monsoon season but what it saw on 26 July 2005 was unprecedented. In a period of twenty-four hours starting at 8.30 a.m. the city received 99.4 cm of rainfall. Trains, roads, airports, mobile networks were all thrown out of gear as the city collapsed under the volume of this rainfall. Many were stuck in traffic for close to more than twenty-four hours. Other parts of the state of Maharashtra were also flooded because of this downpour. More than 1,000 people lost their lives in Maharashtra; many of them in Bombay. Cars were stranded on the flooded roads and many people were electrocuted. All services were disrupted and the next two days were declared public holidays by the government.

Monsoons came and went and India recovered and prepared to celebrate Diwali in October. Two days after Diwali, on 29 October, Delhi was struck by three bomb blasts that hit a railway station, a bus and a busy market. The three blasts killed sixty-two people. A Pakistan-based group, Islamic Inquilab Mahaz, claimed responsibility for this terrorist attack.

Three Indian states went to polls in 2005. Haryana saw the incumbent government of Om Prakash Chautala being thrown out as the Congress party won a landslide victory. Bihar and Jharkhand, however, saw hung assemblies. No government was formed in Bihar after the polls, held in February, so a repeat election was organized in October–November. This saw the JD(U)–BJP alliance come to power in the state under the leadership of Nitish Kumar.

The Pakistani cricket team was visiting India in a return series. The series comprised three Test matches and six One-Day International matches between the traditional rivals. The Test matches were played in Mohali, Calcutta and Bangalore. The first Test at Mohali was drawn while a century in each innings by Rahul Dravid helped India beat the visitors at Calcutta in the second Test match. The third match was won by Pakistan at Bangalore and the Test series was drawn 1–1. The six-match One-Day International series was won by Pakistan 4–2.

The year also saw a twenty-year-old Pankaj Advani become the World Billiards Champion with a rare feat of winning in both the point and time formats. He was the first player to achieve that distinction.

In January 2005, India lost the services of former foreign secretary and national security adviser (NSA) to the Manmohan Singh government, Jyotindra Nath Dixit. 'Mani', as he was known to his friends, had been a career diplomat who rose to become India's foreign secretary, retiring in 1994. A brilliant diplomat with a formidable grasp and recall of things, he had been India's NSA under Manmohan Singh for only seven months when he died. He was succeeded by M.K. Narayanan for the post.

With its highs and lows, 2005 was a mixed bag for India, as if living up to the words:

*Pal mein hasaaye*
*Aur pal mein rulaaye yeh kahaani*
*Kaisi paheli hai yeh*
*Kaisi paheli zindagaani*

# 2006: *Roo-ba-roo Roshni Hai*

*Dhuan chhata khula gagan mera*
*Nayi dagar naya safar mera*
*Jo ban sake tu hamsafar mera*
*Nazar mila zara*
*Roo-ba-roo roshni hai*

Lyrics: Prasoon Joshi
Music: A.R. Rahman
Singer: Naresh Iyer
Film: *Rang De Basanti*

CHANNEL V, which used to be a music channel till 2015, launched a talent-hunt show, *Channel V Super Singer*, in 2004. Judged by singer Adnan Sami, one of the episodes also had a guest appearance by A.R. Rahman. One of the singers who performed in front of Rahman, Naresh Iyer, impressed Rahman so much that he asked Iyer to work with him. Iyer did not win the competition but started his career with Rahman in Chennai. In 2006, he crooned '*Roo-ba-roo*' for the film *Rang De Basanti* and became a well-known name. He went on to win the Filmfare–R.D. Burman Award for Upcoming Music Performer, instituted in 1996. The first winner of this award was Rahman himself, thanks to the success of his first Hindi soundtrack, *Rangeela* (released in 1995).

*Rang De Basanti* was one of Rahman's most refreshing soundtracks in a few years and was loved for its fusion of folk and Western music sung by new voices like Iyer, Mohit Chauhan and Harshdeep Kaur. Rahman won his sixth Filmfare Award for Music for *Rang De Basanti*. The song '*Roo-ba-roo*' is about a man's awakening, of becoming aware of his self-worth. The song was used to depict a moment in the film when the young characters become aware of their own capability and stand up for what they believe is right. Naresh Iyer also won the National Award for this song.

Himesh Reshammiya, whose star had been on the ascendancy the previous year, also had one of the biggest musical hits in 2006 with *Aksar*. The song '*Jhalak dikhlaja*' was a crowd favourite thanks to its beats and the repetitive hook of '*Jhalak dikhlaja*' in the lyrics. Even as purists scoffed at Reshammiya's style of music, he managed to find success by using these catchy, repetitive hooks to great effect in many of his songs and the listeners loved them. '*Jhalak dikhlaja*' was a rage at weddings, in clubs and among the youth. The song was so popular that when BBC's famous show *Strictly Come Dancing* was launched in its Indian avatar in 2006, they called it *Jhalak Dikhla Jaa*. The show has seen nine seasons since then.

Another musical success in 2006 was *Fanaa*, an Aamir Khan film that had music by Jatin–Lalit. The duo was nominated for the Filmfare Award for Music eleven times in their sixteen-year run, without ever winning the trophy, not even for their biggest hit, *Dilwale Dulhaniya Le Jayenge*. *Fanaa* was their last film together.

While the youth in *Rang De Basanti* was awakening and coming to terms with themselves in '*Roo-ba-roo*', the Indian government was launching an ambitious rewiring of the Indian welfare state set-up. Passed late in 2005, the National Rural Employment Guarantee Act (NREGA) was launched in 200 districts in the country in February 2006. NREGA, which later came to be known as MGNREGA after Mahatma Gandhi, sought to guarantee work under the 'Right to work' to all Indians. It sought to provide at least '100 days of guaranteed wage employment in a financial year, to every household whose adult members volunteer to do unskilled manual work'. Workers were supposed to be provided employment within 5 km of their residence with minimum wages to be paid to them. MGNREGA was designed as a self-targeting scheme, as only the poor chose to do manual labour for minimum wages.

It was created to provide economic safety to the poorest sections in rural India and over the years has had a budgetary outlay of ₹35,000 crore to 40,000 crore. In 2014, the World Bank termed it as a 'stellar example of rural development'. One of the biggest successes of the programme was the high participation of Scheduled Castes, Scheduled Tribes and women. One of its biggest contributions was the push it gave to rural consumption in the country as it pushed rural wages upwards, which led to a reduction in urban migration. A study by the National Council for Applied Economic Research (NCAER) said that it helped reduce poverty by almost 32 per cent from its launch to 2011–12 and prevented fourteen million people from falling into poverty. More than these numbers, MGNREGA's success lay in taking the benefits of liberalization to the rural poor in India. Its signal contribution was to make economic growth more inclusive as it sought to provide succour to the poorest in the country.

Three states went to polls in 2006: West Bengal, Tamil Nadu and Kerala. The year turned out to be a good one for the communist parties in the country as they won elections in both West Bengal and Kerala. In West Bengal, the Left Front, which had been in power since June 1977 beat the Trinamool Congress, led by Mamata Banerjee, to retain power in the state under Buddhadeb Bhattacharjee. In Tamil Nadu, the DMK led by M. Karunanidhi trounced the All India Anna Dravida Munnetra Kazhagam led by J. Jayalalithaa to regain power, while in Kerala the Left Democratic Front (LDF) beat the Congress-led United Democratic Front (UDF) to capture power.

As the Congress party stood strong, having regained power in Delhi in 2004, the opposition seemed to be in a disarray. Even as the BJP struggled to get over its improbable loss in 2004, it was struck by another calamity: the death of its general secretary. Pramod Mahajan was the first among equals in the second generation of BJP leadership. Known for his management skills in the BJP, Mahajan was in charge of their 2004 electoral campaign, which ended in a loss. The Maharashtra politician was shot by his younger brother Pravin Mahajan on 22 April 2006 at his home in Bombay. Pravin drove to Pramod Mahajan's house on that day and after a heated argument with him, shot him using a licenced revolver. He later drove to the police station and surrendered. Fifty-six-year- old Pramod Mahajan died thirteen days later in a hospital in Bombay.

Bombay was the centre of more horror when seven bombs set in pressure cookers went off in suburban trains on 11 July 2006. It was eleven minutes of horror on the western line of the Bombay suburban train network and claimed 209 lives while 700 more were injured. Indian security authorities claimed that 7/11, as it came to be known, was the handiwork of Pakistan's Inter-Services Intelligence (ISI). National Security Adviser M.K. Narayanan said that India had very good evidence of ISI's involvement in the blasts.

The year 2006 also saw the departure of Hindi film stalwarts Naushad and Hrishikesh Mukherjee. Naushad Ali hailed from Lucknow and mesmerized Indian film lovers with his compositions steeped in Hindustani classical music. His ageless music in *Ganga Jamuna*, *Pakeezah*, *Mughal-e-Azam* and *Baiju Bawra* continues to enthral listeners. Hrishikesh Mukherjee, or Hrishi-da as he was popularly known, made forty-two films as director including some Hindi film classics like *Anari*, *Satyakam*, *Anand*, *Abhimaan*, *Chupke-Chupke* and *Golmaal*. He walked the middle road between mainstream commercial and art cinema.

The year was also rocked by protests in institutes of higher education when the Union government decided to reserve 27 per cent seats for OBCs in institutes of higher learning. This included institutes like the Indian Institutes of Technology (IITs), Indian Institutes of Management (IIMs), National Institutes of Technology (NITs) among others. As students protested in Delhi, the government stuck to its guns and the constitutional amendment was passed unanimously in parliament with only two members abstaining. The Supreme Court upheld the law in 2008 but asked for the exclusion of the 'creamy layer'.

Did the reservations clear the skies for the country's youth? Would it help them realize their own self-worth?

*Ujaale main, pee gaya*
*Roshan hua, jee gaya*
*Kyun sehte rahein*
*Roo-ba-roo roshni hai*

# 2007: *Aao Milo Chalein*

*Aao kho jayein hum, ho jaye gham yun laapata*
*Aao milo chalein, jaana kahaan na ho pata*
*Hum jo chalne lage, chalne lage hain yeh raaste*
*Aa ha ha ha manjil se behtar lagne lage hai yeh raaste*

Lyrics: Irshad Kamil
Music: Pritam Chakraborty
Singers: Shaan and Ustad Sultan Khan
Film: *Jab We Met*

USTAD Sultan Khan (1940–2011) became popular with the generation of music lovers who grew up around the turn of the century with his album *Piya Basanti*. A famous sarangi player, his earthy vocals were also much in demand to spice up compositions in many Hindi film songs after *Piya Basanti*. In the film *Jab We Met*, the composer Pritam Chakraborty chose to use both Sultan Khan's sarangi and his vocals for a song for the road, '*Aao milo chalein*'. Picturized on the lead pair in the film, the song is about how the odd pair brought together by circumstances starts enjoying their journey. A tantalizing combination of melody and rhythm, the song marries Sultan Khan's folksy bits with Shaan's more modern vocals just as it fuses the traditional sarangi's sounds to the more modern sounds of a synthesizer. Irshad Kamil's lyrics detail the journey of two people discovering the joys of an aimless journey and each other's company.

*Jab We Met* was a success at both the box office and music charts with its soundtrack becoming very popular. For Hindi film music, 2007 was a good year with many high-quality soundtracks vying for ear space. Pritam had another successful film album with *Life in a ... Metro* while there was the redoubtable A.R. Rahman with *Guru*, sweeping all the awards. Then there was Monty Sharma with his compositions in Sanjay Leela Bhansali's *Saawariya* – Ranbir Kapoor's debut film.

When Shaan sang '*Aao milo chalein*', he might have been singing about India in the seventh year of the twenty-first century – and in its sixtieth year of independence. It seemed to be enjoying the journey as well. In the financial year 2006–07 the Indian economy grew by 9.6 per cent with a 14 per cent increase in per capita income. This was underlined in April 2007 when the country joined an elite club of ten countries with a trillion-dollar economy. The growth was happening at such pace that there were signs of overheating.

Inflation rose to uncomfortable levels of around 6–7 per cent but that didn't seem to matter to Indian industry: they seemed to be humming '*Mauja hi mauja*' from *Jab We Met*. This was true for Tata Steel, for sure. The Tata Group company was celebrating its hundredth year in business and decided to mark it by acquiring Corus Steel, the largest steel company in Europe, for a price of US $12 billion. Corus was four times bigger than Tata Steel when it was acquired and the acquisition made Tata Steel the fifth largest steel company in the world. This was a big acquisition which signalled to the world the strength of the Indian economy and industry.

Three Indian businesswomen, Naina Lal Kidwai of HSBC, Chanda Kochhar of ICICI and Kiran Mazumdar-Shaw of Biocon, were also singing '*Mauja hi mauja*' as *Fortune* magazine included their names in its list of fifty most powerful businesswomen in the world.

The year 2007 was special for another Indian woman and for Indian democracy. On 25 July 2007 the Chief Justice of India swore in Pratibha Devisinh Patil as the twelfth president of the Republic of India. With this, Pratibha Patil became the first (and so far the only) woman to hold the highest office. She had been governor of Rajasthan since 2004 and had been a career politician.

Patil was not the first candidate for the ruling United Progressive Alliance though. The Congress party had suggested many names, including that of Shivraj Patil, the then home minister, for the presidential election, but the Left Front, led by CPI(M) general secretary Prakash Karat, did not approve of the names. Eventually Pratibha Patil became the candidate and defeated former Rajasthan chief minister and senior BJP leader Bhairon Singh Shekhawat in the election.

While Pratibha Patil found a new home in Rashtrapati Bhavan, the voters in Uttar Pradesh decided that it was time to give Mayawati a chance to lead the state. The leader of the Bahujan Samaj Party devised a clever strategy to combine her Dalit vote bank with the votes of the Brahmins in the state. Her strategy paid rich dividends as she romped home winning 206 seats in the 402-seat state assembly. In Gujarat, Narendra Modi made the state assembly polls all about Gujarati asmita (pride) and was re-elected.

While Mayawati and Modi were having a good time in 2007, the chief minister of West Bengal, Buddhadeb Bhattacharjee, burnt his hands as he tried to make a push for industrialization in the state. A proposal was made by the Central government for a petrochemical hub in Nandigram, 160 kms from Kolkata. People of the locality thought their land would be acquired for it. Agitated locals protested and the police fired on the mob, killing fourteen persons. The police maintained that the Maoists had provoked the locals to attack them. This was the biggest challenge faced by the Left Front government in the state in its thirty-year rule. Nandigram became a lightning rod for political opposition in the state and put Buddha Babu, as he was called, in the toughest situation of his political life.

In February 2007, a day before the Pakistani foreign minister was supposed to visit India for talks, bomb blasts ripped through the Samjhauta Express train service between New Delhi and Lahore. The twin blasts killed sixty-seven passengers and injured fifteen others.

In the world of sports, 2007 was the year when India decided to take a new form of cricket more seriously. This was T20 and not only did India win the inaugural ICC T20 World Cup held in South Africa, but it also announced a new T20 cricket league that was to change the economics of the game forever. The T20 World Cup was a consolation for the Indian team after it had a torrid time in the One-Day International World Cup held in West Indies earlier in the year. India had failed to make it past the group stages.

In the T20 World Cup, the Indian team won a thrilling final against arch-rival Pakistan to lift the trophy. The Board of Control for Cricket in India (BCCI) subsequently announced the Indian Premier League (IPL) with a prize money of ₹35 crore to be held every year, with the inaugural tournament to be held in the year 2008. The announcement of IPL was a major event in itself, and no one could have predicted what the future held in store for the domestic T20 cricket league.

It was also the year when the Indian government decided that the challenge that state-owned airlines faced could be countered by merging Air India and Indian (formerly Indian Airlines). Would the future bring *mauja hi mauja* for the merged entity and for India in general?

# 2008: *Haule Haule Ho Jayega Pyaar*

*Tu sabar to kar mere yaar*
*Zara saans to le dildaar*
*Chalfikar nu goli maar*
*Yaarhai din jindai de chaar*

Lyrics: Jaideep Sahni
Music: Salim–Sulaiman
Singer: Sukhwinder Singh
Film: *Rab Ne Bana Di Jodi*

AROUND the turn of the new millennium, the Hindi film industry was hit by a new wave. This was the emergence of middle-class lyricists, writers and film-makers, from non-film backgrounds. Hailing from different towns across north India and armed with a more modern vocabulary, new metaphors and different perspectives, these artists brought with them a freshness to Hindi cinema. One such artist from Delhi was Jaideep Sahni. He was an engineering graduate who stumbled into the world of film and found his calling in writing. Sahni wrote some of the most memorable Hindi films made in the first decade of the new millennium.

Whether it was diving into the management operations of the Bombay underworld in *Company* or narrating the hardships of a middle-class family as it tries to get rid of squatters on its property in *Khosla Ka Ghosla* or how the redemption of a fallen hockey player comes about as he coaches Indian women to sporting glory in *Chak De India*, Sahni's work as a writer and lyricist grabbed attention. For Aditya Chopra's directorial venture *Rab Ne Bana Di Jodi*, Sahni's lyrics gently conveyed the budding romance between the unlikely couple of Surinder and Taani, brought together more by circumstances than design. '*Haule haule ho jayega pyaar*', the mukhda, tells the protagonist that love will happen, slowly.

The lyrics are a combination of Hindi and Punjabi expressions which is suitable, given that the film is based in Amritsar. In one of the stanzas Sahni pays tribute to old Indian poetry about love with the line, '*Kya keh ke gaya tha shaayar wo sayana, aag ka dariya doob ke jaana*'. The songs in the film were composed by Salim and Sulaiman Merchant who had earlier been noticed for their melodious work in *Iqbal, Dor* and *Chak De India*. In '*Haule haule ...*' Salim–Sulaiman use a more traditional arrangement with a kind of staccato harmonium base and then allow the talented Sukhwinder Singh to glide on the vocals. With the 'ordinary' Surinder (played by Shah Rukh Khan) to enact the song on screen, the composers seemed to have made an additional effort to keep it simple – something that made the song stand out.

Aditya Chopra might have been looking for an extraordinary love story in an ordinary pair in *Rab Ne Bana Di Jodi* but India didn't have to look hard for the extraordinary in 2008. It was anything but ordinary. In 2006, the Manmohan Singh government had brought in the Central Educational Institutions (Reservation in Admission) Act, 2006, that reserved 27 per cent seats in government-funded institutions for candidates who belonged to Other Backward Classes (OBCs). The Act had been challenged in the Supreme Court and in April 2008, the SC upheld the Act. The court also held that the exclusion of minority institutions from the ambit of the quota was valid. OBC quotas in government jobs had been brought in by the V.P. Singh-led government in 1990, OBC quotas in educational institutions also came into force in 2008, the same year that V.P. Singh passed away – an event that was barely covered although his tenure had been so turbulent, full of upsets.

The Manmohan Singh government faced extraordinary turbulence in July as it pressed forward with the Indo-US nuclear deal signed in the previous year and approached the International Atomic Energy Agency (IAEA) with a safeguards agreement. The UPA government enjoyed the support of the Communist Party of India (Marxist) but the CPI(M) leadership led by General Secretary Prakash Karat was strongly opposed to India signing the deal with the United States of America. The Congress refused to back down and the CPI(M) withdrew support from the government.

In July 2008 the Manmohan Singh government faced a no-confidence motion. In his speech in the Lok Sabha, Prime Minister Manmohan Singh asked the leaders of the Left parties whether L.K. Advani, the architect of the Babri Masjid demolition, was acceptable to them as prime minister. The government was able to win the confidence of parliament by nineteen votes. The trust vote became sensational when some BJP MPs jumped into the well of the house holding wads of currency in their hands and said that they had been offered bribes by Samajwadi Party leader Amar Singh to vote in favour of the UPA in the House. The UPA had won the trust vote and remained in power despite losing the support of the Left.

Earlier in the year, India and the US had signed their biggest ever arms deal, estimated at approximately US $1 billion, for the purchase of six C-130J Super Hercules aircraft to help improve troop movement. The same year the Indian Air Force reopened an airstrip in the cold desert in the far north of the country. Named Daulat Beg Oldi (after a Yarkandi nobleman and literally translated as 'Daulat Beg died'), the airstrip had last been used in the 1960s and sees temperatures dip to −55 degree Celsius in the winter months.

In the world of business too, 2008 was anything but ordinary. The house of the Tatas finally launched their ₹1 lakh car, Tata Nano. Having been pushed out of West Bengal due to violent protests against land acquisition, the Nano was finally rolled out of Sanand in Gujarat. The Nano was the most affordable car in the world at its launch and was expected to revolutionize the way Indians travelled. The same year, Indian pharmaceutical major Ranbaxy was bought by Japanese giant Daiichi Sankyo in an all-cash deal for $4.6 billion.

In November, India faced events which made the year even more extraordinary. It all started around 8.00 p.m. on 26 November when ten terrorists of the Lashkar-e-Taiba landed on the seashore in Colaba, Bombay, in inflatable boats and then proceeded to attack various places in the heart of the financial capital. These included the Chhatrapati Shivaji Maharaj Terminus, Taj Mahal Place hotel, Oberoi-Trident and Nariman House. The security apparatus was caught off-guard and found wanting. The attackers had been planning this for months in Pakistan under expert supervision, and inflicted maximum damage. The attacks lasted till 29 November, leaving 164 dead and 308 wounded. Nine of the attackers were killed and one, Ajmal Kasab, was nabbed. The dead included twenty-eight foreigners belonging to ten countries. Hemant Karkare, head of Maharashtra's anti-terror squad, was also killed.

The attacks were broadcast live on Indian television news channels, often to the detriment of security operations being conducted to flush the terrorists out. While the attacks were still on, the chief minister of Gujarat, Narendra Modi, arrived in Mumbai and visited three places where the security forces were still fighting the holed-out terrorists. Addressing the press at one of the spots, Modi attacked the Manmohan Singh government's handling of the crisis. The CM was chastized for this boorish behaviour at a time when the country was facing an unprecedented challenge. The 26/11 attacks were unlike any previous terror attacks in the city of Bombay. It was a cruel attack on a city's vulnerable residents.

In June the same year, a Hindi film depicted a day in the life of Dr Aamir Ali who becomes a pawn in a terrorist attack on the city of Bombay. When Bombay woke up the day after the real-life operation to flush all the terrorists out, people could have been humming Amitabh Bhattacharya's lyrics from the film *Aamir*:

*Aani jaani hai kahaani, bulbule si hai zindagaani*
*Banati kabhi, kabhi bigadti, tez hawa se ladti-bhidti*
*Ha reham, ha reham farma aye khuda*
*Mehfuz har qadam karna aye khuda*

# 2009: *All Izz Well*

*Koi na jaane apna future kya hoga*
*Honth ghuma, seeti baja, seeti bajaake bol*
*Bhaiyya aal izz well, are bhaiya aal izz well*

Lyrics: Swanand Kirkire
Music: Shantanu Moitra
Singers: Shaan, Sonu Nigam and Swanand Kirkire
Film: 3 *Idiots*

THE first time that lyricist and singer Swanand Kirkire got noticed was for his song '*Bawra mann dekhne chala ek sapna*' in the 2005 film *Hazaron Khwaishein Aisi*. It was a song he had written during his theatre days in Delhi. Composer Shantanu Moitra decided to record the song in Kirkire's voice. Moitra and Kirkire formed a team and went on to collaborate for various film soundtracks. 3 *Idiots*, the most successful Hindi film of 2009, was their third film together with film-maker Raju Hirani. The peppy, philosophical song '*All izz well*' stuck out.

The year 2009 was good for Hindi films and an even better one for Hindi film music. While 3 *Idiots* regaled audiences with its humour, *Delhi-6* had A.R. Rahman weaving his magic once again with his sound and melodies. The album was a great fusion of folk, classical and modern influences that made it one of Rahman's best works till then – from the vivacious '*Masakali*' to the slow burner '*Rehna tu*' (with Rahman using the continuum fingerboard to accentuate the feel of the song). The year had Vishal Bhardwaj teaming up with Gulzar again for his film *Kaminey* and adding some memorable songs to the Hindi film music library.

While A.R. Rahman, Vishal Bhardwaj and Pritam were expected to belt out good music, another star started shining bright in Hindi film music skies this year. This was in a film that was a modern take on an old Bengali and Hindi classic, *Devdas*. Amit Trivedi had been noticed for his work in his first film *Aamir* in 2008 but with *Dev.D* in 2009, he literally burst on to the charts.

*Dev.D* was the cliched 'breath of fresh air' for Hindi film music as Trivedi brought his modern sensibility and understanding of sound to the table. He added music to his old friend and collaborator Amitabh Bhattacharya's lyrics and created magic in the album. *Dev.D* became a cult film and the music remains popular even a decade later. The quirky, wedding-band-inspired '*Emosanal atyachar*', sung by Trivedi and Bhattacharya themselves, became a big hit. Bhattacharya, who had come to Bombay to become a singer, wrote the lyrics for *Dev.D* (and *Aamir* in 2008) reluctantly.

'*Rehna tu*' or '*Masakali*' or '*Pardesi*' were perhaps greater musical accomplishments in 2009 but it was '*All izz well*' that truly reflected what the Manmohan Singh government might have been feeling; especially after the results of the general elections to the fifteenth Lok Sabha were declared in May. In the 2009 polls, the Indian electorate stood at 71.4 crore. Electronic voting machines were used for polling at 8.28 lakh polling booths across the country. When the United Progressive Alliance (led by the Indian National Congress) and the National Democratic Alliance (led by the Bharatiya Janata Party) went to polls, the result was anything but certain. NDA's prime ministerial candidate, Lal Krishna Advani, chose to attack Prime Minister Manmohan Singh for what he termed as devaluing the office of the PM. According to the NDA, the PM was being remote-controlled by the Congress president, Sonia Gandhi.

The Congress party bought the rights to use A.R. Rahman's popular song '*Jai ho*' and made it the theme song for its campaign. The UPA had faced turbulence the previous year when the Left parties withdrew support from it over the nuclear deal with the US. The results of the general elections, however, laid to rest any worries for the UPA as the voters reaffirmed their faith in the leadership of Manmohan Singh. The Congress party improved its tally from 145 seats in 2004 to 206 seats. The UPA won 262 seats, just a few seats short of the majority mark. CPI(M) leader Prakash Karat discovered that his decision to leave UPA the previous year had backfired as his own party suffered major reversals in the polls and this led to a diminished role for the Left in national politics.

In parliament, the year 2009 was marked by the UPA pushing through the Right to Education Act in August. The Act made education a fundamental right for all children between ages six and fourteen. This Act made it legally obligatory for the Central and state governments to implement this fundamental child right enshrined in Article 21A of the Constitution.

While the government was busy trying to improve the deal for children, the courts were not to be left behind. In a landmark judgment, the Delhi High Court gave a new lease of life to the lesbian, gay, bisexual and transgender (LGBT) community in the country when it ruled that criminalization of consensual gay sex violated the fundamental right of life and liberty and the right to equality as guaranteed under the Constitution. This was a major relief to the LGBT community and a big win for progressive values.

While the Congress could use '*Jai ho*' in its poll campaign, the song brought laurels to A.R. Rahman. Rahman made a huge mark on the global stage when he picked up two Oscar awards for his work in *Slumdog Millionaire*, an English film made by Danny Boyle, based on a book by Vikas Swarup named *Q&A*. He won the awards for best original music score and best song. Having dominated the Hindi and Tamil film music scene over the last two decades, this was international recognition for Rahman's genius. *Slumdog Millionaire* was a global sensation and Rahman was now a global celebrity.

In the corporate world, all was not well as India was shocked when the chairman of an information technology major, Satyam Computers, based in Hyderabad, confessed that the company's accounts had been falsified. The scale of the fudging was huge. B. Ramalinga Raju, the chairman, said that the accounts had been manipulated to the tune of $1.47 billion. The auditors were found to be guilty as well. India's IT industry had been a model success of India's liberalized economy and the Satyam scandal shattered the country's faith in this industry. The scandal led to 50,000 employees across the globe losing their jobs. The government took control of the situation through the Company Law Board and in a few months, Satyam was acquired by Tech Mahindra, a part of the Mahindra & Mahindra Group.

In the same year, the Border Security Force recruited 178 women to protect India's international borders. This was the first time that women were inducted into the BSF. The same year the Indian Navy inducted two women in combatant roles for the first time as well.

All was well for Indian cricket in the year: the Indian team ended the year as the top Test team in the world. On balance, 2009 was a good year for the country. As it entered the last year of the decade, it might have been humming Prasoon Joshi's lyrics, composed by Rahman in *Delhi-6*: *'Rehna tu, hai jaisa tu.'*

# 2010s

# WhatsAppening

## Jo Bhi Main Kehna Chahoon

India gets its first majority government in thirty years. Ubiquitous smartphones make the communications revolution leap exponentially. Census establishes that the young outnumber the old. A generational shift in the leadership of most political parties.

1.

2.

3.

4.

5.

1. World champions again: Mahendra Singh Dhoni leads the Indian cricket team to another cricket world cup win in 2011.

2. The bubble that burst: The anti-corruption protest by Anna Hazare, though a spectacular success initially, fizzled out by the end of 2011.

3. Candle-light processions and display of public outrage after the 2012 brutal gangrape in Delhi led to the enactment of tough anti-rape laws.

4. Narendra Modi, who became the prime minister after the NDA, led by the BJP, won the elections in 2014, greets Prime Minister Nawaz Sharif of Pakistan.

5. Aamir Khan wins over China: The film *Dangal* becomes a rage in China.

# 2010: *Geet Mein Dhalte Lafzon Mein*

*Geet mein dhalte lafzon mein*
*Taal pe chalti nabzon mein*
*Naya, kuchh naya toh zarur hai*

Lyrics: Amitabh Bhattacharya
Music: Amit Trivedi
Singers: Amit Trivedi and Amitabh Bhattacharya
Film: *Udaan*

WHEN Amitabh Bhattacharya arrived in Bombay from his hometown Lucknow, all he wanted was to be a playback singer in Hindi films. He had no interest in literature, poetry or writing. Like all outsiders looking to make a mark in the competitive and tough film industry in Bombay, Bhattacharya also struggled for years. A chance meeting with Amit Trivedi, who was a member of Om The Fusion Band, led to what became a long partnership with him later in life. Initially Bhattacharya helped Trivedi with dummy words for tunes that he wanted to present to others.

This became more serious when Trivedi started working on *Aamir* and *Dev.D* as a solo music composer. With singing still weighing on his mind, Bhattacharya was a reluctant lyricist. *Dev.D*'s dark, folksy and trippy soundtrack had won people's admiration (and a National Award for Trivedi). With *Udaan* in 2010, the partnership confirmed to the world that *Dev.D* wasn't a fluke. *Udaan's* was a soundtrack completely different in its sound, expression and genre from *Dev.D*'s. This was an album about hope and freedom. Bhattacharya's lyrics in the album highlighted his mastery over songwriting. The reluctant songwriter gave some modern classics to listeners with the use of fresh metaphors while Trivedi's fusion of traditional melody with alternative rock sound (a first for Hindi films) made it one of the best albums of the decade. *Udaan* confirmed Trivedi as a master composer.

Trivedi was the most original addition to the list of great film music composers since A.R. Rahman burst on the scene in the early 1990s. It wasn't a coincidence that Trivedi won the R.D. Burman Award for New Music Talent at the 2010 Filmfare Awards function (for *Dev.D*) – the same award which was won by Rahman in its first year, 1995.

While this new talent was making waves with its music, that genius of a lyricist, Gulzar, was writing about a young heart and its escapades in '*Dil toh bachcha hai ji*', for *Ishqiya*, another collaboration of his with Vishal Bhardwaj. This soft, melodious, romantic song was made even better by Bhardwaj's uncomplicated sound arrangement and Rahat Fateh Ali Khan's uncharacteristically soft rendition.

While *Udaan* and *Ishqiya* were a break from the masala Hindi film music genre, *Dabangg* was the very epitome of it. In this decidedly 'filmy' album, composers Sajid–Wajid and Lalit Pandit created some memorable songs as well. While '*Munni badnaam hui*', an item song, became the most popular, there were some other remarkable songs as well. In '*Humka peeni hai*', Sajid–Wajid were able to create a peppy song about consuming alcohol, which was rooted in a very folksy sound and rendition (sung by Master Saleem, Wajid and Shabaab Sabri).

*Udaan* might have been about freedom, escape and coming of age but for Indian politics 2010 was neither of those. The year became *annus horribilis* for the UPA government as it was hit by one scandal after another, each denting its reputation. The dominoes started falling in March when the Comptroller and Auditor General (CAG) alleged that there had been large-scale irregularities in the 2G spectrum allocation and licensing in 2007–08.

Humongous sums in projected losses to the exchequer were mentioned by the CAG report. The CAG, Vinod Rai, questioned the policy choices made by the government. Facing scandal, the telecom minister, A. Raja, resigned.

While the 2G scandal was hurting the government, another storm was brewing in New Delhi. This was related to the organization of the Commonwealth Games in the city in 2010. The games were marred by mismanagement as the preparations were not made in time. The infrastructure was not ready and the organizers rushed to finish the works in the face of mounting criticism in the media. There were allegations of widespread corruption and the Central Vigilance Commission released a report showing irregularities in various games-related projects. The day after the games were over, the Indian government set up a committee to probe into the allegations of corruption against the organizers. The government had to suffer a loss of public confidence because of the corruption allegations.

While the government was losing the perception battle in the media, it was able to make some positive moves as well. The Rajya Sabha passed the Women's Reservation Bill in March. The Bill sought to reserve one-third of the seats in parliament and state assemblies for women. In Delhi, the swanky new international terminal T-3 at the Indira Gandhi International Airport was inaugurated. This was a huge improvement over the bottlenecks that the international airport in the capital faced earlier. In August, the Nalanda University Bill, 2010, was passed by both the Houses of parliament, setting in motion the revival of the ancient university.

The scars of the 26/11 attacks by Pakistani terrorists two years ago were beginning to heal as well. The Taj Mahal hotel, the epicentre of one of the attacks, reopened. The iconic hotel, built in 1903, had suffered extensive damage and lost staff members and guests in the attack. On 3 May 2010, the trial court also found the lone terrorist nabbed after the carnage, Ajmal Kasab, guilty on eighty counts, including murder and waging war against India. He was sentenced to death three days later.

Lal Krishna Advani, Uma Bharti and Murli Manohar Joshi of the BJP were exonerated of conspiracy charges in the Babri Masjid demolition case by the Allahabad High Court. The high court also pronounced its verdict on the sixty-year-old land dispute. The Supreme Court ruled controversially that the land would be partitioned between three parties: one-third of the land was given to each of them – the deity Ramlalla Virajman, Nirmohi Akhara and the Sunni Waqf Board.

While it was terrorism originating in Pakistan that hurt India in 2008, it was Maoist violence that hurt in 2010. The Left-wing terrorists – described as 'the single biggest internal security challenge' for India by Prime Minister Manmohan Singh in 2006 – targeted Indian security forces in separate instances and inflicted major losses of life. In April, the Maoists killed seventy-six CRPF personnel in Dantewada, Chhattisgarh, in an ambush. That was not the only Maoist attack in the year. This was also the year when Kanu Sanyal, one of the founders of the Naxalbari insurgency in 1967, committed suicide. He was found hanging at his home. Towards the end of his life, Sanyal had taken to criticizing the violent ways of Maoist insurgents.

India was in a strange zone in 2010. It was neither happy nor sad, but perhaps more cynical. It was only humming along, adding a new page every day to its story, '*Naya kuchh naya toh zarur hai.*'

# 2011: *Jo Bhi Main Kehna Chaahoon*

*Jo bhi main kahana chaahun*
*Barbaad kare alfaaz mere*
*Kabhi mujhe lage ki jaise*
*Saara hi ye jahaan hai jaadu*

Lyrics: Irshad Kamil
Music: A. R. Rahman
Singer: Mohit Chauhan
Film: *Rockstar*

THE song starts with what seems like an electric guitar being tuned. The singer then joins with a chorus following him closely. The sound transports you to a concert. All this before a word of the lyrics is uttered. The drums then join the party with their gentle rhythm and almost unwittingly listeners start to sway. Mohit Chauhan then slowly starts to burn the lyrics in your head and you are transported to another world, with your eyes closed.

With *Rockstar*, A.R. Rahman, 'the Mozart of Madras', returned to Hindi film music with a bang. This was a new Rahman; now he was high on rock music. In Imtiaz Ali's *Rockstar* his old friend Irshad Kamil wrote '*Jo bhi main kehna chaahoon*' as a cry of the protagonist, Janardan Jakhar or Jordan (played by Ranbir Kapoor) about his inability to express what was going on inside. If *Udaan* in 2010 was 'alt-rock', Rahman's *Rockstar* was more 'grunge' with Sufi music fused in it. The soundtrack found instant acceptance. From the gentle '*Jo bhi main*' to the angsty '*Sadda haq*' to the fun '*Shehar mein*' to the memorable qawwali, '*Kun faaya kun*', Irshad Kamil matched Rahman's musical genius with his expressive lyrics.

Kamil, a student of Hindi literature from Punjab, says that he felt commerce had distanced art from Hindi songwriting and with his work in *Rockstar* (or *Chameli*, *Jab We Met* and *Love Aaj Kal* before it), he had shown that the art of songwriting didn't need to sell out to commerce. Most of the songs were sung by Mohit Chauhan. Rahman had conjured up another great film soundtrack. Talking about working with him, Imtiaz Ali spoke about how he was worried by Rahman's odd working style. Rahman's style might have been odd but the results were spectacular. Kamil talks about how trying to write '*Hawa hawa*' was his most difficult experience in songwriting. The strangely structured song that tells a Czech fairy tale did not follow the traditional Hindi song routine of a mukhda and antara.

If Jordan was struggling to express himself and '*Jo bhi main*' was apt for him, the song depicted the situation of the UPA government led by Prime Minister Manmohan Singh perfectly as well. Caught in the miasma of many corruption scandals that were being talked about every day in newspapers and TV news channels, the government found itself tongue-tied. The natural reticence of the prime minister that had been a marker of his quiet work ethic quickly turned into a liability for the government.

The government may have had a different point of view about the fantastic claims made by CAG Vinod Rai, but through its refusal to communicate clearly to the public and through the non-stop negative media coverage, it was driven into a corner. Former telecom minister A. Raja and the DMK MP Kanimozhi, daughter of the Tamil Nadu chief minister M. Karunanidhi, were arrested. The allegations made by the CAG were related to policy choices made by the government and it was unable to defend those choices in the face of the media onslaught. A Joint Parliamentary Committee was set up to probe the '2G scam', as it came to be known.

From February to April 2011, India played host to the ICC Cricket World Cup in the ODI format. India had last won the World Cup in

1983 and had last reached the finals in 2003 in South Africa. Playing at home, India began the tournament as favourites and gained in strength as it progressed. In what seemed like a repeat of the 1996 World Cup held in the subcontinent, India beat Pakistan in the semi-final match held at Mohali (with the Indian and Pakistani prime ministers doing some cricket diplomacy on the sidelines). Just like in 1996, India met Sri Lanka in the next match (although this time it was in the final). In the tournament finale, played at Bombay, India lived up to the 'favourites' tag by beating Sri Lanka. The Indian captain, M.S. Dhoni, finished the match in style by hitting a sixer to cross the Lankan total. India lifted the trophy for the second time, in the last World Cup played by Sachin Tendulkar. Yuvraj Singh played a stellar role not only in the final but throughout the tournament and was adjudged the Man of the Series. The entire country erupted in joy as people came out on the streets to celebrate the win.

The year had turned progressively pessimistic for the nation with the government unable to fend off the challenge from the political opposition, both old and new. The year also saw India lose some of its famous children. Dev Anand, Bhimsen Joshi, Bhupen Hazarika, Sultan Khan and Mansoor Ali Khan Pataudi bid adieu in 2011.

Bombay, which had faced a brutal terrorist attack in 2008, was at the receiving end once again on 13 July as three bomb blasts at different places in the city killed twenty-six people.

In the courtrooms, thirty-one were convicted for the burning of the train in Godhra in 2002. Eleven were sentenced to death while twenty were sentenced to life imprisonment. In the same year, the newly established National Investigation Agency (NIA) charge-sheeted Swami Aseemanand for the Samjhauta Express blast (2007). The NIA also charge-sheeted an American, David Headley, Hafiz Saeed and two Pakistani army officers for the terrorist attack in Mumbai on 26 November 2008.

'*Kun faaya kun*' from *Rockstar* was a qawwali in praise of Hazrat Nizamuddin Auliya, a fourteenth-century saint. The Quranic phrase refers to God's mystical creative powers. Literally translated, it means, 'Be! And it is!' It signifies how God created the universe by just ordaining it. If '*Jo bhi main*' depicted the situation of the UPA government, '*Kun faaya kun*' depicted another phenomenon in the world of politics in India this year. This was the appearance, out of nowhere, of a disparate group under an umbrella of 'civil society organizations' which sought to fight political corruption in the country. Those sympathetic to the Congress party did say that these protests had been engineered by the Rashtriya Swayamsevak Sangh (RSS), though indirectly through 'apolitical' groups. The presence of figures like Baba Ramdev, Sri Sri Ravi Shankar and others added credence to this view.

The old man of Ralegan Siddhi, Anna Hazare, became the mascot of these protests with his hunger strike. With minute-by-minute coverage on TV news channels, the protests played on the disgust which had been built up in the public over the last year and a half. The UPA found itself incapable of dealing with this social-media-savvy, TV-news-aided group of non-party actors. It made the situation worse by deputing ministers to deal with Hazare and his team on one end and Baba Ramdev on the other. In the process, the UPA reduced its own political legitimacy and handed the same legitimacy to these seemingly 'apolitical' figures who seemed to be batting for the opposition by proxy.

The protesters demanded that the Indian parliament enact a law to create an anti-corruption watchdog, 'Lokpal', so that corruption could be rooted out of the country. The protests were done in three rounds through the year (April, August and December) with Anna Hazare sitting on a hunger strike. In December, the crowd turnout was low which forced Hazare to abandon the fast within three days.

This may not have been much of a consolation for the UPA government, however, as it limped to next year, only making Kamil's lyrics come alive, '*Barbaad karein alfaaz mere*'.

# 2012: *Abhi Mujh Mein Kahin Baaki Thodi Si Hai Zindagi*

*Abhi mujh mein kahin*
*Baaki thodi si hai zindagi*
*Jagi dhadkan nayi*
*Jaana zinda hun main toh abhi*

Lyrics: Amitabh Bhattacharya
Music: Ajay–Atul
Singer: Sonu Nigam
Film: *Agneepath*

IN *Agneepath*, a remake of the film made in 1990, the song '*Abhi mujh mein kahin*' plays in the background in an emotional reunion of an estranged brother and sister. The song begins with a soft tune on the piano, which is accompanied by the strings of a santoor. Sonu Nigam then softly starts with the lyrics to establish the melody. Nigam keeps raising the pitch with every word, reaching a crescendo towards the end of the first stanza, and the song then suddenly drops back to the pace and softness of the beginning. The piano base is then accompanied by a symphonic interlude of violins. The song keeps transitioning from soft hums to high-pitched singing, from symphonic interludes to highly Indian interludes of santoor and tabla.

The song reestablished Sonu Nigam as one of the foremost proponents of playback singing in Hindi films. Amitabh Bhattacharya's songwriting is able to paint a vivid picture of the emotions that Vijay (the lead character played by Hrithik Roshan) goes through in this scene. And finally, the song announces the arrival of a new talent in Hindi film music world. This is in the form of the composer duo, Ajay and Atul.

Brothers Gogavale, Ajay and Atul were born in a family that had no interest in films or music. Their father was working for the revenue department of the Maharashtra government. They did not have any formal training in music. It was composer Ilaiyaraaja's music in Kamal Haasan's *Appu Raja* that got them hooked. Starting with putting school poems to their own tunes in school, the brothers progressed to finding work in religious functions in small towns across Maharashtra. They learnt to play different instruments by befriending people who owned them, as their family couldn't afford to buy those.

A big event was when their parents agreed to buy a 'keyboard' for them at a cost of ₹1 lakh. In an interview to *The Indian Express*, the brothers recalled that they couldn't sleep that night, worried that the money would go waste if they didn't find any work. They worked hard to rise in the Marathi film industry with their original work. One major hit was '*Kombadi palali*' in the 2006 Marathi film *Jatra*. The song was used in *Agneepath* as '*Chikni chameli*' (and became the biggest hit of the album).

While Ajay–Atul shone in *Agneepath* with their more conventional Hindi film music, Sneha Khanwalkar did that by breaking most conventions in *Gangs of Wasseypur* and *Gangs of Wasseypur* 2. Quirky is too mild a term for the soundtrack of Anurag Kashyap's five-hour masterpiece with thirty-five songs (released in two parts). Kashyap wanted the feel of Bihari folk in the soundtrack and allowed Khanwalkar complete artistic freedom. It took two years, multiple trips to Bihar, Jharkhand, and Trinidad and Tobago for her to be able to create this soundtrack. She travelled to Trinidad and Tobago to research 'Chutney music' – a fusion of various genres created by Indo-Caribbean people whose ancestors hailed from Bihar and nearby regions. The song '*Hunter*' was a result of these travels. Lyricist Varun Grover told us that for him the challenge was to be authentic to the world depicted in the film, free of Hindi film music clichés in the use of language, and to try and achieve the musical sensibility of Indian folk. He did succeed in achieving this with songs like '*Bhoosa*' and '*Keh ke loonga*'.

While '*Abhi mujh mein kahin*' was still a song about hope, for the UPA government in 2012, the song could have been about how little life was left. The government had forfeited its own legitimacy to the proxy opposition and it continued to sleepwalk through this year. This legitimacy was further weakened when in February the Supreme Court cancelled the allocation of 122 2G telecom licences given by the UPA government. This only helped cement the perception that the UPA government was corrupt.

As the Indian economy slowed down and the government was trapped in a vortex of scandals coupled with strong political opposition, it reacted by turning even more reticent. The finance minister had come in for criticism from economy watchers and industry. But after a dramatic turn of events involving the TMC's Mamata Bannerjee and SP's Mulayam Singh Yadav, Finance Minister Pranab Mukherjee ended up as the UPA's presidential candidate. Home Minister P. Chidambaram replaced Mukherjee when he became the president of India.

It was not just corruption scandals that hurt the UPA government this year. It was also caught in a dirty fight with the army chief, Gen. V.K. Singh, who dragged the Central government to court in trying to prove that his age (as mentioned in his enrolment documents by himself) was recorded incorrectly. He wanted it to be changed, which would have allowed him a longer tenure as the army chief. The Supreme Court politely told him to withdraw the case to prevent any embarrassment to him. While this was a victory for the government, the media environment was hostile to the government and it continued to be lampooned despite being right in principle. After his retirement in May 2012, V.K. Singh joined hands with the same 'apolitical' actors who had been agitating against the government and joined Baba Ramdev at Ramlila Maidan in Delhi to protest against corruption and black money.

In November 2012, a section of the anti-corruption protesters announced that they would form a political party and contest elections to the state assembly in Delhi. The Aam Aadmi Party (AAP) was thus formed under the leadership of the formerly 'apolitical' anti-corruption activist, Arvind Kejriwal. The same year, in the western part of India, the chief minister of Gujarat, Narendra Modi, led BJP to victory again. Modi had run a high-intensity campaign and painted the UPA government at the Centre as his political opponent. Modi's Gujarat campaign was seen as a warm-up to the parliamentary polls scheduled for 2014. His third consecutive victory in assembly elections helped him project himself as a contender for the national stage.

Early in the year, one of the greatest cricketers India had ever produced, Rahul Dravid, retired from international cricket when he played his last Test match against Australia in February. 'The Wall', as he was known, ended with 13,288 Test runs and more than 10,000 runs in ODIs. Famous for his solid technique and sportsmanship, Dravid had been a role model for young sportsmen with his impeccable behaviour both on and off the cricket field.

In March the same year, another cricketing great, Sachin Tendulkar, decided to retire from One-Day International cricket and played his last game against Pakistan. Having achieved his aim of being part of a World Cup-winning squad the previous year, Sachin ended his ODI career with a staggering 18,426 runs. He scored forty-nine ODI centuries.

The world of music lost a legend in 2012 when sitar maestro Ravi Shankar departed in December at the age of ninety-two. The pioneering musician who made Indian music popular globally passed away in San Diego, USA. A couple of months before that Hindi cinema suffered a loss too when film-maker Yash Chopra bid adieu. They may have departed, but their work remained, leaving behind some *zindagi baaki*.

# 2013: *Suljha Lenge Uljhe Rishton Ka Manjha*

*Roothe khaabon ko mana lenge*
*Kati patangon ko thaamenge*
*Haa haa hai jazba*
*Ho ho hai jazba*
*Suljha lenge uljhe rishton ka manjha*

Lyrics: Swanand Kirkire
Music: Amit Trivedi
Singer: Amit Trivedi
Film: *Kai Po Che*

WHEN Abhishek Kapoor was making his second film after *Rock On!!* (2008), he got in touch with Amit Trivedi to hire him as the music composer. His new film *Kai Po Che* was based on Chetan Bhagat's book *The 3 Mistakes of My Life* (2008), dealing with three Gujarati friends who come of age around 2002 when the state went up in flames in anti-Muslim rioting. Kapoor was a little surprised when Trivedi called him back after just two days and hummed three tunes for him to pick. He thought Trivedi wasn't giving him his best. Three days later he found himself humming the tune of '*Manjha*' in the morning and that was the final decision.

The song begins with a guitar and esraj in a jugalbandi. With the rhythm set, Amit Trivedi starts belting out Swanand Kirkire's words about hope, aspirations and friendships that are bursting with optimism. There is a gentle play with claps in the background as the song lifts you up and soars. The esraj interludes weave an evocative pattern while the refrain keeps bringing you back to the song's rhythm. Manjha (kite string) with its propensity to entangle becomes a metaphor for friendships, and showcases Kirkire's songwriting talent while Trivedi, with his mastery over sound and melody, makes it a memorable ode to life.

The biggest shortcoming of the *Kai Po Che* soundtrack was that there are only three songs in the album. Each of the three songs has a different flavour and distinct sound; each one leaving behind its own memories and impressions. If the ethereal '*Meethi boliyaan*' sung by Milli Nair and Amit Trivedi flows like a gentle stream, '*Shubhaarambh*' sung by Shruti Pathak and Divya Kumar makes you feel a part of Gujarati celebrations. In '*Meethi boliyaan*' the sound was softer rock with fantastic use of continuum; in '*Shubhaarambh*' it was more festive and folksy with shehnai and dhol playing a game with bagpipes.

The year 2013 was a good year for Hindi film music. If *Kai Po Che* left one wanting more, Amit Trivedi and Amitabh Bhattacharya teamed up to satisfy this desire in *Lootera*. The music tried to revive memories of the 1950s as the film was a drama set in that period. Its folksy, sweet compositions and Bhattacharya's words made it a classy album; one of the best of the year.

While *Kai Po Che* was recreating 2002 on-screen, the main protagonist from the events of that year, Narendra Modi, was writing his own play, on a national scale. Having been out of power for nearly a decade, the BJP and the RSS were desperate to do well in the general elections to be held in 2014. Modi, who had won his third assembly elections in Gujarat the previous year, decided to project himself on the national stage. In June, the BJP made him the chief of their campaign committee for the 2014 polls. This was Modi's return to a national position after having served the party as a general secretary in the past.

Modi's rise was the result of a long campaign to promote him as an able administrator. This was done with a well-funded public relations machinery. This enabled Modi to score over rivals within the party when it came to the post of the campaign committee chief. His rise was not smooth though, as senior leaders L.K. Advani and Sushma Swaraj decided to boycott the BJP national executive meeting in Goa. It was suspected that Modi would not be acceptable to allies of the BJP and this was proved right when a week later Bihar chief minister Nitish Kumar's Janata Dal (United) parted ways with the NDA.

In July, the *Wall Street Journal* reported about Rajesh Jain and B.G. Mahesh who were working with a large team to spearhead Modi's campaign on the web. The previous year, Jain had written in a blog about the need for the BJP to create a wave election (in which the party makes major gains) in 2014 for it to emerge victorious. Modi's digital campaign, especially on social media, took India by storm and became the pioneer in terms of using technology for election campaigns. Three months later, in September, Modi was elevated further and declared the BJP's prime ministerial candidate. A big apparatus to promote Modi as India's next prime minister was already working.

While the BJP's campaign for the big elections was getting ready, the UPA government continued its slow struggle. Loss of public support and media campaigns on corruption had eroded the government's political legitimacy and a slowing down economy added to its woes. In 2013, the Indian economy grew at its slowest in over a decade at under 5 per cent.

The Modi campaign sought to compare a floundering UPA government with the image of an efficient Gujarat CM, an image that Modi's PR push had helped build over the previous few years. The economic slump had brought a sense of loss of hope in the country. Modi's team decided to borrow from Barack Obama's presidential campaign in the USA and wove a narrative of hope and change.

Even as the UPA government was weakened politically, it tried to push its legislative agenda in parliament. In September, the National Food Security Act, 2013, was passed which sought to provide subsidized foodgrain to two-thirds of India's population. In December, the Supreme Court struck a blow to individual freedom when it overturned the Delhi High Court's 2009 judgment and upheld Section 377 of the Indian Penal Code. By upholding Section 377 – framed in 1860 – the apex court criminalized homosexuality again. The court argued that parliament could annul the law through legislative action.

The 'apolitical' anti-corruption movement, that had been on since 2011 finally turned political when the Aam Aadmi Party (formed by some leaders of the movement) won twenty-eight seats in the seventy-seat Delhi assembly in December. Arvind Kejriwal took oath as Delhi's chief minister. It was ironical that his government was formed with the support of the Congress party against whose government Kejriwal had led the movement.

The Rajya Sabha also passed the Lokpal and Lokayuktas Act in the same month. The big demand of the anti-corruption movement was thus fulfilled.

The year also saw some departures. In October 2013, one of the greatest playback singers, Prabodh Chandra Dey, bid goodbye to the world at the age of ninety-four. Manna Dey, as he was popularly known, was famous for singing classical Hindi songs that were often too difficult for others to sing. Mohammed Rafi once said that while people listened to his songs, he only listened to what Manna sang.

While Manna departed from this world, another kind of departure made India sad this year. Between 14 and 16 November, Sachin Ramesh Tendulkar played his two hundredth and last Test match at Wankhede Stadium, Bombay. He scored 74 runs in his last innings. His career of twenty-four years had come to an end. Cricket writer Peter Roebuck had called Tendulkar a blend of the sublime and the precise. The man who had come to symbolize Indian cricket, its ambition and its success ended his career with a hundred international centuries. The national hero chose to walk away from it all, leaving millions with tears in their eyes. For India, 2013 was over and 2014 was about to unfold and it may have hoped that perhaps this year it would: *Suljha lenge roothe rishton ka manjha.*

# 2014: *O Jugni Ho Pataakha Guddi O*

*Nashein mein udi jaaye re haaye re*
*Sajje khabbe dhabbe killi ho*
*Pataakha guddi O*
*Nashein mein udi jaaye re haaye re*
*Sajje khabbe dhabbe killi ho*

Lyrics: Irshad Kamil
Music: A.R. Rahman
Singers: Sultana Nooran and Jyoti Nooran
Film: *Highway*

AFTER their successful partnership in *Rockstar*, the team of director Imtiaz Ali, composer A.R. Rahman and lyricist Irshad Kamil got together once again for *Highway* in 2014. '*Pataakha guddi*' with its free-spiritedness became the centrepiece of this soundtrack. The song, written in a mix of mainly Punjabi and some Hindi words, is about rebellion, freedom, liveliness and a vagabond girl. The song starts in a heavy techno mode and turns more and more folksy as it progresses. Full-throated and deliberately unpolished singing by the Nooran sisters only reinforced that this was a song about rebellion and freedom.

Rahman demonstrated his mastery of sound and his ability to weave songs that do not have a definite structure and require an above-average participation from the listener. The song flows like a river with flute interludes rowing the boat energetically. Irshad Kamil excelled with his lyrics about a girl referred to as a 'pataakha guddi' (firecracker kite in Punjabi) and 'jugni' (firefly). The song depicts the protagonist unshackling herself, soaring in the sky like a carefree kite with the strings handed over to the almighty.

While Rahman was composing songs about a free-spirited girl, Vishal Bhardwaj was composing gentle odes to a flirtatious heart in *Dedh Ishqiya*, the sequel to *Ishqiya* (2010). If the heart was a little kid in *Ishqiya*'s '*Dil toh bachcha hai ji*', it had a romantic nature in '*Dil ka mizaaj ishqiya*'. Rahat Fateh Ali Khan excelled as he sang most of the song in a lower pitch, making some pointed excursions to high-pitched parts. The trademark laid-back music arrangement that Vishal Bhardwaj is famous for elevated Gulzar's lyrics and made it a good, romantic song.

Bhardwaj and Gulzar also teamed up for *Haider*, directed by Vishal Bhardwaj himself. Inspired by Shakespeare's *Hamlet*, *Haider* broached a sombre subject compared to *Dedh Ishqiya* and this was reflected in the music. If *Dedh Ishqiya* was romantic and gentle, *Haider* was darker and stronger. While *Dedh Ishqiya* made the listener close his eyes and flow with the romantic mood, *Haider* made one sit up with its rock-music theme, powerful arrangement and poetry. This was best exemplified by the rock song '*Aao Na*', sung by Vishal Dadlani. The song also had a sad version called '*So jaao*', which talked about the lasting sleep of a graveyard.

In 2014, the Republic of India was listening to another type of music too. This was sometimes melodious, often cacophonous and always interesting: the music of the general elections. The polls – held in April and May – to elect the sixteenth Lok Sabha had been a long time coming. The build-up which had been happening for nearly two years reached a fever pitch as political parties and candidates campaigned hard all over India. The Narendra Modi campaign was the first one akin to the US presidential election campaign that India has seen. With reportedly 2.5 million volunteers working all over India, the Modi campaign machinery was able to build an omnipresent and dominant narrative across India. While the UPA was presented as beset with corruption and lacking leadership and its government afflicted with policy paralysis, Modi was presented as the panacea for the nation's problems; the harbinger of the Achche Din (the good days). Modi, the challenger, had a solution to every conceivable ailment that the country and its citizens were facing. Whether it was issues concerning national security, job generation, economic growth or farm distress, Modi presented solutions to these issues in his campaign rallies all over the country. An example of this was when he was asked in a television interview about how Prime Minister Modi's government would deal with adversaries like China when it came to any border troubles. His answer was that his government would 'stare at China with red eyes'.

Modi travelled more than 300,000 km for nearly 500 rallies. The Modi juggernaut was not just a political campaign but an immersive 24/7 experience that bombarded potential voters from all directions. Whether it was television, radio or newspapers, Modi and BJP dominated, both in news coverage and advertising. Their dominance in the social media sphere was absolute and the build-up for Modi the messiah was a success. When votes were counted on 16 May, this massive campaign resulted in the BJP winning 282 parliamentary constituencies. This was the first time in thirty years that a party had won a majority on its own. The voters had decided to hand over the strings of the Indian kite to Narendra Modi.

The Congress party was reduced to just forty-four seats. Manmohan Singh's ten-year-long tenure as prime minister of India had come to an end. While his government was decidedly unpopular towards the end of his tenure, that doesn't take away from its many achievements. The period between 2004 and 2014 was a period of rising prosperity and relative calm in the country. Indian agriculture grew at a fast clip and nearly 140 million Indians were lifted above the poverty line during this period. While the government lost public support, this loss hid the fact that India's GDP increased threefold under Manmohan Singh. The average GDP growth rate in this decade was 7.7 per cent.

The government was castigated for its pro-welfare stance by many commentators but this ignored the fact that programmes under the National Rural Employment Guarantee Act ensured protection to the weaker sections of the population in rural India. As Mihir Sharma wrote in his article in *Business Standard* on 11 May 2014, this decade represented a golden age for independent India, one which was overshadowed by the media narrative in the last years of the UPA government. In a comment on how his government and he personally was portrayed in this narrative, Manmohan Singh commented in January this year that history will be kinder to him than the media.

While Modi had been able to secure the public's support, another politician appeared to be losing it in the state of Delhi. Arvind Kejriwal, who had been sworn in as the chief minister of Delhi, resigned after a period of just forty-nine days. The Aam Aadmi Party leader, who had come to power on the back of his agitational politics, refused to change gears after becoming the CM. For the Jan Lokpal Bill in the Delhi assembly his government clashed with the BJP and lost the support of the Congress as well. Kejriwal, who had won power after a lot of struggle and had projected the AAP as a new kind of political movement, decided to call it quits in February 2014.

In south India, Andhra Pradesh was finally split into two on 2 June and the state of Telangana came into being. Telangana's creation was the result of a long struggle and the division of the state was not devoid of acrimony. To keep peace between the states, it was decided that Hyderabad would continue to be the capital of the two states for ten years during which Andhra Pradesh would build its own new capital city.

While India was contending with big political changes through the year, its space programme was scaling bigger heights. The Mars Orbiter Mission launched by ISRO in November 2013 finally entered the planet's orbit on 24 September 2014. This was a proud moment for India and Indian scientists as India had succeeded in its Mars mission on the first attempt. This pataakha guddi was not going here and there but had its strings in control as Indian scientists guided it to ever higher skies.

# 2015: *Moh Moh Ke Dhaage*

*Yeh moh moh ke dhaage*
*Teri ungliyon se ja uljhe*
*Koi toh toh na laage*
*Kis tarah girah yeh suljhe*

Lyrics: Varun Grover
Music: Anu Malik
Singers: Papon and Monali Thakur
Film: *Dum Laga Ke Haisha*

DUM *Laga Ke Haisha*, directed by Sharat Kataria, is a film set in the 1990s. It is about an odd pair, Prem Prakash Tiwari and Sandhya (played by Ayushmann Khurrana and Bhumi Pednekar), who have an arranged marriage with little romance between them. Prem runs an audio cassette shop and is a big fan of Kumar Sanu, the playback singer whose songs are synonymous with the 1990s. The film-makers tried to recreate the 1990s in Haridwar and chose composer Anu Malik for the soundtrack. Malik, a successful but now past his prime composer, had some big successes in the 1990s and was the perfect fit for this film. The lyrics were written by writer and lyricist Varun Grover. Malik and Grover did try to recreate the '1990s song' with Kumar Sanu singing songs like '*Dard karara*' and '*Tu ...*' in the film but it was '*Moh moh ke dhaage*' that was the star of the album.

The song depicts the evolution of the relationship between the lead pair who are brought together by circumstances but then find their own romance eventually. While usually the expectations from Anu Malik are of filmy, catchy tunes, with this song he went the semi-classical way. The song begins with a tune based on raga Yaman Kalyan and then segues into the antara with a change of raga. While the song is beautifully arranged with a gentle interplay of bansuri, shehnai and guitar, it is Grover's words that breathe life into this song. His work earned him the National Award for Best Lyrics for this song. Papon with his husky timbre and Monali Thakur with her emotive singing elevate the song even further. Like Grover, Monali Thakur also won the National Award for Playback Singing (female) for this song.

For Varun Grover, '*Moh moh ke dhaage*' was one of the many significant achievements this year. If his lyrics in *Dum Laga Ke Haisha* evoked Haridwar of the 1990s, his script of *Masaan* painted a real picture of the city of Varanasi on the silver screen. *Masaan*, directed by debutant Neeraj Ghaywan is a film set in modern-day Varanasi which weaves together two separate stories that converge in the end. In this film, Varun was able to dip into his own experience of having studied in the city to paint its different hues on this canvas while telling a captivating story. He also wrote the lyrics for the songs in this film.

In '*Tu kisi rail si guzarti hai*', Grover took a ghazal written by the famous Hindi poet Dushyant Kumar as inspiration. The song begins with Dushyant's thought to which Varun adds his own thoughts to tell a tale of the protagonist falling for a girl. In another song, Varun takes a philosophical flight with his words and talks about the heart not finding closure. In the song '*Mann kasturi re*', kasturi mrig (musk deer) becomes the metaphor for a restless heart. The songs were composed by the rock band Indian Ocean.

While '*Moh moh ke dhaage*' was a song about getting entangled in love, in the year 2015, India was getting entangled in hatred. In his 2014 election campaign, Narendra Modi had berated the UPA government for 'promoting a pink revolution'. This was a reference to rising meat exports from India. As a representative of the RSS family, protection of cows was an important objective for Modi and his government. With the BJP firmly in power in

Delhi and large parts of India, Sangh Parivar supporters and members, especially in Hindi-speaking regions, felt emboldened to act against what they considered atrocities on cows.

Violent incidents by gangs of gau-rakshaks (cow protectors) were reported from various places, but India was truly shaken on the morning of 29 September 2015, when news came in from village Bisara, near Dadri in Uttar Pradesh, of a mob of villagers having stormed into the home of another villager, Mohammed Akhlaq, the father of an Indian Air Force employee, lynching him on the suspicion of 'slaughtering' a calf. His twenty-two-year-old son, Danish, was seriously injured. Even more shocking was the response of the police and elected representatives. The police collected meat samples from his fridge to verify whether it was indeed beef while BJP MP (and Union minister) Mahesh Sharma came out in support of the killers.

In the world of politics, the ruling BJP suffered two major electoral reversals this year. The first was in the elections to the Delhi assembly when the Aam Aadmi Party, led by Arvind Kejriwal swept nearly all the seats in the elections held in February. AAP won sixty-seven out of seventy seats in the assembly while the BJP won the remaining three. The other and even more significant electoral blow was in November in Bihar, where an alliance between Nitish Kumar's Janata Dal (United) (JD[U]), Lalu Prasad Yadav's Rashtriya Janata Dal (RJD) and the Congress party grounded the BJP's high-stakes campaign spearheaded by Narendra Modi and Amit Shah. The grand alliance, known as the Mahagathbandhan, trounced the BJP-led alliance, NDA, by winning 178 seats in the 243-seat assembly. The NDA won fifty-eight seats. This was a personal blow to Prime Minister Narendra Modi who had staked his personal reputation in these polls and campaigned aggressively. During the campaign, he even attacked the grand alliance for its failure to protect the cow. On the day of voting, newspapers in Bihar carried a BJP advertisement on the front pages, which accused Chief Minister Nitish Kumar of having stayed quiet when his allies were disrespecting cows.

In the state of Jammu and Kashmir, while the results of assembly polls were declared in December 2014, a government couldn't be formed for months. In a most unexpected move, the Hindutva party BJP and its

Kashmiri Muslim counterpart the Jammu and Kashmir Peoples Democratic Party (PDP) came together to form the government. They arrived at an agreement and the PDP chief, Mufti Mohammad Sayeed, was sworn in as chief minister on 1 March 2015. This was a dangerous experiment for both parties as they were at opposite ends of the political spectrum and stood to lose the support of their vote banks if things did not work.

In the world of sports, India saw major success in the world of tennis as both Leander Paes and Sania Mirza won trophies in Grand Slam tournaments. Mirza became the first Indian woman to win a Grand Slam when she partnered with Martina Hingis to win the Women's Doubles Championship at Wimbledon. The pair also won US Open later in the year. Hingis was also the mixed doubles partner for Leander Paes and together they won the Wimbledon, the US Open and the Australian Open trophies in the mixed doubles category. Mirza was awarded the country's highest sporting honour, the Rajiv Gandhi Khel Ratna, this year by the Government of India.

The year ended with all the threads of affection frayed as if the country was wondering, *kis tarah girah yeh suljhe*?

# 2016: *Haanikaarak Baapu*

*Apni kismat ki gaadi ki khasta haalat hai*
*Mhaare baapu is gaadi ke vahan chaalak hain*
*Baapu sehat ke liye tu toh haanikaarak hai*

Lyrics: Amitabh Bhattacharya
Music: Pritam
Singers: Sarwar Khan and Sartaz Khan Barna
Film: *Dangal*

THE film *Dangal*, produced by Aamir Khan, is loosely based on the life of Mahavir Singh Phogat of village Balali, Charkhi Dadri, Haryana. Mahavir Singh Phogat was an amateur wrestler and coach who went against societal norms and taught wrestling to his daughters Geeta and Babita who represented India in international events and won medals too. In the film, Aamir plays Mahavir Phogat who starts training his young daughters one fine day. The song '*Baapu sehat ke liye tu toh haanikaarak hai*' depicts the tussle between two reluctant kids being pushed by their father to train hard, against their wishes.

Composer Pritam set lyricist Amitabh Bhattacharya's quirky words to tune in this situational song for the film. While the song talks about a torturous situation, the words and the playful singing make it a vivacious one. Pritam auditioned twenty kids in Rajasthan to sing the song before he zeroed in on twelve-year-old Sarwar Khan and eleven-year-old Sartaz Khan Barna. The two kids belong to the Manganiyar community, famous for its mastery over Rajasthani folk music.

In the song, the haanikarak baapu (injurious father) acts against the wishes of his daughters but his push results in them becoming world-class wrestlers. Geeta Phogat won the gold medal in the 2010 Commonwealth Games while her sister Babita Phogat won the silver.

While a father's hard push yielded positive results in the world of sports, this was not proving to be true in the real world. It was a haanikarak turn that India took when the prime minister addressed the nation on the evening of 8 November 2016. Ever since Modi was sworn in as PM on the back of the promise of prosperous times, his government had been criticized for its lack of gumption when it came to economic reforms. On this day, the prime minister chose to answer this criticism about the lack of any big-bang reforms with an unprecedented decision. He announced that starting midnight, currency notes of ₹500 and ₹1,000 would cease to be legal tender and that people would have fifty days to get their old currency notes exchanged. In his address the prime minister claimed that this move was aimed at tackling the scourge of black money in the economy. By forcing people to deposit cash, the government imagined that existing black money would be dealt with. Currency notes of ₹500 and ₹1,000 denomination represented 86 per cent of India's total cash by volume. Most of the Indian economy, especially the informal sector, depended upon cash transactions to sustain trade, business and earn a living, and overnight this was thrown into jeopardy. Indian banks experienced never-seen-before pressure at all their branches as people rushed to deposit all their cash holdings in these two denominations. The worst hit were the daily wagers who had to forego their potential earnings as they were forced to spend their working hours standing in queues outside banks.

This demonetization move faced widespread criticism as it threw life out of gear. Many economists like Amartya Sen and Kaushik Basu questioned the rationale behind such a move while former prime minister Manmohan Singh referred to it as 'organized loot and legalized plunder'. He argued that this would shave 2 per cent off India's GDP. The problem was made worse by a number of factors. Farmers were hurt in the middle of the sowing season and lack of cash impeded their ability to purchase seeds. The wedding season made life difficult for parents. The Reserve Bank of India was not able to print enough new currency at high speeds to be able to replenish the old, useless notes in the economy. As evidence piled up of the misery caused by demonetization from all over India, the government responded by turning a blind eye to it. The government kept giving different reasons for why it took such a drastic step.

Security-wise, the year had not begun on a good note: terrorists attacked the Pathankot air-force base on 2 January. The fortified airbase was penetrated by the terrorists without much difficulty and the forces were caught off guard. The cleaning-up operations were mishandled as it took the forces three days to sanitize the area. Seven security personnel, one civilian and four terrorists were killed. Security forces faced another attack on 18 September when four terrorists attacked the brigade headquarters of the army in Uri in Jammu and Kashmir. Seventeen army personnel lost their lives in this attack while all the four terrorists were killed after a six-hour-long gun battle. On 29 November, three terrorists attacked an army base in Nagrota, J&K, which led to the death of seven more soldiers.

The terrorist attacks showed the heightened challenge that the Indian security forces faced in the state of J&K. Things had turned volatile after twenty-two-year-old militant Burhan Wani, a commander of Hizbul Mujahideen, was killed by the security forces on 8 July 2016. Violence erupted in the Kashmir Valley as thousands came out protesting his killing. Things had gone downhill after the formation of the BJP–PDP government in the state and the situation deteriorated after the death of chief minister and PDP elder, Mufti Mohammad Sayeed, on 7 January. By allying with the BJP, Sayeed had lost public support in the Kashmir Valley and after his death, his daughter Mehbooba Mufti waited for months before she took over as chief minister of the state on 4 April 2016.

In the rest of the country, the communal hatred provoked by cow protection squads continued to spread. If it was Akhlaq in 2015 who was lynched in his home, it was the image of two cattle traders hanging from a tree in Latehar in Jharkhand that shocked the country. Thirty-five-year-old Mohammed Majloom and twelve-year-year old Inayatullah Khan were hanged from a tree by gau-rakshaks.

The year also saw riots in the state of Haryana as the state government failed to prevent the protesting Jat community in the state from going violent. The community wanted OBC status for themselves and the state government failed to tackle this demand. Despite warnings, the government failed to move in security forces on time and parts of the state went up in flames as violent mobs went about some towns burning public and private property.

While in *Dangal*, haanikarak baapu was trying to create sporting talent, an Indian sportswoman was making her mark in the world. P.V. Sindhu made the country proud when she won the silver medal in the Badminton Women's Singles final at the Rio Olympics. It looked as if Sindhu was strutting about the badminton court with another song from *Dangal* playing in the background. Her coach, a strict disciplinarian and former badminton star Pullela Gopichand had a big role in making Sindhu a world-class player. In 2016, India could have been grateful to these great coaches, even if it sang '*Haanikaarak baapu*'.

# 2017: *Safar Ka Hi Tha Main Safar Ka Raha*

*Jab se gaon se main shehar hua*
*Itna kadwa ho gaya ke zehar hua*
*Safar ka hi tha main safar ka raha*

Lyrics: Irshad Kamil
Music: Pritam
Singer: Arijit Singh
Film: *Jab Harry Met Sejal*

WHEN Imtiaz Ali makes a film, there are certain features to be expected: a lead couple with a complicated, hard-to-define relationship; a journey; and Irshad Kamil as lyricist. *Jab Harry Met Sejal* in 2017 was another one of their collaborations and unlike his previous three films, Ali chose Pritam to compose the music for his film, and he did not disappoint.

In '*Safar*', Irshad Kamil wrote a contemplative, philosophical song that did not have the structure of a usual film song. Only the refrain, '*Safar ka hi tha main, safar ka raha*', keeps the listener grounded as Kamil expresses the internal fears of an individual's never-ending journey. The lyrics reflect Kamil's skills as he weaves deep lines like '*Jab se gaon se main shehar hua, itna kadwa ho gaya ke zehar hua*' (as I evolved into a city from a village, I became so bitter, got toxic) with consummate ease. Composer Pritam allows the thoughts to run unhindered in the song as he gives it a gentle cloud of guitar and percussion to float on. Arijit Singh then sings it as if intoxicated and it becomes a song for the ages.

For India, the year 2017 started in a daze as the country was still suffering from the effects of demonetization of ₹500 and ₹1,000 currency notes, announced on 8 November 2016. Even as evidence kept piling up about the ill effects of this move, the Narendra Modi government kept devising new justifications for it. From the initially declared aim of fighting black money and corruption, the government moved to fighting terrorists, expanding the tax base, pushing for a cashless economy, formalizing the informal economy, bringing 'idle' savings into the banking system and fighting the menace of counterfeit currency. In August, the Reserve Bank of India (RBI) released figures that showed that 99 per cent of all demonetized currency had been deposited in banks.

Even as the aim of this exercise remained fuzzy, its effects were clear. With cash sucked out of the economy for a prolonged period, all economic activity came to a halt or slowed down considerably. This was reflected in India's GDP growth, which slowed down to only 6.1 per cent in the fourth quarter of the financial year 2016–17. The impact was the worst on investment demand in the country as it contracted by 2.1 per cent in the last quarter. The Indian economy had been dealt a severe and entirely man-made shock whose negative effects were felt all over.

The year also saw keen electoral battles in various states across the country. Uttar Pradesh, Uttarakhand, Punjab and Goa went to polls in February while Himachal Pradesh and Gujarat voted in the month of December.

In Uttar Pradesh, the ruling Samajwadi Party allied with the Congress while the BJP and BSP went alone. In Punjab, the battle was a three-way fight between the ruling SAD–BJP combine, AAP and the Congress party. In Uttarakhand and Goa, the real battle was between the Congress and the BJP. In UP, Prime Minister Narendra Modi campaigned aggressively and the BJP romped home with a huge majority. Adityanath, the Gorakhpur MP and head priest of the Gorakhpur math, became the chief minister of the most populous state in the country. In Uttarakhand too, the BJP trounced the incumbent Congress party comprehensively.

The story was different in the states of Punjab and Goa though. In Punjab, the Congress won a hard-earned and big victory over the AAP against predictions while in Goa it emerged as the single largest party with seventeen seats in the forty-seat assembly but was not allowed to form the government. The BJP with thirteen seats was invited to form the government. Defence Minister Manohar Parrikar returned to state politics and became the chief minister of Goa.

As the BJP kept adding states to its kitty, it also caused a rethink in other political parties about their prospects. The biggest example of this was set by the Bihar chief minister, Nitish Kumar. In July, Nitish Kumar terminated his grand alliance with the RJD and the Congress party. He resigned as chief minister and then joined hands with the BJP in the state. He was sworn in as the chief minister again with BJP members as part of the cabinet as well. This was a significant setback to opposition politics barely two years before the next general elections.

After years of planning, debate and bargaining, India saw the Goods and Services Tax (GST) being introduced in the country in the month of July. The GST had been in the works for a long period. It was ironical that the Narendra Modi-led BJP government pushed for the rollout of the tax though the BJP had resisted its implementation when in opposition. The objective of introducing the GST was to simplify the indirect taxation regime in the country, which was considered to be one of the most complex in the world. GST was supposed to simplify filing tax returns and thereby improve compliance but that was not to be as the government pushed for a more complex GST regime than what was prevalent in the rest of the world.

Experts warned that the IT systems required to ensure a smooth rollout were not in place and the structure was too complicated to understand or comply with but the government chose to ignore these protests. The result was a mess as businesses tried to comply with the new regime. The Indian economy that had not yet recovered from the jolt of demonetization suffered yet another setback with the hasty implementation of GST. Small and medium enterprises suffered the most.

In the month of June, India got embroiled in a border faceoff with China. The stand-off began when China started constructing a road in the Doklam plateau. The area was a disputed territory between China and Bhutan.

Indian troops entered the area to prevent the Chinese from constructing the road. China asserted that the area was its territory and asked India to withdraw. After a tense seventy-three-day stand-off, India and China announced a disengagement from the site. Indian troops withdrew to Indian territory while Chinese troops started building temporary and semi-permanent infrastructure a couple of kilometres from the area. The stand-off ended only to give way to a more permanent one with increased Indian and Chinese troop presence in the region.

The lines '*Itna kadwa ho gaya ke zehar hua*' from the song '*Safar*' might have been written about how bitter India had become. The hatred that had come to fore with the lynching of Mohammed Akhlaq in Dadri, UP, in 2015, reared its ugly head repeatedly in 2017 as well. Fifty-five-year-old Pehlu Khan, a dairy farmer from district Nuh, Haryana, was lynched by gau-rakshaks in Behror, Rajasthan, as he was returning to his village with cows that he had purchased in Jaipur. Six others were injured. The police charged the victims with cow smuggling. In June, seventeen-year-old Junaid and his two cousins were attacked in a train near Palwal in Haryana. Junaid was killed in a dispute over carrying meat in the train. The victims in such incidents were mostly Muslim. Dalits too faced the brunt of increasing atrocities. As the frequency of communal and caste violence increased, it led to an increasing sense of unease and insecurity among the minorities and deprived sections of society.

For India, another year had ended, adding another chapter to its long history. A new one awaited, with new hopes, new aspirations and new challenges. Leaving memories behind, 2017 had ended perhaps with these words: '*Safar ka hi tha main safar ka raha*'.

# Epilogue

In Amitabh Bhattacharya's lyrics for *Udaan* (2010), '*Geet mein dhalte lafzon mein, taal pe chalti nabzon mein, naya kuchh naya toh zaroor hai*', he might have been writing about Hindi film music and India itself. Note by note, songs have been composed; songs that portrayed a different and changing India and Indians.

Hindi film music's importance needs no new testimonials but it probably deserves more credit when it comes to its contribution to original art. With hundreds of new films made every year, stories, plots, situations kept repeating themselves ever so often and with it arose the need for composers to devise new ways to fill them with new music and for lyricists to give words to those feelings. It is a testament to their original thought and effort that composers and lyricists have managed to give us new songs for similar situations over decades. Instead of churning out cover versions or remixes of old or folk songs, these artists have produced works of art that have entertained generations and given vent to their deep thoughts.

With his 'ancient palimpsest of many layers' statement, Nehru may have unwittingly described the phenomenon of Hindi film music as well. Hindi film songs and film music have flowed like a river since 1947; changing their colours at each corner with a different tempo at every other turn. Except, this river doesn't meet the sea; it just flows. But like the palimpsest of Nehru's imagination, the Hindi film song too changed with each new layer, retaining something from the previous one. Change with continuity.

Hindi film songs have moved from the times when all the musicians and singers had to be present together at the same time in the same studio to a time when an A.R. Rahman can have an orchestra in Germany perform an interlude in a song while the singer may arrive a week later to record his part.

In 2017, Hindi film songs might have had a different language compared to 1947, with a greater influence of Western music, but it also had songs that are steeped in Hindustani classical music and singing.

If the gramophone was how the listeners enjoyed Hindi film songs in 1947, they are now doing it on their headphones plugged into their mobile phones. A variety of music apps now stream music 24/7. This has also led to changes in how the Hindi film music album is viewed. Over the last few years, the focus has shifted to individual songs rather than a music album. This will bring its own changes to the Hindi song and it will evolve into something new – *kuchh naya*.

The Hindi film song only mirrored what India, a young constitutional republic, did. From 1947 onwards, Bombay cinema played a huge role in shaping the sense of India being a nation. The link between its words, tunes and the Indian people is deeper and stronger than we acknowledge. This book is a small attempt to underscore this point, note by note and page by page.

India left behind its many pasts, it chose a new path in 1947 and reaffirmed it in 1950. It embarked on a new journey, summoned the people to join and they joined this experiment cheerfully. From the hopeful days of the 1950s to the dark clouds of the 1960s to the restlessness of the 1970s to the upheaval of the 1980s to the manic energy of the 1990s to the assuredness of the new century, the Indian experiment has endured and the Indian people have embraced the change.

With its progressive Constitution, India's founding fathers made some choices for us and perhaps imperfectly, not wholly or in full measure, but very substantially, we have tried to keep this pledge. India has endured. India will abide.

# Select Bibliography


Alam, Mohd. Sanjeer and K.C. Sivaramakrishnan (eds), *Fixing Electoral Boundaries in India: Laws, Processes, Outcomes, and Implications for Political Representation*, New Delhi: Oxford University Press, 2015.

Anantharaman, Ganesh, *Bollywood Melodies: A History of the Hindi Film Song*, New Delhi: Penguin Books, 2008.

Austin, Granville, *Working a Democratic Constitution: A History of the Indian Experience*, New Delhi: Oxford University Press, 1999.

Aziz, Ashraf, *Light of the Universe, Essays on Hindustani Film Music*, New Delhi: Three Essays Collective, 2003.

Basu, Jyoti, *Memoirs: A Political Autobiography*, Calcutta: National Book Agency, 1999.

Bhatia, Gautam, *Offend, Shock, or Disturb: Free Speech under the Indian Constitution*, New Delhi: Oxford University Press, 2016.

Bhattacherje, S.B., *Encyclopaedia of Indian Events and Dates*, New Delhi: Sterling Paperbacks, 2008.

Bose, Mihir, *Bollywood, A History*, New Delhi: Roli Books, 2007.

Burman, Khagesh Dev, *R.D. Burman: The Prince of Music*, New Delhi: Rupa Publications, 2015.

Chandra, Bipan, *Communalism in Modern India*, New Delhi: Har Anand Publications, 1984.

———, *In the Name of Democracy: JP Movement and the Emergency*, New Delhi: Penguin Books, 2003.

Chandra, Bipan, Mridula Mukherjee and Aditya Mukherjee, *India Since Independence*, New Delhi: Penguin Books, 2008 (Revised and Updated).

Chatterji, Shoma A., *100 Years of Jump-Cuts and Fade-Outs: Tracking Change in Indian Cinema*, New Delhi: Rupa Publications, 2014.

Chaudhuri, Rudra, *Forged in Crisis: India and the United States Since 1947*, New York: Oxford University Press, 2014.

Dasgupta, Sunil and Stephen Cohen, *Arming without Aiming: India's Military Modernization*, Washington: Brookings Institution Press, 2010.

Desai, Meghnad, *Nehru's Hero, Dilip Kumar, In the Life of India*, New Delhi: Roli Books, 2004.

Diettrich, Brian, Jane Freeman Moulin and Michael Hugh Webb, *Bollywood Sounds: The Cosmopolitan Mediations of Hindi Film Songs*, New York: Oxford University Press, 2011.

Dreze, Jean and Amartya Sen, *An Uncertain Glory: India and its Contradictions*, New Delhi: Penguin Books, 2013.

Frank, Katherine, *Indira: The Life of Indira Nehru Gandhi*, London: HarperCollins, 2001.

Gandhi, Rajmohan, *Rajaji: A Life*, New Delhi: Penguin Books, 2000.

Guha, Ramachandra, *India After Gandhi: The History of the World's Largest Democracy*, New Delhi: Picador India, 2008.

Gupta, Shubhra, *50 Films that Changed Bollywood, 1995–2015*, New Delhi: HarperCollins India, 2016.

Hasan, Zoya, *Congress after Indira: Policy, Power, Political Change (1984-2009)*, New Delhi: Oxford University Press, 2012.

———, *Quest for Power: Oppositional Movements and Post-Congress Politics in Uttar Pradesh*, New Delhi: Oxford University Press, 1998.

Jayal, Niraja Gopal and Pratap Bhanu Mehta, *The Oxford Companion to Politics in India*, New Delhi: Oxford University Press, 2010.

Joshi, Prasoon, *Sunshine Lanes: A Poetic Journey*, New Delhi: Rupa Publications, 2013.

Kabir, Nasreen Munni, *Talking Films and Songs: Javed Akhtar in Conversation with Nasreen Munni Kabir*, New Delhi: Oxford University Press, 2005.

Khilnani, Sunil, *The Idea of India*, London: Penguin Books, 2012 (With a new introduction).

Khosla, Madhav, (ed.), *Letters for a Nation: From Jawaharlal Nehru to His Chief Ministers*, 1947-1963, New Delhi: Penguin Books, 2014.

Kudaisya, Gyanesh, *A Republic in the Making: India in the 1950s*, New Delhi: Oxford University Press, 2017.

Malone, David M., *Does the Elephant Dance?: Contemporary Indian Foreign Policy*, New York: Oxford University Press, 2011.

McGarr, Paul M., *The Cold War in South Asia: Britain, the United States and the Indian Subcontinent*, 1945-1965, New York: Cambridge University Press, 2013.

Menon, Shivshankar, *Choices: Inside the Making of Indian Foreign Policy*, New Delhi: Penguin Random House, 2016.

Menon, V.P., *Integration of the Indian States*, Madras: Orient Longman, 1985 (with new appendices).

Morcom, Anna, *Hindi Film Songs and the Cinema*, New York: Routledge, 2007.

Mukherjee, Rudrangshu, *Nehru and Bose: Parallel Lives*, New Delhi: Penguin Books, 2014.

Namboodiripad, E.M.S., *History, Society and Land Relations: Selected Essays*, New Delhi: LeftWord Books, 2010.

Nehru, B.K., *Nice Guys Finish Second: Memoirs*, New Delhi: Viking, 1997.

Nehru, Jawaharlal, *The Discovery of India*, New Delhi: Penguin Books, 2006 (Modern classics).

Palanisamy, P.K., *Kalaignar, A World Poet*, Annamalai Nagar: Annamalai University, 2014.

Palshikar, Suhas, Sanjay Kumar and Sanjay Lodha (eds), *Electoral Politics in India: The Resurgence of the Bharatiya Janata Party*, London: Routledge, Taylor & Francis Group, 2017.

Rafi, Yasmin Khalid, *Mohammed Rafi, My Abba, A Memoir*, Chennai: Tranquebar Press, 2012.

Raghavan, Srinath, *1971: A Global History of the Creation of Bangladesh*, Cambridge, Massachusetts: Harvard University Press, 2015.

———, *War and Peace in Modern India*, Basingstoke: Palgrave Macmillan, 2010.

Ramesh, Jairam, *To the Brink and Back: India's 1991 Story*, New Delhi: Rupa Publications, 2015.

Ranchan, Vijay, *Story of a Bollywood Song: Evolution of Hindi Film Music Through Stories*, New Delhi: Abhinav Publications, 2013.

Sabharwal, Gopa, *India Since 1947: The Independent Years*, New Delhi: Penguin Random House India, 2017.

Sonthalia, Vinod and Kamal Beriwala, *The Legacy of The Legend – K.L. Saigal*, Kolkata: V. Sontholia, 2005.

Saran, Shyam, *How India Sees the World: From Kautilya to the 21st Century*, New Delhi: Juggernaut Books, 2017.

Sen, Amartya, *The Argumentative Indian, Writings on Indian Culture, History and Identity*, London: Penguin Books, 2005.

Setalvad, Motilal C., *My Life: Law and Other Things*, Bombay: N.M. Tripathi, 1970.

Shani, Ornit, *Communalism, Caste and Hindu Nationalism*, New York: Cambridge University Press, 2007.

———, *How India Became Democratic*, New Delhi: Cambridge University Press, 2017.

Shivkumar, Nalini and Rema Mahalingam, *Unforgettable: The Iconic Women of South Indian Cinema*, New Delhi: Rupa Publications, 2014.

Singh, Daman, *Strictly Personal: Manmohan and Gursharan*, New Delhi: HarperCollins India, 2014.

Singh, Sushant, *Mission Overseas*, New Delhi: Juggernaut Books, 2017.

Somaaya, Bhawana, *Once Upon a Time in India: A Century of Indian Cinema*, New Delhi: Penguin Random House India, 2016.

Srinivas, M.N., *Social Change in Modern India*, New Delhi: Orient Longman, 1995 (New Indian edition).

Thakur, Sankarshan, *The Brothers Bihari*, New Delhi: HarperCollins India, 2015.

Vittal, Balaji and Anirudha Bhattacharjee, *Gaata Rahe Mera Dil: 50 Classic Hindi Film Songs*, New Delhi: HarperCollins India, 2015.

Wilkinson, Steven I., *Army and Nation: The Military and Indian Democracy since Independence*, Cambridge, Massachusetts: Harvard University Press, 2015.

# Acknowledgements

IT takes a village to bring up a child. *Note by Note* owes its life to the village of our times. We thank each of our friends, colleagues (very specially our bosses at *The Indian Express* and *Business Standard*) and families who bore with us as we struggled with the idea and then its execution.

The book would certainly not have been possible minus the patience of our publishers, HarperCollins – who stayed with the idea despite the twists and turns in the *aaroh* and *avroh* of our lives, ever since we thought of doing this in 2016.

To Krishan Chopra and Antony Thomas for pushing us ever so gently, a very special thanks.

Hindi films and Hindi film music are topics so vast and varied that it needed special help from those who've been part of the industry to illuminate our path. The same is true of Indian political history where we have benefited from people who have either experienced it first-hand or at least studied it. There are just too many people in both fields to express our gratitude to, and it would not be physically possible to list them all. But each one of you knows who you are. Heartfelt thanks.

A book like *Note by Note* by its very nature cannot be perfect. The responsibility for all errors and mistakes lies with us, and us alone.

We learnt so much during the writing of the book – about ourselves, about Hindi film music and about independent India. We hope that we have been able to convey a part of that at least – the rhythm of history to the beat of music: note by note.